First published 2014

The History Press
The Mill, Brimscombe Port
Stroud, Gloucestershire, GL5 2QG
www.thehistorypress.co.uk

British Library Cataloguing in Publication Data.
A catalogue record for this book is available from the British Library.

ISBN 978 0 7524 8613 0

Typesetting and origination by The History Press
Printed in India

THE HULL BOOK OF DAYS

SUSANNA O'NEILL

The History Press

JANUARY 1ST

2012: Anyone who has lived in Hull for any length of time should recognise the name Pauline Gift. Her son, Roland, became a well-known musician touring with his band The Fine Young Cannibals, but Pauline herself is a character well remembered for her eccentricity and generous nature. Born just outside Hull, she grew up off Spring Bank before moving to Birmingham just prior to the Second World War. Whilst there she became the first woman in Birmingham to get a mortgage! When she returned to Hull, she ran a number of Aladdin's cave-style shops specialising in vintage clothing and bric-a-brac. Her daughter, Helga, commented to the *Hull Daily Mail* after her mother had passed away that, 'She did vintage when the word truly did mean vintage. And she started it in an era when it wasn't socially acceptable.' Pauline's first shop was on Cave Street in 1974, followed by Grafton Street and she then spent twenty years in Pauline's Gift Shop on Princes Avenue after Roland had bought the premises. Pauline died on January 1st 2012 and, as Helga says, 'She was an amazing, eccentric woman who will be missed by a lot of people.'

JANUARY 2ND

1744: Joseph Milner, known as an evangelical divine, was born on this date. A highly intelligent man, he suffered a severe attack of measles at the age of three which left him delicate. His mind, however, was very sharp and he had a wonderfully retentive memory. While he was in deacon's orders he left Thorp Arch, where he was studying, to take up the post of headmaster of Hull Grammar School. Joseph is said to have greatly improved the school during his headship and William Wilberforce was a student there at this time. In 1768, Joseph was chosen as afternoon lecturer at Holy Trinity Church and became a strong supporter of the evangelical movement of the time. He also took charge of North Ferriby parish church, being first a curate, then the vicar for seventeen years. In both Hull and Ferriby he was seen as a prominent moral force and the poor especially flocked to hear him preach. It is said that Hull became a centre of evangelism largely because of him; he was one of the greatest contributors to its success in the city. He has left behind a legacy of published works about the Church, his best known being the *History of the Church of Christ*. On a journey to York in 1797, he caught a cold and died several weeks later. A monument to his memory was erected in Holy Trinity Church.

JANUARY 3RD

1945: Born in Hull on this date, musician and songwriter Philip Goodhand-Tait had a good start, with a natural talent for music, an excellent ear and a mother who taught piano. He and some friends formed their own band, the Stormsville Shakers, in 1961 with the ambition of attracting a record company to sign them up. Philip was inspired to write songs after working with talented songwriter Chris Andrews, and the band thought they had found their hit song when they collaborated with him on a tune. However, the record company Chris worked for would not allow an unknown band to use the song and it was later released as Sandie Shaw's 'Long Live Love', which became her biggest success, a number one record in the UK Top 10. The band, however, did develop an excellent reputation as a backing group and worked with many famous names as well as eventually releasing some of their own music. Philip has written songs for various well-known artists such as Gary Numan, the Blowmonkeys, Steppenwolf, Steve Marriott, Sandie Shaw and Greg Allman. When reflecting on his career, Phillip said, 'I've had the luckiest breaks and known some wonderful people during my life ... music has been a constant companion, one which I hope to have with me until the end of my life.'

January 4th

1828: The Hull City Repository Archives show that on this date the youngest son of Thomas Richardson became apprenticed to his cabinet-making business. Richardson & Sons was founded by Thomas Richardson in 1812 and was reputedly one of the finest cabinet-making enterprises of the day. The archives show that in 1851 they employed sixteen men and eleven apprentices, which is no surprise as theirs was one of the largest manufacturers of furniture in the country at the time, furnishing mansions both in England and abroad. Starting in Dagger Lane, the business was moved to Bond Street as they expanded, then Waltham Street. Reports show that theirs was a first-rate place of employment, the *Hull Packet* stating that in 1860 they afforded upwards of 100 workers a pleasure trip to Bridlington, one of many employee treats. It is said the workmanship of this company was well sought after by the rich and famous and even Queen Victoria had a special set of chairs made for her use when she and Prince Albert visited the city in 1854. One writer described their work as such: 'For quality variety and richness, it bears the palm of excellence over all others. The showrooms contain specimens of the carvers' skills that astonish by their marvellous beauty.'

January 5th

1941: Amy Johnson was one of the most famous women to come from Hull. Born in July 1903, she attended Kingston High School, continuing her education at Sheffield University where she obtained an Economics Degree. She began flying as a hobby – some saying it was during a five-minute ride at a travelling air show in Hull when her interest was first aroused – and she soon showed great aptitude. She made her first solo flight after less than sixteen hours' tuition and gained her pilot's licence after just over a year as a student. By the end of 1929 she had also obtained a ground engineer's licence, the first woman in Britain ever to do so. After this there was no stopping her and she became a pioneer in aviation, setting many long-distance flying records. Her father helped her to buy her own plane, a Gypsy Moth, with which she had a lifelong love affair. During the war she flew for the Air Transport Auxiliary, delivering military aircraft from factories to airbases. She died, aged just thirty-seven, during such a flight on this date, when her plane came down in the Thames Estuary. Her body was never found.

January 6th

1954: Oscar-winning film director, producer and writer Anthony Minghella CBE was born on this date. He graduated from the University of Hull in 1975 with a First Class Honours Degree in English Drama, then returned there to lecture for seven years whilst studying for his doctorate. Anthony was one of the greats of English cinema, his most celebrated works including *Truly Madly Deeply* (1990) and *The Talented Mr Ripley* (1999). The pinnacle of Anthony's career was directing *The English Patient* (1996), which won nine Academy Awards. He returned to the University of Hull in 1997 to deliver some drama masterclasses and to receive an Honorary Degree. He spent ten years at the university in all and was greatly admired and respected by his colleagues and contemporaries. Drama lecturer Tony Meech taught and worked alongside Anthony. He recalls, 'Anthony was a person of extremely high intellect and he had incredible creative flair. Despite his world-wide success, Anthony never forgot about his time at the University of Hull. He was one of the best friends that Hull had and he never missed an opportunity to acknowledge the debt he felt he owed the university and the Department, for the opportunities he was afforded there.' The university named its newly refurbished drama studio after Anthony, opened by Alan Plater in 2008.

JANUARY 7TH

2010: On this day, Hull-born weatherman Alex Deakin appeared on *Celebrity Mastermind*, where he finished second. Apparently the very same day was the coldest of the 2009/10 winter. Alex graduated with an MSc in Physics with Astrophysics at Birmingham University, after which he joined the Met Office in 1997 and worked in the York and Bristol Weather Centres. Alex joined the BBC Weather Centre in November 2000. In an interview with BBC News he confessed to getting nervous before his broadcasts. When asked if he ever made any mistakes, his response was to admit to 'several; the best one was when I pulled my earpiece out by mistake and I rabbited on for about four minutes!' A more infamous incident, however, was reported in the *Sunday Telegraph* in September 2012. 'BBC weatherman left red-faced over on-air "C-word" forecast. A BBC weatherman, Alex Deakin, has been left embarrassed after accidentally broadcasting live one of the most unacceptable words in the English language ... During a BBC World weather forecast, he told viewers: "By and large it's simply [a] lovely winter's day tomorrow, bucketloads of c---, er, sunshine across central and eastern areas".' Fortunately he was not fired over his gaffe, but if he were, his dream job would apparently have been to play as a professional footballer!

JANUARY 8TH

1997: The *Hull Daily Mail* reported the death of legendary Hull man Bob Carver on this date. 'Bob Carver's' is a celebrated name in the city, as the family has run the most renowned fish and chip shop in Hull for generations. The business was started in 1888 by Bob Carver, who handed it on to his son, Bob, in the early 1920s. His son and grandson, also called Bob, carried on the trade. 'He loved the business and enjoyed meeting people,' Bob the grandson told the *Mail*, 'he will be sadly missed but the Carver business will continue, hopefully, for another four generations.' The business is not only famous for its fish and chips but also for the Hull potato and sage 'pattie'. They have, in addition, had a stall at the historic Hull Fair, in the same position, for decades. There was a gap during the war when Bob served in the army, but afterwards he went back to the council and demanded his old spot back. They have been on Walton Street ever since and claim it is the best pitch at the fair.

JANUARY 9TH

1875: On this date Hull's tram route to Beverley Road was opened. Prior to this, and also in competition with it during its operational lifetime, other modes of transport in Hull included wagonettes, omnibuses and hackney carriages. The trams, however, proved popular and by 1882 over 30,000 passengers were using the tram system every week. The early Hull tramway network consisted of a 1,435mm wide tramline following the five main roads out of the city centre. The tramway was horse-powered to begin with; then, in 1896, it was converted into an electric system and changed to double track. There were around thirty vehicles initially – all single deckers – then, later, some double-deckers arrived, being able to seat around forty people. As time went on more lines and further extensions were added to the city tracks, but by the 1930s the trolleybus was beginning to take precedence. The final tram to run in Hull was in June 1945, the journey being celebrated by 800 lights which illuminated the tram. Local dignitaries hopped aboard for the last ride and thousands turned out to witness the occasion.

JANUARY 10TH

1875: Robert Searle was a lucky Hull man who managed to escape the gallows. It was on this date that he entered into an argument with workmate James McConnell. The two men were working in the stoke hole of the SS *Sappho*, which was lying in the Albert Dock. The quarrel must have been particularly heated, as it resulted in Robert stabbing James in the chest, which proved fatal – he died within forty minutes. Robert must have realised what the consequences of his serious crime would be as he turned on himself and cut his own throat. His suicide attempt was unsuccessful, however, and instead he was treated and then sentenced to death. The next month, though, he managed to get a reprieve! Robert was not the only murderer to escape death at the gallows. Jane Crompton apparently also managed to avoid the death sentence, even though the sixty-five-year-old mother had cut off the head of her four-year-old daughter! She even admitted to disliking the girl and often wishing her dead. Another woman, Priscilla Utting, also only received a prison sentence, despite strangling her two-year-old daughter with a handkerchief. A horrific year for Hull.

JANUARY 11TH

1968: The *St Romanus*, skippered by Jimmy Wheeldon, was the first to be lost in the triple Hull trawler tragedy of 1968. Concerns had been raised previously about the safety of the ship, making it more difficult to crew, and it sailed on January 10th without a radio operator. Lack of radio response after this date was not initially seen as significant. The owners, Hamling Bros, did not make any serious effort to contact the trawler again until January 20th. On January 24th, the Inspector of Fisheries was made aware of the situation and immediately ordered a Pan Pan (urgent message) to be sent across the fishing grounds. An Icelandic trawler, *Viking 111*, had received a mayday call from the *St Romanus* on January 11th but ignored it as they were too far away. On January 13th, an inflated life raft was found 265 miles north of Spurn Point, but it was not linked to the *St Romanus* as she had not been declared missing. Not until February 21st were fears realised, when a lifebuoy from the trawler washed up on a Danish beach. The skipper's wife had spoken to her husband on January 10th. He had promised to call the following day. That call never came and the trawler and entire crew were presumed lost on January 11th en route to the fishing grounds.

January 12th

1898: On this date Sir Tatton Sykes was sued by a London moneylender, to whom the Baronet's wife owed £16,000. He claimed he had promissory notes allegedly signed by Sir Tatton, but the latter declared his wife had forged his signature. Sir Tatton and Lady Jessica Sykes were forced into a marriage. Jessica was thirty years his junior and it is claimed he was an eccentric, mean-spirited man, whereas she was a lively eighteen-year-old girl, so they never got on. Seemingly Jessica sought a different life away in London, where she drank, gambled and took lovers. She even earned herself the nickname 'Lady Satin Tights'. When the debt collectors began to call, Sir Tatton despaired and put an announcement in *The Times* newspaper:

> I, SIR TATTON SYKES, hereby give notice that I will NOT be RESPONSIBLE for any DEBTS or ENGAGEMENTS which my wife, LADY JESSICA CHRISTINA SYKES, may contract, whether purporting to be on my behalf or by my authority or otherwise.

When Lady Tatton died, Sir Tatton was overheard leaving the church saying, 'Remarkable woman, but I rue the day I met her.' Jessica was, however, loved by the people of Hull for her good works and kind heart. For twenty-five years she delivered Christmas treats to schoolchildren in Hull and she was held in great affection by them.

JANUARY 13TH

1948: On this date the well-known actor Malcolm Storry was born in Hull. His career began in theatre, but behind the scenes, as an assistant stage manager. Then, in the 1970s and '80s, he became a regular stage actor. Probably most well known for his TV performances, Malcolm has appeared in such series as *Pie in the Sky*, *Heartbeat*, *Dangerfield*, *Midsomer Murders* and *The Knock*. He has also appeared in major films including *The Last of the Mohicans*, *The Scarlet Letter* and *The Princess Bride*, among others. Whilst in an interview for whatsonstage.com, Malcolm confided that his favourite playwright was Peter Flannery. Other favourites later named were Michael Gambon as co-star and Jonathan Kent as his director.

He has appeared in many Shakespeare productions and admits the role he would most like to play would be Iago in *Othello*. Displaying his cheeky Hull sense of humour, when asked who he would most like to swap places with, living or dead, he apparently replied, 'Last week's lottery winner.'

JANUARY 14TH

1892: On this date the deaths of HRH the Duke of Clarence and Cardinal Manning were publicly announced. The Duke of Clarence, the eldest son of King Edward VII, died of pneumonia, a complication of the influenza pandemic which was then spreading across the country. The Lord Mayor at once ordered the bell of St Paul's Cathedral to be tolled, heard up to 20 miles away. Cardinal Manning, the second Archbishop of Westminster, had served as leader of the Catholic Church in England and Wales for nearly thirty years. His death affected many of London's poorest, who came out in force to pay their respects and it is well documented that his funeral was the largest ever attended in Victorian England. A great sense of sadness and mourning fell and towns across the country paid their individual respects to these two notable figures. In Hull this happened on the day of the prince's funeral. The majority of Hull's shops closed and there was an entire cessation of business for several hours. Flags were flown at half-mast on the churches and public buildings in the town, muffled peals were rung, the minute gun was fired by HMS *Audacious*, and, it is said, never since the death of the Prince Consort in 1861 had the town presented such a general appearance of mourning.

JANUARY 15TH

2009: Dr James Bickford died on this date, aged ninety-one. Originally from Devon and qualifying in medicine, James joined the Navy during the war, afterwards finding it difficult to obtain a post in general medicine. His father suggested psychiatric care and in 1956 he became Superintendent at De La Pole Hospital, Hull, where he made radical changes to the way the patients were treated. His approaches and practices were at odds with the mainstream ideas of the day, but his compassion and care drove him on. When he joined the hospital, many of the wards were locked and there was little for patients to do. With the support of the staff, who were swayed by his convictions, patients were encouraged to engage in a variety of physical and mental activities. Basic literacy skills were taught together with singing, sports, gardening, metalwork and woodwork. He arranged summer camps, trips to the sea, sledging in winter and holidays to the Norfolk Broads and the Isle of Man, as well as some abroad. James is quoted as saying that, 'With very little effort and no expense, great improvements in the lives of older people and relief of many debilitating symptoms could be achieved simply by means of compassion.' He was a real pioneer, with nationwide influence.

JANUARY 16TH

1980: David Whitfield, the first British male vocalist to earn a gold disc for selling 1 million copies of the same record, died on this date. He was on tour in Australia when he suffered a brain haemorrhage aged fifty-four, his ashes being flown back to the UK and scattered just south of Spurn Point. Born in Hull in 1926, in a small terraced house without hot water or an inside toilet, David rose to become a big star in both Britain and America during the 1950s. From the age of eleven he sang in pubs to supplement the family income. One night, during the Second World War, he was asked to sing at Perth Street Club. This was his first booking and he was paid *7s 6d* (37p). His big break came in 1949 when he won *Opportunity Knocks*. He then became a regular singer on Radio Luxembourg, which procured him legions of devoted fans. The year 1954 saw David's greatest record, 'Cara Mia', which sold more than a million copies. That same year he sang for Queen Elizabeth II at the London Palladium. During his career he recorded twelve top 10 hits and two No.1s in Britain. He was also the first British soloist to achieve a top 10 hit in America's famous Billboard Hot 100 chart.

JANUARY 17TH

1786: Commodore Edward Thompson was the son of a Hull merchant. Born in Hull in the 1730s, he was sent to sea at a young age. In 1757 he rose to the rank of lieutenant, then on the outbreak of the American War Edward obtained a captain's commission, being appointed commander of the frigate *Hyaena*. It was said that he was always a well-liked and respected man, one friend saying that his popularity in the service was almost unparalleled, 'from the sweetness of his temper, and benevolence of his nature'. In 1785 he had command of the *Grampus*, in which he went out to the west coast of Africa as commodore of the small squadron there. Unfortunately, he contracted a fever and died on board ship on this date. A friend said of him, 'He was considered as a brave and skilfull commander, and had that infallible testament – the affection of his crew.' Despite his prominent career, he is probably better known as a literary figure. His nickname in the navy was 'Rhyming Thompson'. He was famous for having edited an edition of the works of Andrew Marvell and also John Oldham and Paul Whitehead. He was excellent at comic poems but also wrote dramatic works and sea shanties, taking inspiration from his own sea voyages.

JANUARY 18TH

1921: In 1865, the Hull Seaman's and General Orphan Society was established to house children whose fathers had been lost at sea. The orphanage was opened in 1866 for children who had seafaring connections with, or were born in, the port of Hull or its ancient limits of Bridlington, Grimsby and Goole, or within 7 miles of Trinity House. The Wilsons, the well-known shipping family, donated generously to the orphanage, paid for extensions to be built and even organised summer excursions for the orphans. In 1916, the Wilson Company was bought out and so the orphanage lost a major source of its funding. By 1920, it was necessary for it to change premises and it moved into Hesslewood Hall. On January 18th 1921, girls first arrived at this new home, the boys following in February. For over 100 years the orphanage bathed, fed, clothed, educated, housed and took responsibility for the health of hundreds of orphans, whose motto was 'courage to climb'.

JANUARY 19TH

2003: On this day, the bassist for Hull band The Gargoyles tragically died in a collision with a car whilst out on his push bike. Paul Warhurst was one of the members of the off-the-wall 1980s band, along with former members of chart-topping band The Housemartins, Hugh Whittaker and Ted Key. Ted stated that, 'The other band members are devastated, he was much-loved. Paul's death is a tragic loss to the local music scene.' He added, 'I think it's more sad than anything because The Gargoyles had recently reformed and were planning more gigs.' The band, in their own words, were on a 'quest for the absurd'. Their lyrics and song themes were viewed as ridiculous to many, but they had a loyal fan-base and they said the songs made sense to them. Such ideas included travelling around the world on a space hopper! Once, when interviewed by the *Hull Daily Mail*, Ted shared a memory of the day twenty-three Gargoyles fans crammed into the back of the band's van on the way home from a gig in Aldershot. 'Somehow our manager, Marge, managed to drive straight over the top of a roundabout,' he recalled. 'It was better than Alton Towers – but luckily, by the time the police arrived we'd managed to hide everyone.'

January 20th

1920: The *Hull Daily Mail* reported an East Hull blaze on this date, detailing heavy damage caused at a seed warehouse. Apparently several thousand pounds' worth of damage was caused at the warehouse of Mr T. Miller and Mr J. Sisson on Lime Street in the early hours. Fortunately, the blaze was noticed by a policeman out on duty, who called in the fire services directly. The fire, however, was well underway by the time they arrived, with dense volumes of smoke pouring out of the buildings. It spread to the upper part of the building, destroying a cabinet maker's storage, and the fire crew were said to still be at the premises at four in the afternoon, making the area safe. Then, in the evening, they were again called out to a smaller blaze at Stoneferry, where a lobby had caught fire, and then a third fire was reported at a shop premises in Saville Street which, although small, caused the firemen 'an unhappy half hour or so'. The flames here were particularly difficult to extinguish as they had been caused by a pan of burning sulphur, meant as a rat-exterminator. Three fires in the space of a few days. Coincidence?

JANUARY 21ST

1994: First constructed in 1810, then opened in 1847, Hull's Victoria Pier was initially known as Corporation Pier until 1854, when Queen Victoria left the city from this port following her visit to Hull. It had a railway station office, but was one of the few piers in the country with no trains! The station office was used just as a ticket office and waiting room for the Humber Ferry, a ferry service between New Holland and the port of Hull. The building is a handsome red-brick structure, described as including 'a central dormer with shouldered coped gable topped with a finial and containing a clock, and a trefoil with the company's initials'. Fortunately, this grand construction will stay with us for quite some time, as it became a listed building on this date. Originally a two-tier affair, the pier itself was a beautiful creation and became a popular place for a perambulation. The ferry service was also extremely popular until the opening of the Humber Bridge. The last ferry, named the *Faringford*, left the pier on June 24th 1981.

January 22nd

1912: The *Hull Daily Mail* printed a photograph of the stranded RMS *Bayardo* on this date. Built just the previous year, by Earls of Hull for the Wilson Line, she ran aground just off Alexandra Dock on January 21st, whilst returning from Gothenburg on her thirteenth voyage. The caption accompanying the photograph stated how the ship had run aground on the Middle Sand in the Humber and it was feared her back was broken. She was pictured a few more times in the paper, being aided by a lighter and tugs, until being declared a total loss.

The same paper also ran a story on this date entitled 'The Boy and his Mouth' about schoolboy Robert Wilson, who apparently made a bet that he had a larger mouth than any of his friends. As proof he inserted a billiard ball between his jaws, which got stuck, and it took two hours and three doctors to remove it. Poor Robert lost five front teeth for his daring wager!

JANUARY 23RD

1790: World-renowned ship HMS *Bounty*, known for its infamous mutiny, was burned on this date. Originally known as *Bethia*, the ship was built in Blaydes shipyard in Hull in 1784. It was used as a coal transporter until it was bought by the Royal Navy for £2,600 and refitted in 1787. It was sent to the South Seas under the command of Lieutenant William Bligh to collect breadfruit plants. The idea was to try and grow the plant in the West Indies, where it would be a cheap source of food for slaves working on the sugar plantations. It was an arduous ten-month voyage to Tahiti, the cramped crew of forty living in an area that usually housed fifteen. Some say it was the contrast between these living conditions and the five months of freedom, living on land and gathering plants in Tahiti, that led to the mutiny on the journey home. William and those loyal to him were set adrift in the open oceans whilst the mutineers took charge of the *Bounty* and settled in the Pitcairn Islands, where they burned the boat to avoid detection. That area is now known as Bounty Bay and parts of the famous wreck can still be found there.

JANUARY 24TH

1986: On this date the *Hull Daily Mail* ran a story on a legend from the 1800s. The tale concerned Hull's Ha'penny Bridge – otherwise known as South Bridge – opened in the 1860s as a toll bridge, presumably the fee being a ha'penny. The bridge was built to give better access to the newly built Victoria Dock, as it was easier than the ferry system used by workers to reach the dock. The newspaper stated that the ghost of a girl apparently haunted the bridge. Hull girl Louise was abandoned by her lover, Robert D'Onston, for a rich heiress. He is said to have finished their affair on the bridge at midnight one night in August 1867, but Louise made him promise that, alive or dead, they would meet there again in one year's time. Robert kept his promise but when he arrived at the bridge one year later he was greeted by the ghost of his former lover, pacing the bridge. The newspaper reported that the bridge disappeared from records during the war and no one seems to know quite what happened either to the bridge or the ghost of poor broken-hearted Louise.

JANUARY 25TH

2008: Tracy Seaward was born in Hull and attended Wolfreton School, followed by Hull College. She then went on to study film and cultural studies at Leeds, forging a successful career thereafter as a well-known film producer. Considered as one of the film industry's most respected producers, Tracy has worked on a number of acclaimed films including *Dirty Pretty Things*, which was nominated for the 2003 European Film Award and the 2003 Alexander Korda Award for Best British Film. She produced *ExistenZ* (1999), *The Good Thief* (2002), *The Constant Gardener* (2005), *War Horse* (2011) and *The Queen*, which was awarded the BAFTA Award for Best Film in 2007. Tracy was also trusted with the honour of being the producer of the Summer Olympics Opening Ceremony in London 2012. On January 25th 2008, she was awarded an honorary degree from the University of Hull in recognition of her work. This also cemented the university's reputation as one of the country's premier universities for drama and film studies. It was the first university in the world to launch a Master's Degree in British Cinema in 2007.

JANUARY 26TH

1968: The *Kingston Peridot* was the second Hull trawler to be lost during the triple Hull trawler tragedy of 1968, news of her loss reaching the city just as the realisation of the *St Romanus'* demise was dawning. *Kingston Peridot* set sail on January 10th – the same date as the *St Romanus* – and, like her, was lost without trace, taking the crew of twenty with her. The *Kingston Peridot* was in contact with her sister ship, the *Kingston Sardius*, who received information on the morning of January 26th that *Kingston Peridot* was to try and head east, closer towards her because of the severe gales which had increased to Force 9, causing a serious build up of ice. This, however, would not be possible until the crew had spent time de-icing the ship. Despite repeated calls from *Kingston Sardius* over the next twenty-four hours, the *Kingston Peridot* was never heard of again.

A full-scale alert and search followed but nothing was found. The ship had vanished. One of her life rafts washed ashore on January 29th and on January 30th Hull citizens were made aware of her loss. An official inquiry deduced that the most likely explanation was that *Kingston Peridot* had capsized on January 26th, or even January 27th, due to severe icing up in the terrible weather conditions.

JANUARY 27TH

1990: On this date The Christians' album entitled *Colour* entered the charts at No.1. The Christians were a band formed by Hull-born musician Henry Priestman. When quizzed about the name of their band, which at first seems overtly religious, it became clear that the name was inevitable, as the other band members were brothers whose surname was Christian – the same as Henry's middle name! Henry wrote the songs but also played guitar, keyboard and accordion, as well as performing some backing vocals. Their band sold over 3 million albums for the Island record label and their debut LP created five UK top 30 singles and became the Island's all-time biggest selling debut album, with UK sales alone exceeding 1 million copies. Henry said that the band had a sponsorship deal with Cheetah who, in the early '90s, at the height of their success, donated various drum machines, synths and mother keyboards to them. Cheetah were involved with developing a hard-disc recording system and The Christians were asked in 1991 to help demonstrate this revolutionary new product on BBC TV's peak hour programme *Tomorrow's World*. Henry has had a full and varied career and he has been used as a session musician by various top names.

JANUARY 28TH

1904: The *Hull Daily News* reported the sad story of the loss of two Trinity House boys on this date. H.S. Woodroffe, aged sixteen, and R. Richardson, aged fourteen, were both apprentices on board the *Routenburn*, a four-masted ship bound for San Francisco. The paper reported that:

> The *Routenburn* was only three days out, when she encountered a fierce gale. Tremendous seas boarded the iron ship, and washed the decks fore and aft. Woodroffe was caught and swept through one of the portholes into the surf and drowned. No one for the moment appears to have been aware of the loss of the lad. Later the weather developed into a hurricane. Immense volumes of water leaped on board, and Richardson was washed overboard. The crew raised the alarm, and a line and life-buoy were secured and thrown to the drowning young fellow. He clutched the line and was dragged through the sea safely until he was alongside of the ship's side. They were hauling him on board when, from sheer exhaustion, he dropped the rope and was drowned. Both lads were well conducted, and most popular with all the crew. Their untimely end cast a gloom over the entire ship.

JANUARY 29TH

1883: On this date the SS *Lord Cardigan*, one of numerous ships built at Martin Samuelson's shipyard in Hull, was lost at sea. The SS *Lord Cardigan* was built and launched in the first year of the shipyard's business, named after the commander of the Light Brigade in the Crimean War in 1854. Martin set up his shipyard in 1849, which eventually covered 12 acres and forever after the area has been known locally as Sammy's Point. The *Hull Free Press* described Martin as a man full of energy, 'who bowled along like an express train'. One of the highlights of his career was in 1863, when he launched four vessels from his shipyard, drawing thousands of spectators to watch the spectacle. Martin was an honourable man and was both Mayor and Alderman of Hull in his time. In the first ten years of his business he built ninety-five vessels, mostly steamers, and it is said by 1863 'the firm built a larger number of vessels than any other firm in the kingdom'. The land was subsequently bought by a succession of owners, all in the ship business, and was then used by the Humber Conservancy as a buoy depot, but was abandoned in the 1980s. The Deep aquarium now stands on the site.

JANUARY 30TH

2009: The *Hull Daily Mail* interviewed Keith Herd on this date. Keith was responsible for creating Hull's first recording studio, Fairview Studios, in the 1960s, before even Leeds or Sheffield had one. It became a real success and recorded such bands as The Housemartins, Def Leppard, Shed Seven and guitarist Mick Ronson. He also recorded Hull's first ever girlband Mandy and the Girlfriends. Mandy began her career aged just thirteen, later forming Mandy and the Girlfriends with four others. They began to practise in Mandy's garden shed and as news of them spread, the novelty of an all-girl band ensured them various gigs around Hull. Their fame became more widespread and they received invitations from London. On their first gig there they supported The Animals. In 1967, they were asked to perform a tour of US air bases in Germany, which the girls accepted. They became such a hit that they recorded an LP of covers for the men to listen to after their departure. When Keith, aged seventy-two, released a double CD of some of Fairview's early recordings, Mandy and the Girlfriends opened it with the first two tracks.

January 31st

1952: On this date the Hull-based healthcare firm Seven Seas Ltd was founded. The company explained that cod liver oil had a long history as a popular folk medicine among Nordic and Scottish fishermen. In the eighteenth century, scientific research apparently endorsed its reputation as it was conclusively demonstrated that cod liver oil could help to fight the effects of malnutrition. It quickly became accepted by the medical profession as a mainstay in combating the diseases of poverty. By the early twentieth century, cod liver oil was a vital tool in the battle against the crippling bone disease rickets, after it was discovered that it was a rich source of bone-building vitamin D, vitamin A and polyunsaturated fats. A consortium of East Yorkshire trawler owners invested in the commercial production and by 1935 they launched their brand Seven Seas. From then on the company went from strength to strength, being especially sought-after during the Second World War rationings and again with the discovery that cod liver oil was a rich source of Omega-3 nutrients, an important discovery in the treatment of heart conditions. The company was recognised the world over and more than 250 people were employed at the Hull branch, until its closure in 2012.

FEBRUARY IST

1902: This was the date that seventy-eight-year-old Anne Todd died. The unfortunate lady was almost beaten to death by two intruders who broke into her Cottingham home in February of the previous year, but she survived until nearly a year later. Apparently, the law states that if a victim dies of their injuries within a year of their attack, it is classed as murder. Her injuries were most severe but she did manage to tell police that her attackers had been a man and a woman. After that her memory failed, which was a shame as the intruders left Anne's purse, containing £8, untouched, leaving a large question mark over the motive.

— ◆ —

1960: On this date the countryside magazine, *Dalesman*, attempted to explain that aged ditty connected with Hull; *From Hell, Hull, and Halifax, Good Lord, deliver us*. Dating back as far as the 1600s and named the Beggar's Litany, it is said to be a thief's plea to be spared the harsh punishment these three places all offered. In Hull, criminals were hanged and sometimes tied to gallows in the Humber Estuary at low tide and left to drown as the sea returned, and Halifax had a device to behead any thief who stole anything to the value of more than 13p!

FEBRUARY 2ND

1911: At a mass meeting of railwaymen on this date, it was decided that a strike was to be called on the fourth of the month. Like other groups of transport workers, many railwaymen worked in poor conditions, receiving low wages and being involved in high-risk occupations. The Board of Trade reported in October 1903 that long periods of duty, up to and exceeding eighteen hours, were still common. Unionisation was considered to be synonymous with insubordination. By 1911, the unions claimed that employers constantly refused to recognise the voices of the union at negotiations. This particular strike in February was called in support of six fish porters and four casual workers at Paragon Station, who had been dismissed over wage disagreements. There was also strong resentment for the increasing substitution of boys for adult male labour in fish-portering. The strikes meant that a general stoppage on the railway system would take place. Initially, on the Friday night goods and passenger traffic was kept running but as men came off their shifts they joined the strike, until both skilled and unskilled workers were picketing side by side. The strike lasted three days, ending with the promise that the points at issue would be addressed at the next conciliation meeting.

FEBRUARY 3RD

1999: Charles Bronson, known as Britain's most disruptive prisoner, took a hostage in Hull Prison on this date after hearing that his grandmother had died. Friends postulate that Charles was distressed because he had missed his father's funeral and felt he had let his mother down by not being present. Phil Danielson was taking a tutorial in the prison when Bronson burst in and took him hostage at knife-point for forty-three hours. It is said that during the ordeal, Charles carried a makeshift spear and tied a leather skipping rope round the neck of Mr Danielson. However, this was not the first time that Bronson was involved in a jail hostage-taking. Charles was originally given seven years for armed robbery in 1974 but stayed in prison – spending twenty-two years in solitary confinement – due to repeated attacks on prison staff. Mr Danielson was awarded £65,000 compensation from the Home Office and Bronson was given a further life sentence.

February 4th

1988: The *Hull Daily Mail* published an article on this date to commemorate the twenty-year anniversary of Hull's triple trawler tragedy, where nearly sixty fishermen were lost. This terrible disaster sent shockwaves through Hull and the wives of Hessle Road's fishing community rose up in protest, as explained in the article. One woman in particular, Lillian Bilocca, or 'Big Lil', fought tirelessly to make working conditions safer for fishermen, becoming a local folk hero and known county-wide. Her father, husband and son had all worked at sea and her campaigning gained immense support. Between 1948 and 1964, over 750 fishermen died at sea. A trawlerman was said to be two and a half times more likely to lose his life at work than a miner. The triple trawler tragedy was the final straw and Big Lil and the headscarf campaigners took a 10,000 signature petition down to London for a meeting with the Prime Minister. New safety measures were agreed upon, such as keeping vessels away from Iceland in extreme weather, tighter regulations on reporting procedures and making it compulsory for every trawler to have a full-time radio operator. In recognition of her achievements, a plaque was placed down Hessle Road, reading 'To Lillian Bilocca and the Women of Hessle Road'.

FEBRUARY 5TH

1968: 'I am going over. Give my love and the crew's love to the wives and families.' This was the final message from the stricken trawler *Ross Cleveland*, broadcast by skipper Phil Gay in the early hours of February 5th. The weather had deteriorated alarmingly and the trawler was attempting to shelter in Isafjord, Iceland, but it was crowded with vessels and the *Ross Cleveland* had to remain in the main fjord. The only contact ships had with each other was by radar. Hurricanes and snow blizzards had obliterated visibility. Harry Eddom, the first mate, had the job of chipping ice from the radar of the *Ross Cleveland* to keep it working. For his survival on deck in these conditions, Eddom wore a waterproof duck suit over his clothes. Gradually being buffeted towards rocks on the eastern side, it was decided to turn the trawler westwards. As the ship turned, a huge wave sent her onto port side and she could not right herself. Waves 40ft high continued to batter her and she filled with water. Eddom managed to release a life raft and two other crewmen reached it. They were the only survivors from a crew of twenty: the ship vanished. Eddom survived, probably because of his waterproof clothing, and was washed ashore and found on February 6th by a young farm lad. His two shipmates died of hypothermia.

FEBRUARY 6TH

1901: William Bernard Traynor was born in Hull in 1870. His family lived on Moxon Street and he went to Pryme Street School. In November 1888, William joined the Second Battalion West Yorkshire Regiment, in which he served in India and South Africa. It was on this date, whilst serving in South Africa, that he was involved in an act of bravery which saw him receive the Victoria Cross. William, then aged thirty, and his regiment came under intense fire during the night. The casualties were heavy and, seeing a fellow soldier wounded, William jumped out of a trench and ran for the man, under concentrated fire. Whilst trying to reach him William was shot in the thigh and took a splinter in his chest. He could not carry the injured man alone so he called for assistance. Lance-Corporal Lintott came to help and they all managed to get to safety. It is said that despite his own injuries, William remained on duty and was most cheerful in encouraging his men. William's injuries had him sent home, much to his wife's relief, and as he could not get to London to receive his reward from the King, he instead made it to York, where Colonel Edward Stevenson-Browne presented it to him.

FEBRUARY 7TH

1979: On this day, Hull lass Gloria Bielby disappeared. It was never discovered what happened to this girl, who worked at Reckitt and Colman, but her family and friends all maintained that she was not the sort to just run off without a word. She had separated from her butcher husband and was rumoured to have a salesman boyfriend, Mike Walker. Neighbours reported seeing her loading cases into a red Ford Escort late in the morning on the day she vanished. Some say they saw a man known as 'Dapper Dan' pick her up from her house frequently, so suspicion naturally fell upon him. Her jealous husband also had motive and, according to some, he minced the poor woman up at his butcher's shop! Two bodies were found around the time, one in the watercourse in Holderness, the other on the North York Moors, but neither of these turned out to be Gloria. Her disappearance remains a mystery.

FEBRUARY 8TH

1974: The trawler *Gaul* was launched in 1972 and eighteen months later was lost at sea, on February 8th 1974. As no distress signal was received, a search was not precipitated until February 10th, after two failures to report in. The thirty-six crewmen were lost and until a lifebuoy was washed up three months later, no trace of the ship was uncovered. For such a modern fishing vessel, the loss was difficult to comprehend and the fishing community harboured suspicions of conspiracy and espionage, alleging that she could have been sunk or captured by the Soviet Union. The Formal Inquiry of 1974 decided heavy seas had capsized the ship, but in 1975 a Norwegian trawler reported snagging her nets underwater near where the *Gaul* had gone missing. In 1997 the wreck was found at this spot. DNA tests on human remains established that they came from the *Gaul*'s crew. In 2004, a new inquiry found that some chutes and hatches left open on the *Gaul* had accentuated the effect of the heavy seas and as the ship had attempted an emergency turn, the surge of water had compromised stability, causing her to capsize. Many relatives, however, still believe this is not the whole truth of the tragedy and suspect politics and espionage had a part to play. It was the worst peacetime loss of life in the UK fishing fleet.

FEBRUARY 9TH

1904: On this date the *Hull Daily News* reported that the retailers of Hull were raising the price of flour by 1*d* per stone. 'We ought to have gone up three or four weeks ago,' a leading tradesman apparently told the paper. The reason was due to the millers having advanced the price to the retailers by 1*s* per 20-stone sack. 'That brought the price to 24*s*, and we were selling it at 25*s* ... we were bound to increase the price to our customers,' the source explained. He also said that the wet weather had spoiled the English crop that year and so the millers had to rely on foreign wheat. 'Millers,' he said, 'are inundated with speculative inquiries, and they have no doubt increased the price to protect themselves.'

In the same paper there was mention of a body found in Hull's Queen's Dock the previous morning. The man had been identified as Thomas Merrycroft, and a Dr Hemmans believed he had been in the water between five and six weeks. After some deliberation, the jury returned the verdict that Thomas had drowned.

FEBRUARY 10TH

2001: The *Guardian* newspaper printed an article on this date, interviewing the four creators of *The League of Gentlemen*. Reece Shearsmith, one of the main writers and actors, was born in Hull in 1969. At school he showed great aptitude for drawing, but instead of moving on to the planned graphic arts course, he had a last minute change of heart and went on to do a drama degree at Bretton Hall College. It was here he met the three other members and they achieved their first big break with a show at the Edinburgh Festival in 1996. By 1999, BBC2 had commissioned their comedy-drama and *The League of Gentlemen* appeared on television. Classed as a strange and sinister programme, the four wanted to capture the oddities we all occasionally exhibit: 'Royston Vasey and its idiosyncratic inhabitants have caught the strangeness of Britain – its insularity, hypocrisies and freakishness – in gloriously minute detail.' Their odd humour obviously stirs something in us all, as *The League* won the Sony Silver Award for their radio show, *On The Town with The League of Gentlemen*, as well as the Perrier, a Royal Television Society Award, the Golden Rose of Montreux in 1999, and a Bafta for Best Comedy in 2000. The video of *The League's* first series sold some 100,000 copies.

FEBRUARY 11TH

2006: On this date indie rock band the Red Guitars performed in a single-show reunion at the Winterlude Festival in Hull. Starting from humble beginnings the lead singer, Jerry Kidd, and lead guitarist Hallam Lewis became friends whilst attending a Community Arts Programme in Hull in 1979. Their first band was called Carnage but changed to The Czechs when Mark Douglas joined. Their style then was an eastern European reggae sound, but after Mark left and others joined, they became the Red Guitars, concentrating more on blues, punk and folk music. The band favoured quite an anti-corporate ideology, reflected in their songs and the left-wing benefit shows at which they performed. They had a fairly small but loyal national fan base and their third single, 'Marimba Jive', reached No.1 in the UK Indie Chart in 1984. The band also produced their own record label, Self Drive Records, but the added pressure of this was too much for Jerry, who left in 1984. The others carried on for a couple more years, with a new vocalist, but finally disbanded in 1986 until their one-off reunion in 2006.

FEBRUARY 12TH

1724: On this date Hull poet William Mason, described by Coleridge as 'the most considerable Yorkshire poet since Marvell', was born. In 1785, he was William Pitt the Younger's choice to succeed William Whitehead as Poet Laureate, but he refused the honour. Obviously talented, he was also a busy man. In 1754, he was ordained at St Margaret's Church, Westminster, and in 1765 he married Mary Sherman, who sadly died two years later. He was a royal chaplain between 1757 and 1572 and Precentor of York Minster from 1762. He published a book on the poems of his friend Thomas Gray and composed his epitaph after Gray's death. His famous work was *The English Garden* and he was also known as a garden designer. At Nuneham Courtenay in Oxfordshire he designed a walled garden for Lord Harcourt. William has a memorial in Poets' Corner in Westminster Abbey. The mural monument of white marble shows a mourning woman, personifying Poetry, leaning on a profile portrait medallion which is supported on a low pedestal decorated with a lyre, mask and chaplets. The Latin inscription was written by William's friend Bishop Richard Hurd and, translated, reads: 'Sacred to William Mason, poet, master of arts, the best of men, cultivated, chaste and pious. Died 7 April 1797 aged 72.'

FEBRUARY 13TH

1944: Hull-born Flight Engineer John Pulford died in a tragic flying accident on this date. As a youngster John was apprenticed at the Paragon Motor Company, on Anlaby Road, but when war broke out he left to join the RAF and ended up on one of the most famous British missions, that of Guy Gibson's 106 Squadron, the Dambusters. The story of how that brave crew in their AJ-G Lancaster bomber completed their mission to bomb the Mohne and Eder Dams is world famous. John joined the 617 Squadron a year later, on a mission to bomb the Antheor Viaduct in Italy. The operation was a success and the men landed safely back in Sussex to be debriefed, but tragedy struck on the short trip back to Woodhall Spa on February 13th. A thick fog descended, creating poor visibility, and the aircraft crashed into a hillside in Upwaltham on the Sussex Downs. Sixty-five years on, in 2009, the people of the small hamlet of Upwaltham raised £10,500 for a memorial for these men plus those from an American aircraft, which crashed there in 1945. 'These young men were not just the faceless casualties of conflict,' said one resident. 'We shall remember them.' John and his fellows were heroes who met a heartbreaking end.

FEBRUARY 14TH

1927: This date saw the worst railway crash in Hull's history, when twelve passengers were killed and another twenty-four seriously injured. The disaster struck when the 08.22 Withernsea to Hull train collided head-on with the 09.05 Hull to Scarborough train. An inquiry found that one of the signalmen had pulled the wrong lever, intending to set the points for the incoming train but instead setting the points ahead of the Scarborough one. Locking bars should have prevented these points from being changed. Unfortunately, one of the other signalmen was setting different signals, and in contravention of the rules, this was done whilst the train was still passing. A combination of these two failings led to the disaster. The driver of the Scarborough train, realising he was on the wrong line, had brought his own train almost to a standstill. However, the Withernsea train driver, with his view obscured by the Argyle Street Bridge and still travelling at about 15mph, could not avoid the catastrophe that ensued. Having heard the noise of the impact, nursing sisters and doctors arrived from the Victoria Hospital for Sick Children in Park Street, as well as staff from what was then the Hull Institution Hospital, today's Hull Royal Infirmary. They were later joined by members of the St John's Ambulance Brigade and staff from the Hull Royal Infirmary, then situated in the city centre. Eighty-five years later, in 2012, a new plaque was unveiled to remember those who died.

FEBRUARY 15TH

1871: Dr Frank C. Eve is one of Hull's forgotten heroes. Born on this date, he went on to pursue a career in medicine, working at Cambridge and Leeds before settling in Hull. He was a physician at Hull Royal Infirmary from 1906 to 1952 and became famous for his newly devised method of respiration, which lifesavers now acknowledge as a highly valuable technique in keeping victims breathing indefinitely. His idea was a simple yet effective method of tilting the sufferer up and down in a see-saw type action, which allowed the diaphragm to move up and down, helping air to pass in and out of the lungs. No machinery was required so the system was ideal in emergency situations, of which Frank no doubt had his share, throughout the war years. His procedure has now been adopted and refined, using machines to perform the same task, and this equipment can be found in every intensive care unit and operating theatre in the world. Frank's work on artificial respiration was acknowledged in the *London Times* newspaper, where it stated he lived to the grand old age of eighty-one.

FEBRUARY 16TH

1915: Initially launched in September 1914, HM Submarine *E13* was sent to patrol around the Maas Lightvessel on this date. This was the start of the submarine's course of bad luck. When she arrived at this station, the weather was so poor that she had to turn home, but was reported as a hostile submarine on the way back! Surviving this situation she was later involved in battle with Zeppelin *L9*, as well as being sighted by a German fleet. Enduring all this she sailed on, in August 1915, to the Baltic, where her magnetic compass failed and she ran aground off Saltholm. Here she was fired upon by a German destroyer, despite Danish intervention, and tragically fifteen of the *E13*'s crew were killed, the news causing worldwide outrage and condemnation. SS *Vidar* transported the bodies back to Hull, where thousands lined the streets for one of the most remembered funeral processions in the city. The people of Helsingor also showed their respect to the dead. Three Danish submarines stood out from the harbour and lay in line while their crews stood out on parade. All buildings on the harbour and at Kronborg Castle dipped their flags to half-mast as the *Vidar* passed by. The crews on submarines and torpedo boats stood with their heads uncovered, and the sentries presented arms. In Hull many wreaths had been sent, including one from the Danish colony in London which contained over 800 carnations. Queen Alexandra sent fourteen magnificent wreaths of white arum lilies.

FEBRUARY 17TH

1937: On this date Hull firm Smith & Nephew rose to become an associated limited company after starting life back in 1856, when Thomas Smith opened his first shop in Whitefriargate, Hull. A trained pharmacist, Thomas' shop sold wholesale bandages and related material, and, taking advantage of his position near the docks, he began to supply hospitals with cod liver oil, respected for its therapeutic worth in cases of rickets, tuberculosis and rheumatism, as vitamins had not then been identified. A few months before Thomas died, his nephew became a partner and the company went from strength to strength, especially during the war years, when bandages were very much in demand. In addition, legislation in the early 1920s, which stipulated that miners and factory workers have access to first aid kits in the workplace, offered Smith & Nephew a natural opportunity. The firm is now described as a multinational medical equipment company, being the world's second-largest producer of advanced wound management products. At one point they had almost 11,000 employees and a presence in more than ninety countries.

FEBRUARY 18TH

1973: On this day Maureen Lipman married Jack Morris Rosenthal, a producer, director and playwright who sadly died of cancer in 2004. Maureen was born into a Jewish family in Hull on May 10th 1946. Her mother encouraged her gift for drama and Maureen attended Newland High School, where she took the lead in all school productions. She went on to study at the London Academy of Music and Dramatic Art. Always a prolific worker, her career has spanned four decades and she has appeared in films, TV and the stage, including several West End productions.

Her film career began in 1967 with her appearance as Sylvie in *Up the Junction* and in 1979 she famously starred on TV as Jane Lucas in the ITV comedy series *Agony*. Her marriage lasted thirty years until her husband's death and they had two children, son Adam and daughter Amy, who is a playwright herself and wrote *Sitting Pretty*, in which her mother starred in 2001 at the Nuffield Theatre, Southampton. In 1999, Maureen received a CBE from the Queen. She supports the work of The Burma Campaign UK and speaks out strongly about human rights issues there. Despite her long and varied career, she is still remembered by many people for her BT adverts, in which she appeared as Beattie with the famous catchphrase, 'You got an ology?'

FEBRUARY 19TH

1801: Sir Samuel Standidge died on this date, aged seventy-six. Born in Bridlington, he moved to Hull at a young age, driven by his love of the sea and his search for adventure and fortune. By nineteen he was mate and later master of vessels, making voyages to North America. He certainly found adventure on his travels, being captured by privateers off Hispaniola in 1744 and nearly shipwrecked on the Nantucket coast in 1749. He already had a good knowledge of trading, but it was here he saw how profitable whaling could be. Britain had lost interest in the trade by the 1660s, but Samuel believed wealth could be found. The government encouraged the idea, offering 20s per ton, which rose to 40s in 1740, for ships fitted out for whaling, as they desired more skilled seamen, important to the Royal Navy in wartime. Samuel sent numerous ships to Greenland, which came back with both whales and seal skins. He was the first man in Britain to have seal skins tanned instead of thrown overboard, with which he had shoes made. With his wealth he owned a 130-acre farm in Preston and a 200-acre property at Thorngumbald, plus a house in High Street. He is remembered as one of the founding fathers of the Hull whaling trade, being knighted by George III, and holding the offices of Sheriff, Mayor of Hull, and Master Warden of Trinity House during his lifetime.

FEBRUARY 20TH

1967: The headline of an article in the *Hull Daily Mail* on this date declared, 'Man snatches children from blazing Hull home'. Pregnant mother-of-four Mrs Rustill, taking her youngest, had gone to sit with a neighbour until her taxi driver husband returned from work at midnight, as she had been frightened by a fused light at home. When Mr Rustill returned home he found his living room ablaze and dashed across the road to his friend's house to call the fire brigade. While he did this, his friend, Mr Thornton rushed to the house and smashed the kitchen window to get in, running up the stairs, waking the five-, four- and three-year-old boys and carrying them to safety. 'The house was full of smoke,' he later explained, 'it was dark and I had to feel my way upstairs. The children were sleeping in the front bedroom – directly above the fire.' Mr Rustill had recently changed his shift pattern from all night to finish around midnight, which was lucky, as had he been away all night Mrs Rustill may have gone to bed and the whole family could have died in the fire!

FEBRUARY 21ST

2001: Born in Hull in 1926, 1950s crooner Adrian Hill, known by his stage name Ronnie Hilton, died on this date. Ronnie is said to have left school aged fourteen and went to work in an aircraft factory in the early years of the war. He was eventually called up to fight and when he was demobbed in 1947 he moved to Leeds, working in a sewing machine factory. He had always had a passion for singing and it was during this time in Leeds that he performed in the evenings with the Johnny Addlestone band. It was apparently here that he was talent spotted by HMV's A&R manager, Walter Ridley. He approached Ronnie and persuaded him that he had real talent and that if he perhaps changed his name and had an operation to reconstruct his hare lip he could offer him a recording contract. Ronnie accepted and went on to become one of Britain's most popular romantic crooners of the time. During his career he made hundreds of recordings and had more than twenty hits, his signature tune being May 1954's No.1, 'No Other Love'. Another popular favourite of his was 'A Windmill in Old Amsterdam'. In 1989, Ronnie was awarded a gold medal for services to popular music from the British Academy of Song Composers and Authors. He was also a regular on BBC radio programmes and pantomimes, especially when the rock 'n' roll era began.

February 22nd

1542: The foundations for the Hull Castle and the Blockhouses were laid on this date, in accordance with the orders of Henry VIII, who wished for Hull's fortifications to be made 'mighty strong'. Henry's persecution of Catholics affected the whole country and the Blockhouses at Hull saw many Catholics tortured, starved, beaten and robbed for their faith. There were three great religious institutions in Hull that were completely destroyed on the orders of the king. The area of the Blackfriary, the Whitefriary and the Carthusian Priory had existed for more than three centuries before this: all we are left with today are street names to remember them by. It was the very stones and mortar of the Blessed Virgin of Carmel, the Carthusian Priory and the Saint Augustine friary that were used to build the dungeons and torture chambers of the Castle and Blockhouses. It has been suggested that Henry spent £23,155 17s 5d on the construction of the Castle, the Blockhouses, the walls, the North Bridge and a canal for fresh water. The Castle and Blockhouses were intended as gun platforms to return fire at any ships firing from the Humber and were said to have been tremendous fortifications for their time. The aquarium, The Deep, now stands on the site.

FEBRUARY 23RD

1791: On this date, the *Hull Packet* newspaper included a mention of two dogs which were apparently stolen from the stable of one Mrs Hales:

> STOLEN – A Black and White greyhound dog, which answers to the name of Snail; also a Red and White greyhound bitch, which answers to the name of Whimsey. Whoever will give information so that they may be had again, shall be handsomely rewarded.

Whether or not the dogs were returned is unknown.

———◆———

2010: On this date the *Hull Daily Mail* reported a story concerning a spooky photograph taken at the site of Anlaby Primary School. John Fores, who was involved in the demolition of the school building, took the photograph, in which the ghostly image of a young boy aged around eight, with short hair and wearing a dark top, appears, looking into the camera. He told the newspaper, 'I took the pictures just after noon. I took a few and at the time didn't notice anything. When I put the pictures on the computer and I saw the figure, the hairs on the back of my neck stuck up.' The school was built in 1936 and caretaker Gordon Bradshaw said it had a reputation for being haunted. The photograph in question caused much controversy over its legitimacy, some claiming the boy must have been an ex-pupil revisiting to watch the destruction of his school.

FEBRUARY 24TH

1941: Buried in Hull on this date, John Cunningham was one of the brave soldiers from the First World War who received the Victoria Cross for his heroism during action. The Victoria Cross is the highest and most prestigious award for gallantry in the face of the enemy that can be awarded to British and Commonwealth forces. John was just nineteen and a private in the Hull Sportsman's Pals Battalion, the East Yorkshire Regiment, when on November 13th 1916, his division was sent on a treacherous mission into enemy trenches. Their bombing section was ordered to a German communication trench, but was met with heavy opposition and all but John were wounded or killed. After collecting all the bombs from his fellow soldiers, John single-handedly went on, using them all up, and even returned a second time for more bombs. Apparently this time he was met by ten Germans but somehow managed to kill all of them and carry on to clear the trench. Fortunately, this courageous and clever young man made it home alive and married Eva Harrison in Hull, where they settled and had two children. He died relatively young, aged just forty-three, but at least he lived longer than his companions on that fateful mission.

FEBRUARY 25TH

1971: At 12.30 p.m. on this day Hull's BBC Radio Humberside was officially opened. The launch took place from the bridge of the British trawler fleet's mother ship, the *Miranda*, stationed more than 1,000 miles away in Reykjavik, Iceland. The station covered the largest geographical area of any station in the BBC local radio network, including North Lincolnshire, the East Riding of Yorkshire and the City of Hull. The Hull studios were situated above a post office on Chapel Street, with transmissions from the 250ft-tall mast at High Hunsley. Dorothea Desforges recounts one caller ringing into the helpdesk line one time to tell the presenter that a seagull had stolen his false teeth from the garden chair next to him whilst he had been sitting out. He requested that if anyone along the Hedon Road area found a bottom set of dentures to please return them to him.

There was originally a Hull station, opening on August 15th 1924 at Bishop Lane, with a transmitter mounted on a high building in the Wincomlee industrial zone. This local programming shrunk to merely presenting the news and eventually finished in 1928. It was another forty years before BBC Radio Humberside was launched.

FEBRUARY 26TH

1847: On this date the *Hull Advertiser* reported a tragic accident which occurred near Hessle on the Hull and Selby railway. The incident happened not 5 miles out of Hull station, on a dark, cold evening. It was a large heavy train, with mail coaches, passenger coaches and fish wagons. It needed two engines to pull it, the *Kingston* and the *Exley*. As the train picked up speed, it rounded a slight curve in the line and somehow slid off the rails. A man called John Spicer was thrown clear of the crash, suffering only minor injuries, so he was able to help rescue others at the terrible scene. He was later called upon as a witness in court to describe what had occurred. He believed it was the speed of the train that caused the derailment, when it came to the curve too fast. An inquiry later found that the track on that part of the line was of weak construction and it was lifted and replaced with a heavier gauge. Unfortunately the inquiry was too late to stop the accident, or to save the lives of the two men, James Brown and George Waring, who died in the crash.

FEBRUARY 27TH

2008: Arco is one of Hull's largest employers, with over 500 people employed in its Waverley Street Head Office. The firm was established in 1884 and originally the company made tennis balls for the Wimbledon tournament. Now it specialises in supplying safety clothing and has forty branches across the country. The company moved from London to Hull in 1890 because of the shipping trade and Thomas Martin became Managing Director in 1907, the business staying in the family ever since. The company reached its 125th anniversary in 2009 and, looking back, it can be seen that it has had a long and loyal customer base. In May 1941, an enemy bomb destroyed all of the company's sales records, which could have easily indicated the end, but apparently not one customer failed to settle their accounts. In 2003, on the retirement of the previous family team, Jo Martin took over as Joint Managing Director, the fourth generation of the Martin family to lead the company, but tragedy struck on February 27th 2008, when she died, aged just thirty-nine, after a prolonged and dignified battle with breast cancer. The Jo Martin Cancer Care Trust was established following Jo's death and has been supported by a number of fundraising initiatives by Arco as well as by donations from suppliers and customers.

FEBRUARY 28TH

1865: On this date the *Eastern Morning News* reported a 'shocking accident', which happened to a man employed on Hull's then new West Dock. The man, William Jones, was apparently 'engaged in driving a tip-truck, laden with earth, over the tramway to the embankment on the Humber side of the dock. After liberating the horse, at the extremity of the rails, the man unfortunately stumbled and fell diagonally across the rails. The truck, which was at full speed, passed over him, almost cutting him in two in the body. He was, of course, shockingly mutilated.' The poor man was rushed to the Infirmary, but there was nothing to be done.

The same newspaper gave a detailed account of the last hours of Elizabeth Cogan, who had been assaulted by her husband whilst they were both in a state of drunkenness. A witness said that she had seen the husband, James Clarke, come home in the early hours of the morning and then Elizabeth had come home later on that same evening, with another man. There was arguing and the other man left, but it seems as though James had attacked his wife and she was very ill the next day. The doctor visited, as did several friends, but the woman did not survive.

February 29th

1968: The *Hull Daily Mail* reported on this date that Hull's suffragettes were to make a march through the city centre the next week. This mock march was in celebration of the fiftieth anniversary of the vote being given to women. Even though women are still not viewed as equal to men in many parts of the world, the triumph of women over the age of thirty receiving the vote in Britain in 1918 was a great victory, and then again ten years later, when the age was reduced to twenty-one. Eighty-four-year-old Mrs E. Wilson, one of the original suffragettes, opened the anniversary exhibition and numerous exhibits had been collected to show to the attendees, including a WSPU (Women's Social and Political Union) belt used to fasten a suffragette to railings during protests. Mrs Wilson was apparently one of the organisers in Hull for women's meetings and she was said to have taken part in 'great marches' in London. One of the pioneers of the suffragette movement in Hull was one Mrs Elizabeth Cawthorne. She was apparently so incensed at the injustices to women that she wrote to Ramsey Macdonald asking for a Labour League of Women to be formed in Hull to advance their cause. Her daughter-in-law remembers her talking about it and recalls being shown a photograph of Elizabeth with Ramsey.

MARCH 1ST

1882: Two crew members who had served with twenty-three-year-old Osmond Otto Brand came forward on this date to inform the police that Otto was a murderer. Otto was the skipper aboard a Hull fishing smack, *Rising Sun*, and fourteen-year-old William Papper had been his apprentice. The ship was away for three weeks and when they returned, Otto apparently visited William's parents' house to tell them that William had been swept overboard in a heavy sea, saying he had stopped the ship and searched for the boy but to no avail. William's mother disbelieved Otto, however, but had no evidence of mistreatment until March 1st, when two of the crew came forward to the Hull police and disclosed that Otto had treated the boy with 'the most revolting cruelty'. Otto had apparently taken a dislike to the boy from the off and once on open sea, would regularly beat him with a thick rope. He subjected the poor boy to torture during their short voyage, forcing him to stand on the stern for hours while he threw mud, stones and buckets of cold water at him. He starved the lad, beat him and ducked him in the freezing sea until, eventually, William died, whence Otto threw him overboard and concocted his lie. At court no mercy was shown to the accused and Otto was sentenced to death, the judge stating that the crime was the most atrocious he had ever heard.

MARCH 2ND

1989: Hull's first ever theme bar caused a buzz of news in the *Hull Daily Mail* on this date. Headlined 'Bar puts robots on tap', the newspaper reported how Hull's newly built Jazzbo Brown's was installing tap-dancing robots to 'dazzle the crowds'. Apparently dressed in period costume, the three robots would perform jazz tap-dancing routines, in keeping with the bar's 1930s American theme. Part of a national chain, Hull's Jazzbo Brown's, named after the semi-legendary jazz founder and singer, was the first of twelve of the themed bars scheduled to be opened across the country. Built by Allied Leisure to complement the company's neighbouring thirty-four-lane Megabowl Centre, the paper also boasted that the bar would contain 'a range of period mannequins, a "magic" jazz keyboard played by a pair of ghostly white gloves suspended on invisible wire and a matching drum kit hanging in mid-air'. Alongside these impressive details the decorations would also include a giant replica Dakota DC-3 plane with a video screen mounted on its nose showing old Hollywood films, and giant saxophones pumping out dry ice. Despite these amazing features, Jazzbo's of Hull only lasted a few years.

March 3rd

1866: The *Hull Advertiser* detailed the 'pitiable plight' of the fishing smack, *Regina*, on this date. Her crew apparently arrived at Grimsby on board another smack, having had to abandon their own vessel. The story was that the ship and crew were just north of the Dogger Bank when a gale mounted. They had their lights on, in accordance with the Board of Trade regulations, and despite the strong wind the night was a clear one. However, just before midnight a barque collided with them, apparently inflicting 'such serious injury on the smack as to cause her to sink in a few minutes, the stern of the vessel being, in fact, cut away.' Somehow the barque did not notice the collision and sailed away, much to the horror and dismay of the sinking crew. They only had time to launch their small boat and get clear of the *Regina* before she went down. 'The sea ran so high that every moment they expected their frail barque would have been overwhelmed, and it was only by constant exertion and good seamanship in keeping the boat's head to the wind that they were enabled to keep her afloat.' This was their state for four hours until another smack finally rescued them.

MARCH 4TH

1782: On this date Thomas Ward and John Firbank, dealers in spirituous liquor, bought a freehold property along Dagger Lane with the intention of creating a brewery. This they did, registering the Hull Brewery Company Limited in 1888 and by 1890 they were recorded to having owned 160 licensed houses. The Hull Brewery Company had an excellent reputation for their beers with respect to quality, purity and flavour. Their four varieties of malt ale included the celebrated XXX ale, XXXXBB best bitter, BS stout and Champagne Bitter. The barrelage was said to have increased from 19,400 in 1887 to around 56,000 in 1901, rising just short of 100,000 barrels over the next ten years. As well as owning licensed houses and other breweries, the company expanded so much that new developments were taking place all over the city. One such advancement took place on Silver Street, where a new 214ft 9in-tall chimney was built in 1903. It was a huge construction, the diameter at the base being 18ft 10ins and the top being 10ft 4ins. They say that in a strong wind the top swayed an amazing 2ft from side to side.

MARCH 5TH

1916: On this day, Hull was attacked by two Zeppelin bombers during the First World War. They had apparently been on course for Scotland but strong winds had diverted them to the east coast. Heavy cloud cover meant that the bombers hovered for over an hour waiting for a clear view and then, as Hull citizens watched helplessly, they dropped their load. The majority of the damage was to the city centre on this occasion, killing seventeen people and destroying the glass roof of Paragon Station.

———— • ◆ • ————

2009: This was the date that Her Majesty the Queen, accompanied by the Duke of Edinburgh, visited Hull for the first time in a decade (apart from a brief secret visit in 2008). Arriving on the Royal Train at Hull Paragon Interchange's platform 7, she unveiled a plaque to officially open the newly refurbished Interchange before they were taken to Castle Hill Hospital. Here, Her Majesty unveiled a plaque to officially open the new £67 million Oncology and Haematology Centre, which was named in her honour. Returning to the city centre, they were entertained at the Ferens Art Gallery by dancers and musicians, before meeting some of the people affected by the floods of 2007. Thousands flocked to catch a glimpse of the Queen in Victoria Square.

MARCH 6TH

1883: It was on this terrible date that more than 360 fishermen and boys from east coast ports died, in what was later known as the Great March Gale. This was one of the most appalling gales that ever swept across the Dogger Bank. One old seadog, a man called Ben, remembered the storm: 'During my life as a North Sea smacksman I saw as much wind and weather on the Dogger as most men; but I never saw anything so savage as the Great March Gale. I have known other breezes as bad in some ways, but never one which brought up such a deadly sea as that, and in such a short time did so much mischief and caused such heavy loss of life.' During this deadly storm twenty-three fishing smacks from Hull were lost, with 135 crew members dead. Over seventy other vessels were said to be damaged. Ben explained that 'when a smacksman talks about a gale he means that's something phenomenal took place; in the ordinary way bad weather means to him a breeze but the weather has to be something of a hurricane before he'll call it a gale.' That March gale was always remembered as being the worst and, sad as it was to see four docks filled with battered and damaged craft, it was nothing compared to seeing the streets where nearly every house had orphans and widows.

MARCH 7TH

2007: Paul Sykes, dubbed the hardest man in Britain, died from pneumonia and liver cirrhosis on this date. Although originally a Wakefield man, he spent time in Hull Prison, A wing, and was well known to the Hull police. His adult life was one long journey of being in and out of prison, for alcohol abuse, petty robberies and especially violent crimes. 'I'm not a violent man but I am an expert at violence,' he apparently told the *Independent*. 'I've had an extra ten years for whacking screws and coppers. I've never hit anybody [who] didn't deserve it.' Paul began his boxing career as prisoner 80857 at Her Majesty's Jail, Hull. He was released in 1973 and began boasting he would win the British heavyweight title by a knockout in 1979. He was very able and the *Glasgow Herald* named him Britain's latest heavyweight hope. When asked to say a few words from the ring after winning a fight, he apparently told the cheering audience, 'I'm more used to speaking to visiting magistrates.' Paul was eventually beaten and ended up back inside jail. It was calculated that by 1990, when he was forty-four, he had spent twenty-one years in prison and had been transferred twenty-five times.

MARCH 8TH

1897: Kathleen Mary Margaret Bryant, known as Margot, a doctor's daughter and a Hull girl, was born on this date. As she grew older she became interested in acting and after finding work with the stage chorus line she moved into musical comedies and films. She had the good fortune to work alongside such figures as Fred Astaire, Adam Faith and Oliver Reed. Then, at sixty-three, she secured a role in a new TV drama, *Coronation Street*. This is the role Margot is best known for, playing timid, cat-loving Minnie Caldwell for over fifteen years. Her character was involved in many varied plot lines during these years, such as money problems, a gambling addiction, involvement in a coach crash, being held at gunpoint by her own lodger and, of course, entanglement in romantic storylines. Minnie carried a torch for her old lover, Handel Gartside, and it was this storyline that helped her leave the popular series. In real life Margot's health was declining and – due to the onset of Alzheimer's – when filming her last few episodes she had to read her lines from prompts and hidden scripts. Margot saw her days out in a Manchester nursing home, living into her nineties.

MARCH 9TH

1984: On this day, nine-year-old Christopher Laverick was abducted. Christopher's brother-in-law was looking after the boy on the evening in question when he popped out of the house, along Harpham Grove, east Hull, to buy him some crisps. When he returned the television was missing, and so was Christopher. The hunt went on for two days until eventually a man out walking his dog found Christopher's body, wrapped in a carpet bag in Beverley Beck. The poor lad had been sexually abused and battered to death. It is Humberside Police's longest-running unsolved murder case and the only unsolved child murder. The *Hull Daily Mail* reported that in recent years police believed Christopher's uncle to be responsible; however, they were unable to gather enough evidence to charge him with murdering Christopher before he died from cancer in Hull Prison in 2008, aged sixty-four.

MARCH 10TH

1869: On this date the *Hull and Eastern Counties Herald* announced that the eminent novelist, Charles Dickens, was to give readings in Hull. In his personal letters he is said to have mentioned that he made more than £50 profit at Hull on his first reading and so had returned by popular demand more than once. He stayed at the Royal Station Hotel and performed his favourite extracts to audiences at the Assembly Rooms and later the New Theatre. There is a lovely story of a visit he made to a drapery shop on Whitefriargate, where he bought six pairs of women's silk stockings, almost certainly for Ellen Ternan, his muse, and whilst there got chatting with the sales assistant about the readings. The assistant, unaware he was speaking to Charles Dickens himself, told him what a fan he was but that he did not have tickets for the readings. On his departure, Dickens apparently left the open-mouthed gent a free ticket and the story even goes so far as to say that Dickens looked out for him in the audience and even read out sections that the assistant had mentioned were his favourites! Dickens was apparently due to return to Hull in June 1870, but this was the very month he died.

MARCH 11TH

1592: The little street in Hull's old town named The Land of Green Ginger has aroused curiosity for years. The actual origin of the name is something of a mystery but there are various theories, including the idea that Hull, as a busy port, was bound to house exotic and unusual goods and perhaps ginger was sold in this street at one time. Some do believe it was grown here, which is a possibility with the right conditions. It is said that ginger was first imported into England in 1530. It was a valuable commodity and apparently a favourite of Henry VIII. The street was then known as Old Beverley Street and a Hull merchant, John Monson, is thought to have planted some West Indian ginger at his home, in anticipation of a visit from the king. There is a manuscript, dated March 11th 1592 in John's handwriting, stating that he had 'sett his exotic roots in the Land of Green Ginger,' a name that stuck and supplanted Old Beverley Street. Sources say John was actually included in the royal entourage when the King did visit, so perhaps his ginger was served at the royal table. The name could equally have grown from the Norman word *Ginge* meaning a spring or stream, issuing from a green. There is archaeological evidence which suggests a watercourse ran nearby, or perhaps it was a corruption of a family name in the area.

March 12th

1863: This date was the last recorded use of the armament on Hull's blockhouses, a salute being fired from the citadel on the occasion of the wedding of the then Prince of Wales. The blockhouses and castle, being built in the 1540s on the orders of Henry VIII, were meant to house prisoners and defend the city from hostile ships in the Humber. However, the Crown had to pay £1,000 a year to maintain the Hull fortifications and by 1552 Edward VI had given custody of the castle and blockhouses to the Mayor and Burgesses of Hull instead, wanting rid of the financial burden. The guns remained the property of the Crown and some were removed to Bridlington and Flamborough, the remaining ones being fired from time to time, to hail ships or on ceremonial occasions, such as the above. The castle and blockhouses had originally been built hastily and on marshy ground; thus repairs and maintenance were needed often and were expensive. The site moved through many stages of use over the years but military presence was gradually wound down in the 1840s, Fort Paull being viewed as a better position to defend the Humber. Much of the citadel was demolished in the 1860s and the land drained and put to other uses.

MARCH 13TH

1989: On this date, Alan Lowe issued a plea in the *Hull Daily Mail* for anyone with original photographs or information about the night Jimi Hendrix topped the bill at Hull's former Skyline Ballroom, in March 1967, to come forward. Alan explained that the Hendrix Information Centre was hoping to publish a book on the twentieth anniversary of Jimi's death, containing photographs from as many concerts he played at as possible. During the Hull concert, Jimi was apparently supported by The Family, The Small Four, The Strollers and The Mandrakes and the cost of a ticket was 12s 6d. Alan said that the drummer with the Hendrix cover band, Nine, had asked Jimi to sign his wage packet, to which Jimi's response was, 'What is it?' The Skyline, initially a ballroom dancing venue, was host to a number of famous acts, such as Pink Floyd, The Drifters and The Temptations. Later it became Bailey's nightclub, then Romeo's and Juliet's. The venue had two halls: the main cabaret room that held 1,200 guests seated and 200 more standing, plus a 700-person discotheque next door. Romeo's and Juliet's closed its doors in November 1991.

MARCH 14TH

2002: The headline in the *Guardian* newspaper on this date read, 'Man had sex with a nanny goat'. All the more shocking was that the man, from Hull, performed his act in a field near to some railway lines and at the precise time a full commuter train from Hull to Bridlington stopped at a nearby crossing and got quite an eyeful! Several of the horrified passengers rang 999 but there were also some members of the public passing by, who grappled the man to the ground and held him until the police arrived. The man, a chef, was apparently on his way home from his sister's house. He had lassoed the poor goat around the neck with the belt of his trousers and had assaulted her for over 10 minutes. The goat was reported to have been 'subdued' by the incident and the judge, Michael Mettyear, had some difficulty sentencing the man. He commented, 'I have got to tell you that I'm very sceptical that there is any programme that has been devised at the moment that will help him.' Jailed for six months, the man refused to comment as he left court.

MARCH 15TH

1786: On this date the dead body of William Swan was found in his bed at a lodging house. William was the only surviving male heir of the late Thomas Swan, who had been Mayor and Alderman of the city of Hull. William had apparently been trying, in vain, to lay his hands on his family's estates, worth up to £20,000 per annum, but it appeared that bad luck ran in the family. His grandfather, Richard Swan, had seemingly fallen out with Thomas at a young age and sent him abroad. En route, however, Thomas' ship was wrecked and he was taken by Algerian pirates, who sold him as a slave. He was freed by friars after four years but all too soon was captured again, becoming slave to a planter in South Carolina, where he suffered terribly. He managed to return to England in 1726 but still his father refused to acknowledge him. At least we know he did have a happy period in his life, marrying a girl and settling near Hull, with their son, the above mentioned William. Legend states, however, that he died of a broken heart in 1735. Better to have loved and lost ...?

MARCH 16TH

1941: Actor Roy North was born on this date in Hull, where he attended Hull Grammar School and supported his hometown football club, Hull City. He began acting in Hull's Amateur Dramatic Society in the late 1950s and changed his name from Roy Stathers to Roy North to show his pride in being a northerner. Having acted in various roles, Roy will be best remembered as the sidekick, or straight man, to his double-act partner Basil Brush. *The Basil Brush Show* was an immensely popular children's TV programme, loved by kids and adults alike and featuring many guest celebrities and multi-talented entertainers. Basil the fox, the glove puppet, was the real star, yet Roy was one of the men who worked with him, interviewing and talking to the show's guests. Roy was working on London's West End production of *Joseph and the Amazing Technicolour Dreamcoat* when he got the audition to replace Derek Fowlds as Basil's companion. He went on to spend four years with Basil Brush and they even toured New Zealand together. Sticking to his northern roots, Roy would sometimes even wear his Hull City shirt on the programme! Since parting with Basil, Roy has worked with Hull-born Barrie Rutter in the Northern Broadsides Theatre Company, acting in Shakespeare plays and other productions.

MARCH 17TH

1932: Dorothy Mackaill was born in Hull, attending Thoresby Street Primary School. As a young woman she worked at the *Hull Daily Mail* headquarters in Whitefriargate. Her father was the manager of Maypole Dairy but in the evenings he ran a dancing academy, where Dorothy became a dance teacher. Her appetite for stardom was whetted and she decided to move to London to pursue her dreams. She started as a chorus girl but was spotted by a Broadway stage choreographer who persuaded her to move to New York City, where she became involved in the *Ziegfeld Follies*. This was her big break, as it was there she was talent spotted by a film director. He signed her up and her first film was *The Lotus Eater*. This was the start of big things for this Hull lass and Dorothy was one of the few who made it through the transition from silent movies to talkies. On March 17th 1932, *Love Affair* was released, starring Dorothy and movie heart-throb Humphrey Bogart. This romantic drama between an adventurous socialite and an aeroplane designer was a huge hit and this era was Dorothy's most memorable. Dorothy eventually died of kidney failure in Honolulu, Hawaii, aged eighty-seven. She was cremated and her ashes were scattered at sea off Waikiki Beach.

March 18th

1924: Sir James Reckitt died on this date and is buried in the Hull Quaker Cemetery. He was born in 1833, the youngest son of Isaac Reckitt, who was the founder of the Reckitt firm. Reckitt & Sons was built up from a small starch-making business to what is now an international pharmaceutical firm. As well as being well known for his involvement in his company, James had a reputation in Hull for helping many charitable causes and bestowing gifts upon the city. He is said to have had a very strong social conscience and spent much time, effort and personal capital improving the quality of life for the people of Hull. James headed the campaign for free provision of public libraries in Hull, and when the local authorities failed to provide one, he himself built one at his own cost. He also assisted in setting up Hull's Royal Infirmary and with his brother, Francis, bought a derelict hotel in Withernsea, which they converted into a convalescent home and donated it to the Infirmary. He was a benefactor of The Sailor's Children Society in Hull and became its first president. James was also instrumental in establishing Hull's Garden Village.

MARCH 19TH

1958: On this day, American singer-songwriter and one of the pioneers of rock and roll, Buddy Holly, came to Hull. The post-war years were a tough time for everyone. Rationing was still in place even into the 1950s and the memory of the terrors and loss of war were still relatively recent. When rock and roll arrived it created a frenzy and diversion like no other and Buddy Holly was at the forefront of this new wave. Holly is described by critic Bruce Eder as 'the single most influential creative force in early rock and roll'. He produced records that were new, exciting and full of energy. Works like 'That'll Be the Day' and 'Peggy Sue' are instantly recognisable to us all, even now. His originality was copied by numerous musicians, notably The Beatles and the Rolling Stones. In his tour of Britain, he visited nineteen cities throughout the country, Hull's Regal Cinema being on this date. By all accounts the cinema was absolutely packed and when Buddy came on stage, with his trademark specs, he is said to have compared Hull's weather to that of his own, in Texas, where, he said, 'It's so hot the trees are a'chasin' the dawgs'. A complete success, anyone who was there will undoubtedly remember the experience forever.

MARCH 20TH

1911: Our very own Hull-born German spy, Max Wilhelm Emil Hugo Schultz, was reported by *The Times* newspaper to have been arrested in Germany on this date. Max's parents had emigrated to England from Prussia during the recession in the 1870s and Max made his way as a successful yacht broker. He married a Hull girl and they went on to have eight children. As the tensions and rivalry between Britain and Germany intensified, both sides were recruiting normal, reliable people to become 'casual agents', as apparently happened in the case of Max. Max's main role was to put himself in contact with men who had specialist first-hand knowledge of how merchant ships might be used in wartime, and then to report back to his commander. He went to Germany in August 1910 to make contacts, but *The Times* reported he had been arrested as a spy by March 1911. This apparently was the first his family knew of the matter! Even though he was interned as a prisoner for two years, he was proud to be the man who 'conducted the naval revolution in Hamburg which really finished the war,' said a *Daily Graphic* reporter.

MARCH 21ST

1955: This was the date that the poet and novelist Philip Larkin took up the post of University Librarian in Hull, aged thirty-two, where he stayed for thirty years, completing many of his most important works. After being initially housed in university accommodation in Cottingham, Larkin soon moved to a second-floor flat in Pearson Park, where he stayed for the next eighteen years. He only moved house, in 1974, to Newland Park, as he was informed his Pearson Park abode was set to be demolished and it was whilst living in this Newland Park house that he died in 1985. In 2010, twenty-five years after his death, Larkin was commemorated in Hull with the Larkin 25 Festival. Sixty-five giant fibreglass toads were positioned all around the city in honour of Larkin's two famous toad poems, costing something in the region of £292,000. One report suggested, however, that the toad trail brought nearly £1 million into the local economy. Each toad sculpture was painted with its own unique design created by local artists and inspired by Larkin's poetry. In 2003, almost two decades after his death, Larkin was chosen as the nation's best-loved poet in a survey by the Poetry Book Society and, in 2008, *The Times* named Larkin as the greatest British post-war writer.

MARCH 22ND

2008: On this date Dean Windass returned to play for Hull City Football Club in a match against Leicester City, making this his 700th career appearance. Dean started his footballing career as a trainee at his hometown club, Hull City, and signed his first professional contract there. He scored 64 goals in 205 games for Hull, initially playing midfield for the Tigers and later as a forward. By all accounts he became a firm fans' favourite, and in a 2005 poll to name the top 100 Tigers, Dean was named the fourth best player in the club's 100-year history – quite an honour! In December 1995, with the club in financial difficulty, he was sold to Aberdeen for £700,000, a record transfer fee at the time. Having returned to Hull by May 11th 2008, he scored his 200th goal in English football, in the Championship play-off semi-final first leg against Watford. His 201st goal was in the play-off final at Wembley Stadium on May 24th 2008, giving Hull City a 1–0 win against Bristol City, which meant that Hull City were promoted to the Premier League for the first time in their 104-year history. His goal was estimated to be worth £60 million to the club because of Premier League television rights gained.

MARCH 23RD

2002: The Deep, Hull's underwater aquarium, opened on this date. It was designed by architect Sir Terry Farrell, who also built the MI6 building featured in many of the James Bond films. He created The Deep in the shape of a capital 'A' on its side, encased in aluminium and black enamelled tiles and situated on Hull's waterfront, overlooking the River Humber. A massive tourist attraction since its opening, it has welcomed over 2 million visitors from around the world. The main feature is a ten-metre deep pool, housing 2,500,000 litres of water, which contains various sharks, rays and other exotic fish. The facility also includes a variety of coral, glow-in-the-dark fish, seahorses and over 3,500 fish in various other tanks and surroundings in the interestingly shaped interior. As well as being an aquarium for the public, The Deep is also a marine research centre, involved in a range of conservation and education projects across the world, such as coral reef research in the Red Sea and Costa Rica. It is a real boost for Hull's reputation and economy to house one of Europe's largest fish tanks. It also brings together the old tradition of Hull's fishing, whaling and shipbuilding – where fisherfolk made a living from the sea – with today's sustainable fishing ethos.

MARCH 24TH

2012: The *Hull Daily Mail* published a story on this date concerning Hull soldier Len Cavinder. During the First World War, Len went to France with the East Yorkshire Regiment. He was told that he was in charge of dishing out the daily rations and one day he realised there was one too many and a man was missing. He made his report but it was not until six months later that the deserter was found in St Omer. He was brought back and Len was given the task of taking him to Ypres Gaol and looking after him until the appointed time of execution. Len described how ten men from his platoon had to go to the gaol every day and practise firing at a small piece of paper. They all knew why but were sworn to silence. The deserter apparently was nearly out of his mind, knowing his fate, and it was up to Len to stay with him the night before the execution, comforting him and praying with him. In the morning the ten platoon men fired, with five firing blanks so no one knew who had actually killed him. 'It was the worst thing that has ever happened to me,' Len said afterwards, as one can well imagine, having to kill a fellow soldier for not wanting to die in battle.

MARCH 25TH

1902: This date saw the very first execution at Hull Prison on Hedon Road. Four months after Arthur Richardson had been found guilty of brutally murdering his aunt, Mrs Hebden, he was hanged by William Billington. Arthur was apparently of a quite slight build and thus was allotted a longer rope than a stouter man would have had. Even though he was the first to be executed here, the gallows were actually built for twenty-one-year-old John Aaron Walker. John had murdered his father but was reprieved from the death sentence because of his youth. Prior to this, prisoners were hanged at York Castle or Armley Gaol, but when the castle was converted into a military prison Hull was chosen for capital sentencing. The types of hanging that occurred in Hull before this decision were hangings from trees or low-slung gallows. Some gallows were erected in 1302, where the Prospect Street Shopping Centre now stands. In fact, there had been quite a gap between the last hanging of this type and Arthur Richardson's death in 1902. John Rogerson was the last known before Arthur in 1778. Other known hangings included Frederick Gottfried in 1575, for forging coins, and Robert Skelton in 1639, for forging a will. A man named Nathaniel Picket faced death in 1684 for scuttling a ship in the Humber.

MARCH 26TH

1921: David 'Magical' Mercer joined the Hull Tigers Football Club in 1914 and began to play with the team just three months after becoming a member. This was the start of his magical run of 218 consecutive appearances. Of these, there were 142 appearances during the war. This was a notoriously difficult time for carrying on life in any semblance of a normal way, including all sports fixtures. When League Football resumed after the war, Hull City continued their perpetual quest for Division One status but had to be content with mid-table existence in the Second Division. As they moved into the 1920s, however, financial troubles began to emerge. To survive, the directors pursued a policy of selling their better players to meet the costs of running the club in an area of the country that was really still dominated by rugby league. Magical Mercer was up for grabs as he was one who would attract substantial transfer fees for his time. Sheffield United moved to strengthen their right flank with the signing of David, who came with a price tag of £4,250. The first high point of his career with the Blades came on March 26th 1921 at Highbury. Without an away win all season, United hammered six goals past the Gunners with Harry Johnson getting a hat trick, David scoring from the spot.

MARCH 27TH

1865: A real claim to fame, it was on this date that Hull inventor James Wright received a missive from Windsor Castle testifying that James' 'Toffy, Myton Toffy', was 'superior to any yet introduced in to the Royal Household'. The story goes that when Prince Albert Victor passed through Hull in 1864, James apparently presented the future king with a box of his 'toffy'. Just a few weeks later an order for a quantity of this Hull 'lollypop' arrived from the chief seat of British royalty after which James received the above mentioned missive. As well as being a confectioner, with his own shop in Osborne Street, James was also something of an artist. He apparently spent a great deal of time on rustic modelling, chiefly in cork. With a royal reputation for making 'toffy', James was also envied for these artistic talents, one writer saying of him, 'There is no exaggeration in asserting that for artistic conception and mechanical completeness, most, if not the whole of Mr Wright's work in cork cannot be surpassed.' Quite a compliment indeed.

MARCH 28TH

1854: Born on Holderness Road on this date, Joseph Rank revolutionised the milling business not only for Hull but the rest of the country too. His father had a flour mill and when he died he left an estate of around £30,000, from which Joseph received £500 and started his own business. In 1883, he first saw a roller mill and realised the huge advantage grinding with steel rollers would give instead of millstones. He thought that if the process could be automated it could change milling forever. Two years later he built the engine-driven Alexandra Mill in Hull, installing steel rollers instead of millstones, enabling him to produce an impressive six sacks of flour an hour rather than the usual one and a half. Soon an extension was introduced and ten bags an hour were being produced. By 1888 he owned another steel-roller plant, which could turn out twenty sacks per hour but had the capacity to expand to sixty. Some of the equipment used in Joseph's mill had never been used before in the UK and his business was seen as the finest in the country. With such prolific production, Joseph's firm was invaluable during food shortages in the war. Bread was the staple food and Joseph was asked to become a member of the Wheat Control Board and build up stocks before the First World War broke out.

MARCH 29TH

1934: Twenty-six-year-old Charles Arthur Banks was committed for trial by the Hull Stipendiary Magistrate on this date, on three charges of larceny. The *Hull Daily Mail* covered the story, explaining how Charles was accused of stealing a bicycle, a woollen jumper suit and some items of underclothing. The bicycle had been taken from a passageway but when first asked about it, Charles told police, 'You are wrong. I bought it from a man in English Street some time ago, and I gave him thirty shillings for it.' However, when pressed for his name and address he cracked, replying, 'It's no use: I'll admit it.' Then when asked about the jumper suit his response was, 'Yes, I took it ... when it once gets hold of you, you can't give it up.' He also admitted to taking the undergarments and selling them on. Not much chance of Charles being found innocent! The same paper gives some figures from the Home Office relating to road accidents in 1933. In Hull there were 1,464 road accidents where twenty-seven people were killed and 1,601 injured. Of these, 'pedal cycles' were responsible for 387. In 2010, official figures showed that the number of casualties involved in road accidents in Hull was 925, 172 of which were cyclists. Road safety has obviously improved to some extent, even though there are far more vehicles on the road today.

MARCH 30TH

1969: Hull-born Karl Bushby was born on this day. In 1998, Karl set out in an attempt to become the first person to walk an unbroken path around the world. He called his trek the Goliath Expedition. His aim was to walk from Punta Arenas in Chile back home to Hull, which is over 36,000 miles. He began his journey on November 1st 1998 and as of 2006 he had covered 17,000 miles, walking through South, Central and North America. He estimated he would be in Hull by 2012 but was delayed by Russian visa rules. He was only allowed to be in Russia for ninety days out of every 180 days and told he must leave the country before each visa expired. This caused much delay as his route took him through an area that can only be travelled on foot via frozen rivers and ice roads, meaning he could only walk during late winter and early spring. Then the Russian authorities denied him a visa for 2012. After many talks and petitions Karl decided to make a 3,000-mile 'detour' in protest, planning to collect signatures on his travels and hand a petition to the Russian embassy in the USA. The saga continues ...

MARCH 31ST

1621: Born on this date, metaphysical poet and politician Andrew Marvell has both a Hull school named after him and a statue erected in his honour in Hull's market place. His clergyman father was at one time lecturer at Holy Trinity Church, moving the family from Winestead in Holderness to Hull. Andrew proved his academic prowess from a young age, attending Trinity College, Cambridge, when only thirteen. He was a well-educated man and much travelled, but came back to his roots and was elected MP for Hull in 1659, and again in 1661. Much of his writing was published either after his death or anonymously, as it was politically risky, and he also wrote prose satires against censorship and Catholic dogma. Quoting from his *The Growth of Popery and Arbitrary Government in England*: 'There has now for diverse years, a design been carried on to change the lawful government of England with an Absolute Tyranny ...' He received much support from fellow dissenters and made such an impact that his name is well known even today and his poem *To his Coy Mistress* is still frequently studied in school exams. It even mentions the Humber!

APRIL 1ST

1299: Originally, as a developing town, Hull was named Wyke on Hull, after the Scandinavian word *vik*, meaning a creek, referring to the point where the River Hull entered the River Humber. Often being referred to as just Wyke or Hull, it was first mentioned in 1193, when the wool, supplied by assorted monasteries, for the ransom of Richard I, was collected at 'the port of Hull'. Being a secure natural haven for shipping, situated mid-country, it attracted the attention of King Edward I who, in 1296, decided to buy Wyke from the monks of Meaux, their abbey lying 7 miles to the north, for the sum of £47 7s. It is said he visited the area twice around 1292 and it is thought that this is when he decided to acquire the town. There is a charter dated April 1st 1299 alleging that King Edward gave the town a new name on this date, Kingston-upon-Hull, granting it also the status of a borough. Transforming an area of wasteland within the area of the Hamlet of Myton, Kingston-upon-Hull eventually became a thriving port and sprawling town, receiving the approval of city status from Queen Victoria in 1897. The monks of Meaux would never have recognised this new city as their old home!

APRIL 2ND

1869: On this date the *Hull Packet and East Riding Times* made a report that the Hull Corporation had 'devoted a portion of the borough fund' to provide a public swimming bath in Hull. They had apparently agreed to a seven-year lease of the Spring Bank reservoir, to allow the good people of Hull to enjoy a public bath, which they expected would be a 'great boon' to the town, thus justifying the expenditure. The paper, however, did state at the end of the piece that, 'We confess we agree ... that it would be better, if possible, to have a salt-water bath ... the Spring-head supply of water is too precious to be lightly diverted from the ordinary domestic requirements of a rapidly-increasing town.' How times have changed, the city now having more than five public swimming baths!

On the same date the paper also made a mention of the activities the people of Hull engaged in on Good Friday, in 1869. 'The Park received a fair amount of patronage throughout the day ... But, although, according to external appearances, pleasure was the order of the day, not a few who responded to the call of the church bells, and allotted a portion of the day to devotional exercises.'

April 3rd

1907: The *Hull Daily News* printed a story on this date about Hull girl Beatrice Bell, who had been charged with stealing a costume, a pair of boots, and a hat from the lady she and her 'husband' were lodging with, valued at £1 10s. Beatrice claimed the clothes had been lent to her but then it transpired the man was not her husband at all!

1934: The *Hull Daily Mail* reported the death of a Hull trawler mate on this date. Stories of men washed overboard or ships lost at sea are unfortunately common, but this gentleman, Mr Charles George Garwood, aged sixty-five, collapsed at the winch of steam trawler *Kite*. He was taken down by the skipper to rest, but died shortly afterwards. Charles had apparently been 'one of the best known of local trawlermen, having sailed out of port as skipper and mate for close on forty years.' The cause of his death was blamed on heart failure, but he was said to be in the best of health when he left Hull two weeks prior and he was intending to retire within the year. His body was brought home, 'the flags of the North Sea fishing fleet flying at half mast.'

APRIL 4TH

1983: The original Hull Truck Theatre, on Spring Street, became home to the Hull Truck Company on this date. The company was founded in 1971 by actor Mike Bradwell when he could not find work. He apparently placed an advert in *Time Out* magazine saying, 'Half-formed theatre company seeks other half,' with the stipulation that the 'other half' must be willing to move to Hull. Within a few years Hull Truck was having success, playing at venues in cities such as Glasgow and London. However, they were still basically working from the back of a van, hence the name Hull Truck Theatre. They were very happy to have a stable home in Spring Street and the next year artistic director John Godber joined the company. He decided that the best way to improve sales and the success of the company was to write a play relevant to its audiences; thus he wrote *Up n' Under*, a play about the rugby league in Hull which proved to be a big success. The Spring Street theatre moved to a new home in 2009, next to St Stephens, but one of Hull Truck's most popular and well-known plays, John Godber's *Bouncers*, was the final one to be performed before the move.

April 5th

1904: The *Hull Daily Mail* printed a letter on this date from a gentleman signing himself 'Hard Up', expressing his utmost dismay at the new restrictions of the proposed regulations being enforced upon advertising in the streets of Hull. He was a man who pushed these boards or carried them on his back as a last resort before having to enter a workhouse.

> There are scores of chaps in the same position as myself that would be deprived of the means of keeping life and soul together, but I hope the gentlemen who have the power of the alteration of things will take a broad, business view of the matter, and remember they are not only going to deprive the shopkeepers, who pay the bulk of the rates and taxes, of advertising their wares, but they are also robbing us of the means of earning our daily bread. I would rather have half a loaf honestly earned than a whole loaf buttered top and bottom, stamped with the three crowns of the workhouse.

On the same date a report tells how a baby fell between the gap of the train and platform, on the way home to Hull from a day trip to Leeds. The frantic mother dived from the train, but found her baby sitting upright, quite unharmed, save a small scratch to the forehead.

APRIL 6TH

1889: The *Hull News* reported the sad story on this date of 'Cruel Desertion of 4 Children in Hull'. Sarah Jane, aged nine, Rebecca Elizabeth, aged eight, Laura, aged six and Benjamin, aged two, were found by neighbour Alice Gill, 'in a most disgraceful and starving condition'. The poor children were apparently left 'completely alone and friendless all Wednesday, and at ten minutes to nine o'clock at night as no one appeared to be coming to look after them,' Alice informed the police of the matter. They found the children in what was described as 'a dirty, filthy, lost condition'. The parents had been parted for some time and on the day in question the mother had left the children alone. A Mrs Dixon 'very kindly volunteered to look after the little friendless ones for the night'. The following day the mother was found and the five of them were sent to the workhouse. The report ended thus; 'Steps will doubtless be taken to compel the father to support his family.' Unfortunately, this kind of story happened all too often and even though there is no longer a workhouse to send people to, the situation is still familiar in modern times.

APRIL 7TH

1906: The *Hull News* on this date enlightens us about the times and concerns of everyday living in Hull in the early 1900s. In the 'Household Hints' column we are told that the following is a good substitute for glue: 'Take a small piece of cold potato which has been boiled and rub it up and down on a piece of paper for about five minutes with your fingers. It will become the right consistency, and stick as well as the strongest glue.' Their 'Woman and the Home' section advertises a new hairstyle: 'The latest aid to hair-dressing is the puff-curl. It is particularly useful for building up the tilt of a hat and artistically arranged, are very charming ornaments.' We are also told that 'Veno's Seaweed Tonic' was the strongest nerve tonic, it being impossible 'to make a stronger or more effective nerve strengthener'.

> It possesses marvellous, purifying, healing, and tonic properties. A rare and edible species of seaweed obtained on the Pacific coast is used. In cases of nervous weakness, lassitude, debility … and especially female weaknesses … it is pre-eminent. Cures permanently. No return. Pleasant to take. You feel better at once.

What more could one ask for?

APRIL 8TH

1992: 'Scared mum fears flat is haunted' – this was the headline in a *Hull Daily Mail* report on this date. Joanne Bulmer feared she may have disturbed a ghost when she made some new changes to her flat, including the installation of a new door. The family of three was terrified after strange things began happening in the flat since the alterations. Joanne reported that the television in an empty room had begun turning itself on and the worst thing was, it was even doing this after it had been unplugged! A decorating knife had seemingly appeared on the other side of the new door, even though the door had been locked! Not only that, but the very same locked door had been found wide open when the family returned home after a day out. Other incidents included bizarre knockings, unexplained footsteps, singing of war songs and candle wax stains. The family became so frightened that they called in a priest and exorcist to try and rid them of the 'restless spirit' that had awoken during the alterations. The saga continues!

APRIL 9TH

1903: On this date Marjorie Rhodes was born in Hull, as Marjorie Rhodes Wise. She has frequently been described as one of those characters, like Gladys Henson and Thora Hird, who were often cast as quarrelsome old bats. Critics say she gave an excellent performance in *Footsteps in the Fog* as the disapproving housekeeper who fell foul of scheming Jean Simmons. One of her best-known roles was as Lucy Fitton, the mother in Bill Naughton's play, *All in Good Time*. She played the role on Broadway, for which she was nominated for a Tony Award in 1965. She is said to have kept the genius of her character in the 1966 film version, *The Family Way*, her superb performance bringing her some concrete recognition, as she was named Best Supporting Actress by both The National Board of Review and The National Society of Film Critics in the USA. For over thirty years her face was regularly seen in countless films and her talent was such that when her name appeared in the credits one knew she would deliver excellent characterisation. She passed away in Hove, Sussex on July 4th 1979.

APRIL 10TH

1912: This was the fateful date that the RMS *Titanic* set sail from Southampton, with Hull's Joseph Groves Boxhall acting as Fourth Officer. Joseph was born into a seafaring family and worked on a number of liners before joining the crew of the 'unsinkable' *Titanic*. His regular duties aboard included scheduled watches, aiding in navigation, keeping the charts up to date and assisting passengers and crew when necessary. When the collision with the iceberg occurred, Joseph was ordered by the captain to inspect the ship. During his fifteen-minute check, a passenger apparently handed Joseph a large piece of ice! Part of Joseph's job was to calculate the ship's position and send out distress signals. He sighted a nearby vessel at the time and tried to signal them with Morse code, but it was a failed attempt. He was in charge of lifeboat No. 2, which apparently only contained eighteen people out of a possible forty. They had to watch helplessly as the *Titanic* went down, Joseph later telling the captain of the ship that rescued them, '...hundreds and hundreds, perhaps a thousand or more ... my God, sir they've gone down with her. They couldn't live in this cold water.' When he died, aged eighty-three, Joseph's ashes were scattered over the site of the sunken ship.

APRIL 11TH

1963: Born in Hull on this date, Karen Briggs is considered one of the UK's most successful competitive judoka. As explained in the *Hull Daily Mail* in 2012, Karen represented Great Britain in the 1992 summer Olympics, the first year that women's judo was included as an Olympic sport. Unfortunately, her gold medal hopes were shattered after dislocating her shoulder and she came fifth, but it was a massive achievement to have competed in Barcelona. On retiring, Karen began teaching and now teaches judo to over 300 children a week. She and her husband Peter run a judo club in Hull and in 2012 Karen was nominated to carry the Olympic Torch through Beverley on its country-wide journey to London. 'The way I look at it,' she told the paper, 'it's a remarkable achievement and the children I teach can put a face to someone who is going to carry the Olympic Torch.' Karen's other successes include being four-time World Champion, six-time European Champion and she also claimed two Commonwealth Games titles and was five times Paris Multi-Nations Champion. Quite a remarkable career for the East Yorkshire lass!

APRIL 12TH

1833: The newspaper, the *Hull Packet*, enjoyed a varied and popular life, including many changes of name and ownership throughout the years. It first appeared in May 1787, under the title the *Hull Packet and Humber Gazette*, publishing political and commercial news, and was apparently quite outspoken against slavery. In 1788 it became just the *Hull Packet* and in 1827 it was renamed the *Hull Packet and Humber Mercury*. Other names have included the *Hull Packet and East Riding Times* and the *Hull Packet and Original Weekly Commercial, Literary and General Advertiser*. On April 12th 1833, it returned to its previous title the *Hull Packet*. At first the paper was weekly, appearing every Tuesday, but then it changed to Fridays. The news was fairly eclectic, running local stories, sports, correspondence and foreign news. Shipping intelligence was always important, with Hull being a port, and it covered agricultural information, literary notices and police reports. As with every paper, it also printed stories to amuse readers; for example, in 1845 there was a half-column story entitled 'A Parrot Admitted as a Witness in a Court of Justice'. The newspaper was incorporated into the *Hull Daily Mail* in 1856.

APRIL 13TH

1743: There was a terrible blaze in the well-known Maister household in Hull on this date, which claimed the lives of mother and child. The family home was occupied by Henry Maister, his wife Mary and their children. The Maisters were one of a number of merchant families who lived on Hull's High Street and traded with ports around the North Sea and Baltic. Over the years the Maisters enjoyed considerable success; family members held offices including Sheriff, Mayor and MP for Hull. It was during the time of Henry Maister, who succeeded to the family business in 1716, that the tragedy occurred. On the night of the fire Henry escaped the blaze, but Mary, the youngest child and two maidservants did not. According to one account, Mary had initially fled the house with her husband but then returned and attempted to save her baby; it is believed that she became trapped on an upper floor of the burning building when the old wooden staircase collapsed. Maister House is now occupied by the long-established firm of architects, Gelder & Kitchen. The staircase is open to the public during office hours and there is a blue plaque on the exterior in remembrance of the family.

APRIL 14TH

1951: This was the date that Hull's 'forgotten star', Duggie Wakefield, died aged fifty-one. He started his life as a showman at a young age, appearing at Bridlington's People's Palace at just eight years old. His talent then was singing. This show lasted for a week, for which he apparently asked to be paid his five shillings wage in coppers, so that it would look like more when he took it home to Hull. He was booked for more appearances on the back of this success and worked as a boy soloist until his voice broke. After a stint in the army he joined a revue and this is where he really came into his own, as a comedian. He worked in many of Gracie Fields' shows in the West End, becoming one of the family when he married her sister. After this Hollywood called, and Duggie appeared in many films, but never forgot his home city of Hull. He returned on numerous occasions, one time in 1941, coming to perform at the Tivoli Theatre in aid of the Mother Humber Air Raid Distress Fund and making a considerable personal contribution. He was acclaimed as one of the country's funniest men and had a heart of gold to go with it.

APRIL 15TH

1935: This was the birth date of eminent playwright Alan Plater, whose family moved to Hull in 1938, where he attended Kingston High School. Alan produced numerous works for the stage and screen, including influential police drama *Z Cars* and an adaptation of *The Barchester Chronicles*. He also penned six novels and was honoured with a CBE in 2005. Plater originally trained as an architect at King's College, Newcastle, but only practised in the profession briefly, at a junior level. He later stated that it was shortly after he was forced to fend off a herd of pigs from eating his tape measure while he was surveying a field that he left to pursue full-time writing. Alan stayed in the north of England for many years after he became prominent as a writer and lived in Hull. In 2008, he was asked to open the University of Hull's Anthony Minghella drama studio. He died in 2010 but will always be remembered for his deliberate portrayal of ordinary people in ordinary settings. He is said to have been pleased when a critic hailed his first TV play as combining the voices of *Coronation Street* and the spirit of Chekov.

APRIL 16TH

1941: It was on this day during the Second World War that Hull saw one of the worst air raids over the city. In addition to conventional bombs, parachute mines were deployed. These fell to earth packed with sufficient explosive to flatten a street with one blast. On this particular night one such bomb landed on the public air-raid shelter in Ellis Terrace and all sixty people inside died. Another 500 were rendered homeless. As the air raids became more frequent, a third of the city's inhabitants left the city centre areas every night and 92,000 citizens, mostly children, were evacuated to rural areas. There were countless news reports from the BBC, but they always referred to Hull as an anonymous 'east coast town'. When the air raids ceased, parts of Hull were like a wasteland and the city suffered more, in proportion to its size, than any other British city. In all, 1,200 people lost their lives and 152,000 lost their homes. From 92,660 occupied houses only 5,938 remained intact, with over 5,000 completely obliterated. Despite its ordeal, Hull had many tales of bravery and heroism to tell, including the proud fact that during the bombing, no ship from the port ever missed a tide.

APRIL 17TH

1931: Hull was lucky to have a generous handful of philanthropists such as Thomas Ferens, James Reckitt and Zachariah Pearson. Joseph Malet Lambert, born in Hull in 1853, was another such figure, passing away on this date. He graduated from Trinity College Dublin in 1879 and that same year he was ordained, becoming curate at Tadcaster. In 1881, he returned to Hull as vicar of Newland, where he stayed for the next thirty years. During this time he was elevated to Dean of Hull, Canon of York and Archdeacon of the East Riding within the Church of England. He had a very active role in social reform and showed particular interest in housing, sanitation and education. Joseph became a member, then chairman, of the Hull School Board and his influence and involvement were such that a school was named after him. He was instrumental in setting up a body to help improve Hull's sewage, refuse and disease treatment systems. Ironically, Joseph and his wife were caught up in a scandal at one point, being accused of cruelty and neglect of a ten-year-old child in their care. The girl in question was removed from the Malet Lambert household and placed in a workhouse.

April 18th

1932: An enquiry report was released on this date showing that Digby Willoughby, a once well-respected Hull councillor, had been involved in a money-making scandal, of which he was so ashamed that he had committed suicide on March 4th of the same year. Found in a hotel room near Glasgow, it is thought that he gassed himself after controversy about him demanding payments from companies and using insider knowledge of land that the council wanted to buy became known. He had been approaching land owners independently and offering to find buyers for a commission. Previous to this Digby had been very passionate about Hull and played a significant role in the expansion of the city in the early decades of the twentieth century. He was Lord Mayor of Hull at one point and played a pivotal role in the tram strikes of 1926. He also became Chair of the Housing and Town Planning Committee and was said to be one of the visionaries behind the scheme to redevelop the area now known as Ferensway. The scandals, however, overshadowed this and cut short the life of a man who could have gone a long way.

APRIL 19TH

1914: On this date the author's maternal grandmother, Mollie Johnson, was born. She was well known in Hull for her fine contralto singing voice. She sang solos at many Musical Union concerts and, at different times, was a member of Hull Savoyards Amateur Operatic Society, West Hull Ladies Choir, the Choral Union and latterly, Hull Ladies Festival Choir, of which she was deputy conductor. She was also a fine pianist who could play by ear – a gift, unfortunately, not inherited by her daughters! Mollie was a Licentiate of the Royal Academy of Music – a diploma gained whilst she was a wife and mother of two small children. In 1940 she married Frank Johnson, who became the Senior Assistant Education Officer in Hull. At that time married women were forced to give up work, but during the war they were needed to replace the men away fighting. She told of going to work and seeing exhausted firemen asleep in the streets and the shock of finding part of the Guildhall missing one morning! Apart from music, Mollie's other ambition was to teach. Personal circumstances prevented training for a career when she was younger, but aged forty she went to the then Hull Teacher Training College and qualified as a junior high school teacher. She taught music at Fountain Road Girl's School and Wold Junior High as well as being a class teacher. Her youngest great-granddaughter is named after her and a star on the wall within Hull Truck Theatre commemorates her and her husband Frank.

APRIL 20TH

1951: Murderer James Inglis was sentenced to be hanged on this date. After leaving the army, due apparently to mental health problems, James moved to Hull, where he befriended prostitute Alice Morgan. The story goes that James had handed in his notice, out of the blue, and spent the rest of the day drinking with Alice. They had apparently had an argument over money and James is said to have snapped and brutally turned on Alice. The body was found by the postman at her house; she had been beaten and then strangled with a silk stocking. James was already known for attacking a woman, his landlady Amy Gray, and when the police found him he confessed straight away. At court his defence tried to plead insanity, but the jury found him guilty and he was sentenced to be hanged. James' actual hanging was unusual. In court, when asked if he had anything to say, he was reported to have said, 'I've had a fair trial from you. All I ask now is that you get me hanged as soon as possible.' As he did not appeal, a date for his execution was fixed for just three weeks later and when the actual day came, it is said James almost jogged to the rope. Records say it took just seven seconds to get him from his cell to the rope – the fastest hanging on record!

APRIL 21ST

1920: The bushy side-burned, grumpy landlord Amos Brearly, well known in the TV series *Emmerdale*, was in fact Ronald Magill, who was born in Hull on this date. He was sent to an orphanage in Birmingham aged nine, after the death of his father, then served with the Royal Corps and Signals during the Second World War, joining a travelling theatre company after being demobbed. Following this he worked at the Nottingham Playhouse for nine years with the likes of Ian McKellen, Michael Crawford and Tyrone Guthrie. When he auditioned for the role of the bachelor licensee in *Emmerdale Farm*, he was rushing from an Edwardian stage play in which he was performing and did not have time to shave off his sideburns! As it turned out, he was told they were perfect for the character and for nineteen years they were Amos' trademark along with his catchphrase 'Nay, Mr Wilks'. Despite Amos being a real country lover and Ronald being more of an urbanite, Ronald admitted he did share a lot in common with his grumpy, pernickety character. He left the regular cast in 1991, saying he did not want to pass his '*Emmerdale* sell-by date' and he went on the BBC's *Wogan* show to shave off his legendary whiskers.

April 22nd

1893: The Dock Strikes were an important event in this year. It was hard, dangerous work with long hours and low pay. Discontent and protests about this began in the 1870s and started a nationwide movement. The strikes caused huge disruption and the Shipping Federation made many attempts to remedy the situation. Where local branches of the union were stronger than the Federation, labourers were imported to work until the union surrendered. At one point Hull was the only remaining union stronghold and there was much confrontation as locals fought the imported workers. On April 22nd 1893, five fires broke out on the Hull timber yards, believed to be rebellion-related arson attacks. The fire brigade arrived quickly but 'strong winds aided the fire in its devastating course,' reported the *Hull Daily Mail*. Some of the timber yards were 'doomed to almost entire devastation … By 6 o'clock a vast area of ground was nothing but a blaze.' The Citadel Hotel succumbed to the flames. 'The building became a mass of ruins in an incredibly short period of time.' The blaze caused several secondary fires in the city and flames could be seen 20 miles away. The dockers refused to assist and over £50,000 worth of damage was caused.

APRIL 23RD

1642: The Governor of Hull, Sir John Hotham, refused to allow King Charles I to enter the City of Hull on this date, duly initiating the English Civil War. Hull possessed the largest armoury of weapons in the north of England; even Holy Trinity Church housed barrels of gunpowder! Sir John had been charged by Parliament to take great care of this arsenal, but the king wanted to commandeer it to assist his battles with the Roundheads. Consequently on this date Sir John convened a meeting at his home, the building now known as Ye Olde White Hart Inn, and subsequently the gates of Hull were closed to the king and he was refused entry and forced to return to Beverley. This reception was very different to the one the king received in Hull just three years previously, when a platform was constructed at the entrance to Hull for the people to view his arrival and he was greeted by the mayor with expressions of loyalty and with gifts. The fateful decision to deny him entry on this occasion triggered civil war and Sir John was branded a traitor, eventually being executed in 1645.

APRIL 24TH

1965: Dr Alexander Hutchinson, Hull's Medical Officer of Health, oversaw the city's emerging paratyphoid epidemic and announced it over by April 24th 1965. The *Hull Daily Mail* front page, on April 5th, reported swift procedures being put in place for five cases of paratyphoid in East Hull. The five casualties were apparently being held in Castle Hill Hospital, although they were diagnosed as 'mild'. All the cases were within a half-mile area of East Hull but doctors believed they stemmed from two completely different sources. One case was that of a nineteen-year-old Merchant Navy seaman on leave after three months in the Med. He had complained of sickness and colic seven weeks previously whilst in Rotterdam. The doctor he visited in Hull on March 24th, the day after he docked at Avonmouth, took tests which showed he had paratyphoid B. Another case was an unrelated fifty-two-year-old man, who had been complaining of not feeling well for two years. His symptoms included occasional rigors and sudden feverish shivering. Tests concluded he also had paratyphoid B. The seaman's sister and parents also exhibited symptoms and a search was launched to trace all the people they may have been in contact with. This particular paratyphoid epidemic was fortunately well-contained and swift to reach a conclusion.

APRIL 25TH

1893: The Dock Strikes caused much disturbance up and down the country and Hull was especially affected, being such a prominent port. Violence was reportedly common and it is said that at its height, a Hull gunsmith alleged selling 200 revolvers and an untold number of knuckledusters in three weeks. It is thought the most serious incident in Hull happened on this date, when Shipping Federation Official George Hopperton and a couple of companions were walking along Waterhouse Lane when, at Osborne Street, they were set upon by about a dozen picketers. They apparently made a run for it but were followed by an ever-increasing mob. After one of his companions had been struck George took out his revolver and shot twice into the crowd. This could have sealed his fate had the police not arrived on the scene, whence George was arrested and the victim of the shooting, Charles Graham, a dock labourer and unionist, was taken to the Infirmary. Upon being searched, George was found to be in possession of a knuckleduster, as well as his six-chambered revolver, which still contained four loaded chambers. The incident caused much ado, but Charles, who had been shot in the thigh, was discharged after treatment.

APRIL 26TH

1884: On this date the *New Zealand Herald* ran a story entitled 'Horrible Murder at Sea' about the tragic death of sixteen-year-old Joseph Rowbottom, who sailed from Hull with the fishing fleet. Joseph had been a cook aboard the fishing smack, the *Sterling*. During this voyage he was treated abominably by the skipper, Joseph Nicholene, and the third hand, Thomas Hardisty. The paper recalled the evidence given by another member of the crew, Daniel Dyall, who was witness to the inhumane treatment meted out on poor Joseph. The youngster had been born in Southampton but, like many young lads, found his way to Hull, drawn by the idea of serving on a fishing vessel. For reasons unknown the skipper and third hand had taken a dislike to Joseph and gave him regular, harsh beatings. Dyall's testimony showed that Joseph was often starved and deprived of sleep, being forced to stay on deck all night. He was kicked with sea boots, beaten with thick ropes, had ice cold buckets of water thrown on him, was ducked into the sea and, on the day he died, Dyall had seen the third hand bashing the lad's head against the side of the cabin. After a two-day hearing a verdict of manslaughter was decided and the two men were sentenced to penal servitude for life.

APRIL 27TH

1885: Hull Labour MP Sydney Smith was born on this day. He was a gentleman who commanded great respect and lived until he was ninety-nine! His family moved to Goole when he was nine years old and Sydney became a paper seller for his cousin's newsagency. At eighteen he moved to Hull, where he began his own newsagent business. His venture eventually expanded to include books especially, by all accounts, the literature of the Fabian Society and through this his interest in politics grew. He joined the Independent Labour Party and was elected to Hull City Council in 1923. He served as Lord Mayor in 1940 and was elected for the South West Hull seat in the Labour victory of 1945. He was made an Honorary Alderman of Hull, the university awarded him an Honorary Doctorate of Law, he became an Honorary Freeman of the city and a Hull school was named after him. The university also ran a lecture series, The Alderman Sydney Smith Lecture, on labour and social history. Sydney never married but he devoted his life to the city he loved.

APRIL 28TH

1999: On this date Beverley-born artist Steven Dews' painting, *Off Cowes*, was sold at Sotheby's for £89,500. For a boy who apparently failed his art A level, gaining recognition in his own lifetime is a great achievement and Steven has become Britain's most sought-after living marine artist, his reputation being recognised internationally. Born in 1949, Steven was allegedly inspired to draw his first seafaring vessel at the age of five, after visiting his grandfather, who was the Assistant Dockmaster in Hull. This was to be the first of many and Dews has built up an amazing portfolio of work. In 1976, his first exhibition was mounted and it is believed that virtually the whole body of work was sold on the first night and seventeen commissions were received. By all accounts he gives meticulous attention to detail and his research for a painting will include long hours studying photos, reference books, model ships and architectural drawings. He is said to have a great love affair with the sea and once he had bought his first yacht, his voyages became his escape from the pressures of his success. He has been quoted as saying, 'There is no escape from reality on a boat, the sea is a great equaliser of all men.'

APRIL 29TH

1844: Foundations were laid for the Stoneferry waterworks on this date. The concern of having a fresh supply of water had long been an issue for the residents of Hull. In 1376, the king had received complaints from the Mayor of Hull that they had no fresh water except that which was brought in every day on boats from Lincolnshire. A ditch was then dug to use the springs of Anlaby, Hessle and Cottingham, which caused problems with these outlaying villages. Then, when the Stoneferry waterworks was introduced, the people complained that the tidal water it used was both muddy and salty, not to mention the pollution from sewerage. In the end it was down to one man, William Warden, who came up with a solution. He spent time doing his own experiments pumping water from the springs of the area and his solution was eventually entertained by the authorities. Once they realised William's ideas worked they established a waterworks at Spring Head and by 1864 it was predicted that Spring Head could supply as much as 7 million gallons of fresh water each day. The water from the boreholes at Spring Head was then used to supply the Stoneferry waterworks and the water supply problem was solved, all thanks to the ingenuity of William Warden.

APRIL 30TH

1931: The *Daily Mail* published a report on this date about the plans for the possible construction of a bridge across the Humber. There had been much discussion about the tides and their effects of the navigable channels in the river and how the building of the bridge would affect these channels. Mr Ralph Freeman, senior partner in the famous engineering company Douglas Fox & Partners, advised Hull Corporation that, unless some circumstances changed, the proposed site for the bridge would 'tend to strengthen the ebb tide and thus help to perpetuate the stable position of the main channel.' Mr Freeman apparently commented, 'These engineers are of such high standing that we must put our bridge in the place which is in accordance with their recommendations.' There was much to decide before the Humber Bridge actually opened in 1981!

In the same paper there was also an interesting report entitled 'How the poor live', which told of one unfortunate lady 'who lives in a house in a back passage off High-street and has been compelled to burn the gas day and night for seven years.' Her window was apparently too small even to let light in, not to mention the damp she suffered, 'and all the evils which follow in the train of these conditions!'

MAY 1ST

1967: Bransholme is an area with a vast housing estate on the north-eastern side of Hull, the first houses being officially opened on this date. It has been widely, but mistakenly, believed to be the largest council estate in Europe, a title apparently more likely to be held by Becontree in Dagenham, but Bransholme is the largest council estate in Yorkshire. The name Bransholme comes from an old Scandinavian word meaning Brand's water meadow (*brand* or *brandt* meant wild boar). Its history is said to go back at least as far as the Domesday Book of 1086, where Bransholme is marked as a little hill surrounded by water. There is evidence of the Romans, the Angles and the Saxons all occupying the area at some time; then later the monks and the Lords of the Manor drained the land with a series of dikes and ditches. In 1939, a barrage balloon defence station was built there and it was used as a RAF station during the Second World War. After the war, when large areas of Hull lay devastated due to enemy bombing, it was clearly necessary to rehouse on a massive scale and so the council made plans for the Bransholme Estate, which now has a population of over 30,000.

MAY 2ND

1810: The Theatre Royal on Humber Street, Hull, opened on this date. The theatre was a replacement of an earlier but inadequate predecessor along Finkle Street in 1770, but the Theatre Royal was not fortunate in its fate. The auditorium consisted of a pit, two galleries, and two tiers of dress boxes, which could hold some 800 people. The middle gallery with its own boxes could accommodate some 700 people, and the upper gallery ran around the whole house. On October 13th 1859, there was a tremendous fire which consumed the theatre, leaving nothing but the containing walls by the time it was extinguished. This was a savage blow to Miss Wilkinson, the proprietor and daughter of the builder of the theatre, who had put it up for sale earlier that year. The building was derelict for six years, after which it was rebuilt in the April of 1865. However, just four years later another fire broke out after a performance of *Robinson Crusoe* and again the theatre was completely destroyed. Fortunately the play had finished and the audience had departed, otherwise a great tragedy could have occurred. The site was not reused as a theatre, the next new one being built in Paragon Street.

MAY 3RD

1980: This was the day of the first ever Challenge Cup Final at Wembley to be contested by two Hull rugby teams, Hull Kingston Rovers and Hull FC. The whole city was in a frenzy of excitement and anticipation, tickets for the game being like gold dust and British Rail provided an extra twenty-eight trains during the Friday and Saturday. Some fans travelled by bus, others by car and everywhere was transformed into a sea of black and white or red and white scarves and banners. Over 60,000 supporters went to London to cheer their team. The half-time score was 8–3 to Rovers after a shaky start by Hull. In the second half they found it difficult to penetrate Rover's defence and despite a plucky effort, they lost 10 points to 5, a magnificent tackle by the renowned Clive Sullivan preventing a late try by Bray. This marvellous Hull sporting day brought great credit to players, supporters and the entire city. On their return home, both teams delighted their loyal fans with an open-top bus tour and an appearance on the City Hall balcony. The thrill of that epic Cup Final day was summed up perfectly by the sign which dominated the fish shop on Boothferry Road, reading, 'Will the last one out please turn off the lights'.

MAY 4TH

1956: On this date a quarrel between Walter Beaumont and four men serving as airmen for the United States Forces broke out in a café in Hull. The circumstances are unclear but resulted in Walter being stabbed with a knife by one of the airmen, James Jordan. Walter was rushed to hospital, where his wound was stitched up, yet he died a few days later and James was tried for murder. At first this seems an open and shut case, but further evidence arose after the trial which shed new light on the cause of death. It appeared that the stab wound had penetrated the intestine in two places, but it was mainly healed at the time of death, so why did Walter die? With a view to preventing infection, it was thought right to administer an antibiotic, terramycin. However, Walter had a bad reaction to terramycin. After the initial doses he developed diarrhoea, which was an indication of his intolerance. The terramycin was stopped, but unfortunately the very next day was resumed by another doctor. This was a regrettable oversight as it was later decided that it was the introduction of a poisonous substance to a patient who showed intolerance that finally killed him. James' conviction of murder was thus quashed.

MAY 5TH

1930: It was on this day that Amy Johnson in her Gipsy Moth biplane, *Jason*, arrived in Australia after an epic 11,000-mile journey. This was a record-breaking solo flight from England to Australia that elevated the Hull girl into the aviation Hall of Fame forever. Up to this point her longest solo flight had been between Croydon and Hull, so it was quite a leap she made, flying this great distance in just nineteen days. She was also the first woman to make the journey alone. She was met with an amazing 20,000-strong crowd waiting for her arrival at Brisbane, but that was nothing compared with the 1 million who turned out to see her arrive back in London, where she received a CBE from King George V. The reception in her hometown of Hull was staggering, with huge crowds lining the streets from the Hedon Aerodrome to the Guildhall. At Hedon, the word 'Welcome' had been spelt out using 1,200 feet of calico, ensuring Amy could see her way home from up to 15 miles away. Her trusty Gipsy Moth is still on display today in the Science Museum in London.

MAY 6TH

1893: The *Hull and East Yorkshire Times* ran a story on this date entitled 'Exciting Event in Waterhouse Lane'. Just after noon on the previous Wednesday, this neighbourhood 'was thrown into a state of intense excitement by the repeated firing of revolver shots from the shop. A large crowd speedily assembled ... and for a time no one raised sufficient pluck to enter the place.' Fortunately two PCs were on duty nearby and went to investigate, whence, 'at a glance they saw that something of an unusual character had arisen'. On entering, they found a seaman lying on a sofa, bleeding from a bullet wound to the head. Then they heard shouts from the crowd outside that a man could be seen at an upstairs window, holding a gun. Upstairs they went and captured the man, Charles Yarling, whom they later established was not responsible for the shooting. However, the crowd 'laboured under the impression that he was the cause of the mischief, and the police had no little difficulty in checking their attempts to do him a bodily injury.' At the police station the injured man confessed the revolver was his, as he had intended on taking his own life. Charles was just a lodger at the house and the angry mob could have caused great harm to an innocent man.

MAY 7TH

1941: The port of Hull was a frequent target for air raids but suffered one of its worst attacks on the night of this date. Over 300 explosive bombs fell, whilst incendiary bombs started around 800 fires. In all, 203 people died, whilst many more were injured. It also destroyed the much-loved restaurant of Yorkshire, Powolny's. Young Ernst Adolf Powolny moved to Leeds in 1858, from Germany, and opened his own restaurant four years later. For thirty years it was one of the best restaurants in Yorkshire, with the delicious fresh ingredients and exciting recipes stimulating the Northern palate. In 1903, the family opened a branch in Hull, on King Edward Street. The Continental style, with marble flooring, mahogany doors and oak panelling became a hit with the affluent Pearson Park and Avenues residents. For the opening the *Hull Daily Mail* advertised 'soups of every description, particularly turtle, hot and cold entrees, fancy ices, aspics, patisserie, pate foie, bonbons, chocolates, savoury and sweet jellies, creams, truffled viands.' Then came that fateful night. Some say the bomb had Powolny's name on it, dropped from a German aircraft, just one weapon in a lethal consignment of 80 tons of explosives that destroyed one of Hull's jewels.

MAY 8TH

1848: This date saw the opening of Hull's Paragon Street train station, although the official date was not until 1851. The railway came to Hull with the opening of its first line, the Hull to Selby route, in 1840. The Hull to Bridlington line was opened in 1846 and the ceremony was remarkable for the meeting for the first time of the corporations of Hull and York at a grand dinner at the Public Rooms, presided over by George Hudson, the 'Railway King'. The original station was at Manor House Street but a more centrally located position was required. Paragon Street station was initially thought to be unreasonably large and extravagant, but the 'Railway King' thought otherwise and the plans went ahead, the station covering an area of two-and-a-half acres. Half a century later it was rebuilt and expanded, creating the last of Britain's great barrel-vaulted glass-and-iron railway stations, being reopened in 1904 with a five-bay train shed and two additional barrel vault bays at right angles covering the concourse. The station has survived two world wars and subsequent decades of redevelopment. The new transport interchange was officially opened by the Queen and the Duke of Edinburgh when they unveiled a plaque on March 5th 2009 after arriving at the station on the Royal Train.

MAY 9TH

1930: Thomas Robinson Ferens died on this date. Born in County Durham, Thomas made Hull his home, moving to the area in 1868 with just two shillings his mother had given him. Through sheer hard work and determination he became one of the richest men in the country, but he was a man with a pure heart, fighting for the causes of others as well as donating gifts to the city – during his life he gave the equivalent of more than £45m to the people of Hull. He joined the Hull firm Reckitt & Sons, helping to establish the business and becoming joint chairman when James Reckitt died. Thomas was the Member of Parliament for East Hull for thirteen years, where he fought for women's rights, orphaned children, the poor and against the trafficking of girls in India. As soon as he began earning a salary he allocated 10 per cent of his earnings to charity and it is said by 1920 he was distributing £47,000 out of his annual income of £50,000. He gave land and money for an art gallery to be built in Hull, the establishment of a university college and a boating lake. When he died he bequeathed his house and its grounds, plus an endowment of £50,000, to be used as a rest home for poor gentlewomen. His name lives on in Ferens Art Gallery and the Ferensway thoroughfare.

MAY 10TH

1941: On this date Chief Warden Robert Tarran issued a document to thank all the members of Hull's Warden Service for their actions during the devastating Luftwaffe attacks on the city earlier in the month. Hull was bombed badly during the war and countless lives were lost. Robert's message to his fellow wardens read: 'Your courage and devotion to duty during and after the two most severe raids yet suffered by this city, can never be excelled by any man or woman serving His Majesty'. Later that year Robert, who was also the city's Sherriff, welcomed King George VI and Queen Elizabeth to Hull, ensuring they were aware that the citizens of Hull demonstrated great resilience in the face of devastation. He stated, 'The men, women and children of this city have been subjected to the enemy's most venomous and brutal attacks from the air. The fortitude shown, not only by all the civil defence workers but by the ordinary folk, is something which has inspired the hearts and minds of all those who have come amongst us. It has also been an outstanding period in the history of Kingston upon Hull ... the spirit of its people would be for ever an inspiration to the world.'

MAY 11TH

2011: The *Hull Daily Mail* published an article on this date reporting that the Hull-born actor, Sir Tom Courtenay, had agreed to be patron of the Creative Learning Team at Hull Truck Theatre, which works with hundreds of up-and-coming actors through its youth theatre. He recently appeared at Hull Truck performing his one-man show, 'Pretending to Be Me', based on the work of Philip Larkin. He was quoted as saying, 'I'm happy to support the theatre in my hometown.' Sir Tom always had a passion for acting and moved to London after his A-levels, choosing University College because it was in the same street as The Royal Academy of Dramatic Art; 'I wanted to look at the students and see if I might fit in one day. I was so focused on my acting at UCL that I failed my English degree, but it didn't matter because by then, in 1958, I had got a scholarship to RADA.' His first film debut was in the 1962 film, *Private Potter*, with a director who had spotted him while he was at RADA. From then he was much sought after and has a string of awards, being knighted for his services to acting. Sir Tom is also the President of Hull City Official Supporter's Club and was awarded an Honorary Doctorate by Hull University in 1999.

MAY 12TH

1948: World-famous mountaineer Joe Tasker was born in Hull on this date. One of ten children from a very close-knit family with a strong Catholic ethos, at thirteen he was sent to Ushaw College to train as a Jesuit priest. Here, the library fired his imagination for climbing and he began practising in the quarry behind the college, with the encouragement of Father Barker. At twenty he realised the priesthood was not his vocation and decided to leave; one of the hardest decisions of his life. He studied Sociology at university and joined the Climbing Club. In 1975, he and university friend Dick Renshaw climbed the North Face of the Eiger, about which he had read so much as a youth. In 1978, he and Peter Boardman joined Chris Bonington on an expedition to K2, where fellow climber Nick Estcourt was killed in an avalanche. Joe participated in numerous climbs and was classed as one of the most talented British climbers during the late 1970s and early '80s. He disappeared with Peter Boardman in 1982 on the Northeast Ridge of Everest. Peter's body was found in 1992, but Joe is still missing. The Boardman Tasker Prize for Mountain Literature was founded in memory of the two climbers.

MAY 13TH

1936: This was the inquest date for the murder of Hull shop owner Oswald Walker, tool merchant. The murder was a violent and bloody one, a sad end to the life of a seventy-year-old. The scene was apparently covered in blood when the police found the poor man partly strangled and then bludgeoned so hard that his skull had been fractured. Suspicion fell immediately upon his son, Norman, as he had been sacked by his father as Oswald allegedly found his ideas 'too modern'. Norman had consequently gone on to open his own shop in competition with his father. Other evidence showed Oswald's wallet had not been stolen during the attack, nor had silver and other valuables left in the shop. Tellingly, Norman was left only a watch in his father's will – the rest going to his daughter. Jealousy? Rivalry? A grudge? We shall never know. Interrogation is said to have shown that father and son had a good relationship, so the inquest decided 'murder by person or persons unknown'.

MAY 14TH

1954: Sadly this was the date actor and comedian Arthur Lucan last appeared on stage, at the Theatre Royal in Barnsley. The following Monday he had been meant to appear in revue at the Tivoli in Hull but he collapsed and died in the wings of the Tivoli whilst waiting for his cue to go on stage. In true music hall tradition of 'the show must go on', the performance went ahead with an understudy playing the lead part. The audience was totally unaware of developments backstage, and only learned the tragic news after the performance. Arthur gained fame as Old Mother Riley on stage, radio and also screen, with a series of comedy films between the late 1930s and early 1950s. He and his young wife, Kitty McShane, became a successful double act and it was apparently after a Royal Command Performance that there followed a successful and highly lucrative film career. In all, Arthur Lucan made seventeen films, sixteen as Old Mother Riley. Legend has it that Arthur's spirit, dressed as Old Mother Riley, haunted the tax building that replaced the Tivoli theatre; an appropriate haunting, as he was hounded by debts from tax right up to his death. His body is buried in Hull's Eastern Cemetery and even over sixty years after his death, his grave is still regularly visited.

MAY 15TH

2006: The Hull-born band The Beautiful South released their final album, *Superbi*, on this date before they announced their split in January 2007. Having had a succession of different band members, the original two who first formed the band were both former members of Hull group The Housemartins. Paul Heaton and Dave Hemingway were the two lead vocalists to begin with but roles changed when other band members were recruited, the role of singer altering numerous times. By the time the band split they had sold around 6,500,000 records worldwide with the famous No.1 hit in 1990, 'A Little Time', from their album *Choke*. Their 1994 compilation album, *Carry On Up the Charts*, was a massive success and became the second bestselling album of that year, securing the Christmas No.1 chart position. In 1995, they were the support act for *REM* and headlined their own stadium concert in 1997. Their musical style changed throughout their career starting as alternative rock, then indie, then changing to folk, but many of the lyrics were love-themed. 'We write about people who've lived together most of their lives,' they're quoted as saying. In 2008, the original duo plus seven reformed under the name, The New Beautiful South, becoming The South in 2010.

MAY 16TH

1916: The *Sappho*, a trawler from the Wilson Line, experienced a dramatic and fatal final journey when it set sail back to Hull from Russia in the winter of 1915. She became trapped in ice and the crew could not free her. By Christmas Eve they had only a week's supply of rations left and Captain Martin made the decision that they should abandon ship and attempt the 18-mile trek to the lighthouse at Cross Island. With only a few provisions and just ordinary sea clothes, only three of the nineteen who set out reached land. These three found help, they were fed and clothed and returned to Hull on February 26th 1916. No trace was ever found of those who did not make it. The *Sappho* was found in the January by the icebreaker *Sadko*, just ten miles from the mainland, but she could still not be reached. It was May when she was next sighted by the Hammerfest sealer, *Alfred Edwards*, drifting in the White Sea. This ship towed her towards the nearest harbour and attempts were made to keep her afloat but a heavy north-west swell caused her to founder on May 16th and she was lost forever.

MAY 17TH

2007: This was the date that South Africa's first black Archbishop, Desmond Tutu, delivered the Wilberforce Emancipation Lecture in Hull, commemorating the life and achievements of the anti-slavery crusader, William Wilberforce. His lecture was part of the city's 700th anniversary celebrations and formed part of Hull's Wilberforce 2007 celebrations of the bicentenary of the abolition of slavery. Dedicated to achieving equal rights for all, Desmond had spent his career campaigning for a democratic and just society without racial divisions. He was best known for his diligent campaign against apartheid in the 1980s, for which he was awarded the Nobel Peace Prize in 1984. During his speech, Desmond commended the people of Hull for supporting him and the South African fight against apartheid, saying, 'In the darkest days of our struggle to show your commitment, you gave me the freedom of your city to proclaim your unswerving support. How appropriate that I should be here today as the recipient of a medal that commemorates an outstanding son of Hull, whose perseverance, whose evangelical faith and fervour made him the leader of the movement to end the awful scourge on humanity; the slave trade and slavery itself.'

MAY 18TH

1957: Queen Elizabeth II and Prince Philip made a visit to Hull on this date. This visit caused much excitement and the streets were lined with hundreds of people waving flags, who had turned out to catch a glimpse of the head of the monarchy. The couple arrived by train, where they were greeted by dignitaries such as Lord Middleton – the Lord Lieutenant of the East Riding – and Lady Middleton, and the Lord Mayor Alderman Kneeshaw, being then escorted off the platform by men in traditional costume, carrying swords and maces. They were taken by car to the University and then on to the Sailor's Children's Society. Here they were greeted by a boy in a pirate's outfit who offered the couple gifts. They lunched at the Guildhall, where an amazing flower display was put out for the occasion and a brass band played outside. Next they were taken to a hostel for the elderly then onto the newly constructed King George Dock. At the Bilton Grange Housing Estate, the Queen apparently paid a surprise visit to one of its residents before they went onto East Park. At Corporation Pier she received a Naval Guard of Honour before embarking on a barge taking them to the Royal Yacht, *Britannia*.

MAY 19TH

1906: The *Hull News* reported the discovery of a William Wilberforce relic on this date. The find was a medal, upon which an inscription read, 'W Wilberforce Esquire returned to the British Parliament the sixth time for the County of York June 1807', and on the reverse side it read, 'The hero of freedom, the pride of his country and ornament of human nature. Africa, rejoice!! Yorkshiremen have acted independently'. The piece was added to the Wilberforce Museum. The same newspaper also commented on the subject of Sunday trading in Hull, as the matter had been raised by the Corporation Committee. The article stated that, 'Hull occupies a somewhat unique position in the matter of Sunday trading, in so much as for the last twenty years it has rigorously put into operation the Lord's Day Act.' Apparently, figures showed that in 1905, 4,132 summonses were issued and convictions obtained, but it seemed to be the attitude of the traders that the 5s penalty incurred each week was part of the nature of the payment for a licence. The Corporation made more than enough to cover court costs and thus it was decided nothing much needed to change.

MAY 20TH

1854: Included in the *Hull Police News* on this date, within the *Hull News*, was a mention of a certain George Douglas who was charged with wilful damage.

> It appeared that a Mrs Brown had often annoyed defendant by shaking a dirty door-mat near his house. A day or two ago, the annoyance was repeated, and the defendant spoke to the complainant about it, upon which the latter struck him with a thick stick, and so exasperated him that he threw the mat into a drain.

Mrs Brown said the mat cost 10s and George was ordered to pay 5s for it. Nothing was mentioned of assault! However, Mary Leonard was charged with assault, by John Bolton, who protested to her that she had hung washing right in front of his home. When she refused to move the clothes John cut the line, whereby Mary struck him with a clothes prop. The court, however, said the line was fixed to a post in a public thoroughfare and so John had no right to interfere and that in fact the 'defendant was justified in striking him. She was discharged.'

MAY 21ST

1816: Benjamin Thompson, famously known for being the translator of *The Stranger*, by Kotzebue, was born in Hull, in 1774. He was educated for the law, but, disliking the profession, he was sent to Hamburg, aged around fifteen, as his father's agent, a merchant, and to finish his education, where he acquired a critical knowledge of the language. Soon after his return to England he translated Kotzebue's well-known play, which was produced at Drury Lane in 1798. Forsaking any other trade, Benjamin became a professional writer, and soon attained considerable eminence in the literary world, especially for his translations of Kotzebue, Schiller, Goethe, Lessing, and Iffland. He produced a number of his own works, but it is said one was to be fatal. *Oberon's Oath* was performed at Dury Lane on this date, but was unfavourably received and the disappointment so affected him as to bring on a fit of apoplexy, of which he died on May 25th 1816, four days after the production of his play.

MAY 22ND

2006: On this date the *Telegraph* newspaper ran a story about 'Britain's richest and most secretive tycoon', Sir John Ellerman of Hull. Described as a reclusive figure, he was, 'according to a 1929 list of millionaires drawn up by the Inland Revenue, so well-off that the next tycoon earned less than half as much as he did.' Having been left some money by his father and grandfather, he started his business empire in 1892, buying up an ailing shipping company. He was described as a genius for such business acumen; 'he could spot underperforming firms and he bought them up and put them back on their feet. He is, in a sense, the ancestor of the people who go to get a MBA in business schools now. When he was doing it there was nobody like him. Now they're a dime a dozen,' commented one university professor. In 1916, he bought up the great Hull shipping company of Thomas Wilson Sons & Company, once the largest privately owned shipping company in the world, for the then staggering sum of £4.1 million. He diversified into brewing, then newspapers, and was a major shareholder of *The Times* and the *Daily Mail*. When he died in 1933 he apparently left over £36 million – over £10 billion in today's values.

MAY 23RD

1853: This date saw the opening of an inquiry into the election process in Hull, at Mansion House. This was because officials at the House of Commons had become somewhat concerned about the rumours they had been hearing in connection with general elections in Hull.

The two parties concerned in the controversy were the Conservatives and the Liberals and the rumours suggested that both these parties had been involved in bribery and corruption regarding votes. The commission, which began on this date, apparently lasted for fifty-seven days, during which time 1,200 witnesses were called to give evidence. When the final report was announced, the findings showed that in 1841 both parties had paid up to 700 voters for their support. This rose to 1,200 in 1847, then 1,400 in 1852. The cost of the whole commission for parliament ran to around £5,000, which was a lot of money in the 1800s and illustrates how important the government believed the problem in Hull to be, especially in a democratic society where the significance of a free vote was paramount.

MAY 24TH

2008: Hull City Association Football Club was founded in June 1904. Previous to this, Hull had been dominated by rugby league teams and indeed the football club's first games were played at the Boulevard, which was the home of the rugby league club. Since then they moved grounds a few times but now have a permanent home at the KC Stadium. This date – May 24th 2008 – is paramount in their history, as this was the day of the 2008 Football League Championship play-off final, between Bristol City and Hull City. The match was won by the Tigers through a 38th-minute goal from Dean Windass. Dean is quoted as having said, 'It feels unbelievable. I don't think there is anyone left in Hull today looking at how many supporters we've got here.' Hull City chairman Paul Duffen backed this up, stating, 'This is fantastic, I think it's amazing. It is something which means a lot to the city of Hull.' Thousands of fans lined the streets of Hull to greet their heroes forty-eight hours later, while behind the scenes preparations for the Club's first ever season of top flight football in the Premier League were well underway.

MAY 25TH

2012: The *Hull Daily Mail* published an unusual report concerning sixty-one-year-old Terry Nolan, who appeared in court on this date. Mr Nolan, who is completely blind, is said to have narrowly avoided prison after being caught with tens of thousands of cigarettes hidden in a secret compartment in his garden shed. After pleading guilty to evading £102,000 of excise duty, he was lucky to escape with a five-month prison sentence, suspended for a year, ordered to pay £680 costs and subjected to a curfew order, requiring him to stay at his home between the hours of 6 p.m. and 6 a.m. Nolan is said to have claimed that he met a man in the pub and agreed to look after the cigarettes for £500 cash and twelve boxes, but that he could not reveal the man's identity to officers from HM Revenue and Customs for fear of reprisals. Nolan apparently had a total of more than 280,000 cigarettes and 140kg of hand-rolling tobacco secreted about his home and garden and after an initial search officers are said to have found a false wall that had been built in Nolan's garden shed, with further tobacco-related goods hidden there.

MAY 26TH

1946: On this day, famous guitarist, songwriter, arranger and producer Mick Ronson was born in Hull. As a child he was encouraged to play various different instruments, including the piano, recorder, violin and harmonium. He soon discovered a love for guitar and joined his first band aged seventeen. After this he went from band to band and strength to strength. In 1970, he was asked to join a new backing group for David Bowie and in February of that year he made his debut with Bowie on John Peel's Radio 1 show. Their first gig was played at The Roundhouse and the group apparently all dressed up in superhero costumes. Mick was Gangsterman, which suited his very masculine attitude. Mick had a very varied career as a session musician and recorded with many great talents, such as Morrissey, Van Morrison, Bob Dylan and Elton John. He also recorded several solo albums, being named as the sixty-fourth greatest guitarist of all time by *Rolling Stone* magazine. Mick died aged just forty-six in 1993, of liver cancer. In his memory, the Mick Ronson Memorial Stage was constructed in Queens Gardens in his hometown of Hull. There is also a street named after him on Bilton Grange Estate, not far from where he lived.

MAY 27TH

1809: Joseph James Forrester was born in Hull on this date. In 1831, he travelled to Oporto in Portugal where he joined his uncle, James, a partner in the house of Offley, Forrester and Weber, wine merchants. Joseph became totally absorbed with the culture and spent much of his first twelve years living there compiling a survey of the Douro wine region and rivers. Its merit was apparently universally recognised and adopted by the Portuguese government. In 1844, Joseph also published an anonymous pamphlet on the wine trade, in an attempt to reform the abuses practised in Portugal in the making and treatment of port wine, and also to change the legislation for trade regulations. He was directly opposing the Douro Wine Company, a government initiative to regulate the trade and production of port wine. He accused their monopoly of causing a depression in the port wine trade and he was victimised for this by the company, although he had a great amount of support from the inhabitants of the wine country. Even now he is remembered as the 'protector of the Douro' and was created a Baron for life by the Crown of Portugal. Ironically, he died in the rivers he had mapped so well. His boat capsized in the rapids and his body was never found.

MAY 28TH

1961: Ask any Hullensian who Roland Gift is and you should not find a blank face anywhere. Although born in Birmingham on this date, Roland grew up in Hull, attending Kelvin Hall School. He has many creative talents, including music, acting and writing, and his first recording, on which he played the saxophone, was with Akrylykz, a Hull ska band. Although this record was unsuccessful, it did bring him to the attention of Andy Cox and David Steele of The Beat. The Akrylykz toured with The Beat and when The Beat finally broke up, around 1985, they asked Roland to be the lead singer of their new band, Fine Young Cannibals. Their 1988 album, *The Raw and the Cooked*, topped the UK and US album charts, and contained their two Billboard Hot 100 number ones: 'She Drives Me Crazy' and 'Good Thing'. Then in 1990 the band won two Brit Awards: Best British Group and Best British Album. After Fine Young Cannibals broke up Roland released a self-titled solo album, featuring the single 'It's Only Money'. It is said that in 1990 he was chosen by *People* magazine as one of the 50 most beautiful people in the world.

MAY 29TH

1875: The legendary 'Gassy' Jack Deighton, founder of modern Vancouver, died on this date. John, or Jack as he was known, was born in Hull in 1830. Whilst in New York he caught gold fever and left to seek his fortune. Unsuccessful at this, he went to sea, becoming a skilled pilot and navigator but the lure of finding gold obsessed him. Simultaneously he ran a small bar called the Globe Saloon, in New Westminster. After returning from yet another failed hunt for gold, however, he found that the saloon's caretaker had absconded with his money; so he and his native wife set off in a canoe with his yellow dog and a barrel of whisky. He landed near the mouth of the Fraser River and on the promise of as much whisky as they could drink, enlisted the local sawmill workers to help build him a new saloon. He named it The Globe, and being the only bar in a 30-mile vicinity, it became very popular, as did his tales of adventures, earning him the nickname 'Gassy'. A settlement, Granville, grew up around his saloon in 1870 but everyone knew it as Gastown. Legend states that on the night of May 29th 1875, his yellow dog began to howl and Jack died soon after, aged forty-four. Gastown continued to grow and today is the oldest part of Vancouver. This city has a statue of Gassy Jack in remembrance of him.

MAY 30TH

1914: This date marked the death of Hull market trader, David Ombler. The case, that of murder most foul, was very high profile as his brother was a councillor. The victim was found in his home in West Parade by his cleaner, Mrs Harrison. The attacker had broken in sometime during the morning, as David's half-eaten breakfast was still on the table. The weapon, an iron poker, had been snapped in two and discarded next to David's prostrate figure. When Mrs Harrison found him he was barely alive and, despite a doctor and the police being summoned immediately, he died a few hours later in Hull Royal Infirmary. The case was classed as a robbery because some of his money was missing, as well as a silver medallion with a sovereign and a silver watch. Two women in the street claimed to have seen a man leaving David's house around ten to eight in the morning. They stated he was in his mid-twenties, short, with a pale face, of thin build, wearing a shabby overcoat and dark cloth cap with muffler. In spite of this detailed description, the attacker was never found.

MAY 31ST

1938: This date saw the birth of the man who was to become Deputy Prime Minister in 1997, John Prescott. He was actually born in Wales, but after graduating from the University of Hull with a BSc in economics and economic history, then becoming involved in politics, he came to represent Hull East as the Labour Member of Parliament from 1970 to 2010. In July 2010, he entered the House of Lords as a Life Peer, with the title Baron Prescott of Kingston-upon-Hull in the County of East Yorkshire. He has been something of a controversial figure during his time in office and has met with some unwelcome receptions. At the Brit Awards in 1998, a jug of iced water was poured over his head, apparently in aid of the Liverpool Dockers' strike. In 2001, an egg was thrown at him and his reflex reaction was to respond with a left hook to the perpetrator's jaw! Tony Blair commented on the event, 'John is John'. He is, however, proud of his northern connections and in the 2011 Red Nose Day event he presented the Shipping Forecast for the Humber, deliberately slipping into his distinctive Humberside accent, saying, 'Umber' without the H as we say it up here!

JUNE 1ST

1829: This date saw the opening of Junction Dock, the site everyone now knows as Princes Quay Shopping Centre. This dock was constructed between the Old and Humber Docks and was renamed Princes Dock in 1854 in honour of Prince Albert, who accompanied Queen Victoria on a royal visit to Hull in 1854. The same visit saw Old Dock renamed Queens Dock. When Princes Dock closed in 1968, after 139 years, the site was redeveloped into a shopping centre, but retained its old name. When the Dock Company built the Humber Dock, it was stipulated that they would build a third dock between the Humber and Old ones when the average tonnage of goods unloaded at the docks reached a certain level. Thus Junction Dock was a consideration for twenty years until it was actually built in 1827. This completed the line of docks connecting the River Hull to the River Humber along the site of the old wall and military fortifications formerly protecting this ancient town. The Princes Quay Shopping Centre was built in keeping with a nautical theme, having 'decks' instead of floors and panoramic views of Hull from its large glass corridors.

JUNE 2ND

1847: This was the date of the official opening of the Hull General Cemetery on Spring Bank. The Mayor, Mr B.M. Jalland, laid the first stone and many people turned out to see the long awaited new plot of ground opened. It was seen as a peaceful resting place, with some 20 acres, filled with a great variety of shrubs and trees, flowers and wildlife. There were five main cemeteries within Hull's boundaries and Hull General Cemetery was privately run by the Hull General Cemetery Company until 1972, when it closed for burials and the council took over its maintenance. It makes for an interesting walk, with a monument erected in 1849 for those poor souls of Hull who lost their lives to the tragic cholera outbreak of the time, where one in forty-three fell victim. There is also a Quaker burial ground in the cemetery, opened in 1855, which contains the graves of 400 Friends including a number of notable Hull Quaker families, such as Reckitt, Priestman, Thorp and Stickney, to name but a few. Said to be haunted, there have been reports of military-looking ghosts and strange children seen flitting amongst the graves.

JUNE 3RD

1875: This is the date of the coroner's report for Thomas Hall, which stated that on the previous day the poor fellow 'accidently, casually and by misfortune received mortal injuries to his legs through being run over by a railway wagon, from which mortal injuries he, the said Thomas Hall, at the Infirmary at the Borough of Kingston-upon-Hull did die.' James Wood was a witness to the accident. He explained how he had seen Thomas Hall's railway shunter early in the morning of the fatal day. He said he saw Thomas riding on the left-hand buffer of a railway truck, pulled by one horse. Thomas was the only driver to haul his full load and was sitting with both legs on one side, feet hanging down. As the wagons crossed the points on the track it 'gave a jerk and he fell off with his body in the four foot and his legs lay upon the rail. The leading wheels ran over his legs and the second wheels stopped on his legs. One of his legs was nearly cut off and the other was hurt.' He was rushed to the Infirmary but died within a minute or two of being brought in. The verdict was death through blood loss.

JUNE 4TH

1972: Hull impressionist Deborah Stephenson was born on this date and began her uncanny knack of mimicking celebrities from as early as thirteen years of age. 'I got into it through my dad,' she told the *Hull Daily Mail*, 'he would write and coach me, while my mum would make costumes.' At fourteen she secured her first big break, winning the TV talent show *Opportunity Knocks*. This natural calling was the start of a prosperous career for Deborah, who went on to land roles in TV's *Coronation Street* and *Bad Girls*. It was, however, her talent for impressionism to which she returned. She met John Culshaw during the 2005 Comic Relief Fame Academy. The two of them whiled away their time doing impressions backstage and later she received a call from his management team proposing a job for her in BBC One's *The Impressions Show with Culshaw and Stephenson*. Initially an eight-episode commission, the show has now run for three series and has proved most popular. Deborah's CV is quite impressive, including appearances in *Blue Peter*, *Playing the Field*, a Catherine Cookson adaptation and *The Friday Night Project*, but it is for her impressions of Cheryl Cole, Amanda Holden and Davina McCall, amongst others, that she is best known and loved.

JUNE 5TH

1985: The talented young actor, Marc Pickering, was born in Hull on this date. He attended South Hunsley Secondary School and was attracted to acting very early on in his life. Aged eight he apparently told his father he wouldn't mind having a go at the audition for *The Sound of Music* and although he did not get this part, it sparked a fire in him and he joined The National Youth Music Theatre. Aged only twelve he was talent spotted by one of the theatre's directors, Jeremy James Taylor, who put Marc forward for the part of Young Masbath in Tim Burton's 1999 film *Sleepy Hollow*.

As well as many stage performances, Marc has made other film appearances, including starring opposite Helen Mirren and Julie Walters in *Calendar Girls* in 2003. In addition to being a successful actor, Marc has a talent for singing and dancing, a role he performed very well in Peter Kay's 2008 talent show parody *Britain's Got the Pop Factor*, in which he played R. Wayne.

JUNE 6TH

1915: The evening of this date saw the first and very unexpected attack on Hull by a Zeppelin bomber. Kapitänleutnant Mathy, the commander of Zeppelin *L9*, was apparently attempting to reach London but by the time he reached the English coast it had become clear that the winds were against him and he would not reach his target. Instead he followed the railway lines to Hull and even though the city was in complete blackout, the Zeppelin dropped flares to light up the docks. He met no resistance as Hull had no anti-aircraft guns, save one which was in a shipyard being repaired. It took a slow route over the city at around 3,000 feet, dropping thirteen high-explosive shells and fifty incendiary bombs. The first two clusters fell over densely packed working-class housing areas, causing many fatalities as well as much damage. More bombs were dropped on the Old Town, where several buildings were destroyed, including the buildings of Edwin Davis & Co., drapers. From the air it must have looked as though the city was on fire and the emergency services, as well as many civilians, worked tirelessly to put out the flames and rescue those trapped beneath rubble. Twenty-four people were killed that night with many more injured.

JUNE 7TH

1837: On this date the people of Hull witnessed a terrible tragedy. The steam packet *Union* was docked just near the pier, preparing to sail to Gainsborough Country Fair. One passenger reported that he had been on board for about twenty minutes when he heard what sounded like crackling and breaking sticks. He said he saw the vessel start to sink and heard what sounded like escaping steam. He believed he saw the captain go to the safety valve and just five minutes later there was an almighty explosion. 'The deck of the vessel was shattered to fragments which flew in all directions.' Corpses were said to be strewn all around, as were parts of the ship and boiler. Thirteen people died and many others were terribly hurt in the accident, said to have been caused by the boiler being overcharged with steam.

———— •◆• ————

1931: On this day, the Dogger Bank experienced an earthquake thought to have been the strongest earthquake recorded in Britain, measuring 6.1 on the Richter scale. Chimneys were said to have collapsed in Hull – even though the epicentre was 60 miles off the Yorkshire coast – and one Hull woman apparently died of a heart attack caused by the quake.

JUNE 8TH

2006: Hull Football Club is one of Hull's rugby clubs, one of the oldest clubs in the Rugby League, formed by a group of ex-public schoolboys from York in 1865. Hull FC were one of the founding members of the Northern Rugby Football Union which was formed in 1895, making them one of the world's first twenty-two rugby league clubs. The club eventually moved into the Hull Athletic Club's ground at the Boulevard, Airlie Street, which gave rise to their nickname, The Airlie Birds. Their first game came in the September of that year, when a record crowd of 8,000 witnessed them defeat Liversedge in the very first season of Northern Union Football. Also known as the Black and Whites, the club's famous anthem is 'Old Faithful'. The song was initially adopted back in 1936, when they claimed a narrow 13–12 victory against Wigan at the Boulevard. Overjoyed with such a dramatic win, the Hull fans began to sing the former chart-topping cowboy song 'Old Faithful' and it stuck! Between April 14th and July 15th 2006, Hull won 13 matches in succession, including a 27–26 defeat of league leaders St Helens on June 8th 2006. The last time they beat St Helens at their ground was eighteen years previously.

JUNE 9TH

1866: The *Hull Advertiser* on this date gave details about the bricklayer's strike in Hull. It stated that, 'Since Monday upwards of 100 bricklayers had left Hull in search of employment,' as other towns were said to pay more and allow a half-day holiday on Saturdays.

On the same date the paper also printed a story concerning a horse that had been frightened by the rain. The poor beast was apparently harnessed to a light cart in George Yard 'when it was suddenly frightened by a heavy shower of rain' and set off at a run. Its 'mad career' was stopped in Whitefriargate by the 'shaft coming into contact with the panel of a cab. Fortunately no one was in the vehicle at the time.'

The same paper gives some interesting figures concerning the inmates of Hull workhouse at this time. 'Adults, not able-bodied, 203; ditto, able-bodied, 18; children, 167. Imbeciles or idiots in the workhouse, 24. Number of pauper lunatics in the borough asylum, 69.' The column also tells of an anonymous benefactor who donated £10 to the workhouse in order for the children to be taken on a trip to Withernsea in July.

June 10th

1893: On this date the *Hull and Lincolnshire Times* reported the story of a free labourer who came to Hull's Railway Dock looking for work. He was granted a ticket for the work but before leaving, he asked if he could leave a parcel in the custody of the registrar, who accepted the trust. The package, a heavy one by all accounts, was forwarded to the Railway Dock where the owner was supposed to be working, but he was not to be found and it was discovered he was actually wanted by the police.

> The contents of the parcel one day were unwittingly exposed to view, and in them was a revelation. A complete burglar's outfit was discovered – a jemmy, dark lantern, bundle of keys, to the number of about two dozen, all sizes and description of keys, some of them specially prepared and filed down, a bundle of letters from inquisitive people wanting to know his whereabouts, a racing calendar and other turfite accoutrements, and everything nice and handy for a midnight haul.

The robber, it is told, never came back for his belongings, obviously fearing the police would catch him there and it is said he was not found. What happened to his burglary outfit is not mentioned!

JUNE IITH

1885: Mrs Rollit, wife of Sir Albert Kaye Rollit, died on this date, during the mayoralty of her husband. The death of a reigning mayoress is without precedent in the history of Hull, apart from the deaths of the Mayor, his wife, and family by the plague in 1478. Mrs Rollit was universally respected, and her funeral was marked with signs of general mourning, over 20,000 persons thronging the Hull cemetery and its approaches. Albert, described as a 'powerhouse of energy and activity, a compulsive collector of offices, accomplishments and honours,' was known for his business mind, as a politician and as a solicitor. In 1886, he was elected as a Conservative Member of Parliament for the South Islington constituency and in his life he received a knighthood for his services to Hull. He served as the Lord Mayor of Hull and at one time he held the office of Sheriff of Hull. He remarried after his wife died, but they had an experience of some misfortune. While travelling by train from Paris to London, her £30,000 jewellery was stolen by the international jewel thief 'Harry the Valet'. When he died in 1922, Albert was hailed as 'a leader of exceptional calibre and a prophet of welfare capitalism.'

JUNE 12TH

1944: The *Hull Daily Mail* during these dark days of war kept a very positive front, always highlighting how well the British troops were doing in battle and how Hitler was 'getting what-for'. On this date the paper printed a column on how Hull did itself proud in the Civil Defence Parade: 'One of the concluding events in Hull's successful Salute the Soldier Week was the parade of the local Civil Defence Services. It was indicative of the strength and spirit of the city, and its determination to meet with courage and resolution anything the enemy might have in store for it.' The same paper also told of comfort parcels it was collecting and sending to the wounded East Yorkshire men returning from France. It described the contents as including cigarettes, books, games, etc. and asked for donations. Along with this there was an article asking firms if they could spare their on-site nurses, as the hospitals needed all the trained help they could get for dealing with battle casualties. 'The services of these nurses would be invaluable at a hospital during a period of exceptional pressure. Arrangements have been made for workers so released to be paid their normal salary by the receiving hospital.'

JUNE 13TH

2008: An article in the *San Francisco Gate* on this date records an interview with Hull-born comic actor Geoff Hoyle. He recalls his childhood as having its share of post-war hardships – ration coupons, one tub of hot water to be shared with his family on a weekly bath night – but the lighter side of life apparently came from his father and uncles, who loved to sing and tell stories. Geoff met his American wife in London when he was doing some work for TV and they moved to the States to settle. His son, Dan, followed in his father's footsteps, as the article highlights:

> Both Hoyles have made their life on the stage, Geoff as a multifaceted actor, solo performer and Pickle Family Circus clown and Dan as creator of bravura solo shows. 'People sometimes say they catch bits of me when they're watching Dan perform,' says Geoff in his deliberate Yorkshire cadence. 'I don't much see that.' For his part, Dan is quick to credit his father's theatrical legacy. 'I have a lot of pride in continuing the family business,' he says. 'I've learned a ton from watching my dad.' But the son, too, finds clear distinctions. 'He imitates everything, I do people. He does dogs and plants – everything.'

JUNE 14TH

1911: On this day, 4,000 men gathered in Paragon Square under a banner proclaiming the Seamen's and Firemen's International Movement 1911. Known as the Transport Strikes, it was a national movement with a series of strikes occurring at most of the principal ports in the country. Hull, the third largest port in the country, was inevitably involved. The working conditions for seamen were dreadful. The wage was inadequate and seamen generally only worked eight months of the year, thus suffering for the remaining unemployed months, having to make their pay stretch even further. Seamen's hours were long and conditions were harsh, with much illness and disease. One source stated that of the 4,304 work people killed in all occupations in 1911, 1,254 of those were seamen. Beatings, bullying and intimidation was rife and union men were unfairly dismissed upon the excuse of medical examinations. These grievances were placed before the Shipping Federation in July 1910 and in Hull on July 14th 1911 the Humber Union organiser, John Bell, began the strikes, as quoted in the *Hull Daily Mail*: 'The men are tired of their employer's non-co-operation, and have determined, internationally, to take a holiday until their demands are recognised.' The strikes in Hull caused turmoil, with workers from all working aspects in the town joining the men, as the authorities refused to yield. A truce was finally reached and negotiations brought a compromise.

JUNE 15TH

1889: The *Hull News Supplement* had a special column in their paper at this time especially for jokes. They advertised that each week a prize of 5s would be awarded for the best joke or anecdote sent to them and below is an example of the humour of the day, from June 15th 1889.

Father (to son): 'What warm weather we are having just now.'
Son: 'Yes, father, that five shillings you gave me has melted into a threepenny-bit.'

'Uncle John,' said little Emily, 'do you know that a baby that was fed on elephant's milk gained twenty pounds in a week?'
'Nonsense! Impossible!' exclaimed Uncle John, and then asked, 'Whose baby was it?'
'It was the elephant's baby,' replied little Emily.

'Ma,' remonstrated Bobby, 'when I was at grandma's she let me have two pieces of pie.'
'Well, she ought not to have done so, Bobby,' said his mother. 'I think two pieces of pie are too much for little boys. The older you grow, Bobby, the more wisdom you will gain.'
Bobby stood silenced, but only for a moment. 'Well, ma,' he said, 'grandma is a good deal older than you are, so I think she ought to know better than you.'

JUNE 16TH

2012: On this day, Hull singing legend Joe Longthorne was awarded an MBE. Aged fifty-seven when he was granted the tribute, he affirmed he was 'extremely glad' that he was still alive to receive it. In 1989, at the pinnacle of his career, Joe was diagnosed with lymphoma, a form of blood cancer that very nearly proved fatal. His career has spanned over forty years and during this time Joe has performed to millions of people, all around the world. He found fame on LWT programme *Search For A Star* in 1981, then soon had his own TV programme, *The Joe Longthorne Show*. He was starring in the *Royal Variety Show* around the time his health deteriorated, eventually worsening into leukaemia and compelling him to have a bone marrow transplant. He slowly recovered and returned to the stage with a sell-out show at the London Palladium in 2006 and, in 2007, the Variety Club's Most Promising Artiste of '83 was awarded the Lifetime Achievement Award, which placed him amongst a host of past recipients such as Sinatra, Garland and Fitzgerald. Joe has been a tireless fundraiser, raising money for organisations including the Variety Club of Great Britain, Cancer Research UK and the Development of Children and Women Centre Nepal. It was for his charity work that he was awarded the prestigious MBE.

JUNE 17TH

1854: The *Hull Police News* in the newspaper the *Hull News* from this date included the mention of Mary Morris, who was charged with stealing a washing tub. She was apparently accosted at about 6 a.m. in the street by a policeman, carrying said tub, which she claimed was borrowed, but in fact had been stolen. William Tomlinn is also mentioned in the paper, having being 'charged with stealing a quantity of old nails. The prisoner was observed leaving Humphrey's shipyard with the nails in his possession ... and was at once apprehended.' After admitting the charge William was 'committed to prison for fourteen days, during which period he is to be once whipped'. Included in the 'Local and Provincial' column was the tragic story of a seven-year-old boy, who had been playing aboard the *Queen of Scotland*, which had been lying in the Humber dock. 'Some of the vessel's bulwarks had been taken out and reared up at the side of the vessel, and while the little fellow was near them, they were either knocked or pulled down, and fell with great violence, carrying the little boy along with them.' He was attended to at once but the poor lad's head was so badly crushed that identification was almost impossible. He had died at once.

JUNE 18TH

1920: Ian Carmichael was born in Hull on this date. He attended a prep school in Scarborough and completed his education in Worcestershire. He was not an academic and studied for a time at the Royal Academy of Dramatic Art, hoping for a stage career. After appearing in several plays he toured in a revue, *Ninesharp*, in 1940 before going to Sandhurst. He was a major in the Second World War but afterwards resumed his theatrical life. In 1949, he believed he received his best training as a light comedian when he was part of a comic double act with Leo Franklyn for a seven-month tour of *The Lilac Domino*. He moved into West End revues, which were then very much in vogue. They satirised the fashions and moods of the day and suited Carmichael's acting style perfectly. He went to New York in 1965, making his debut there in *Boeing-Boeing* and also toured South Africa and Canada. His stage success in *Simon and Laura* in 1955 was made into a film and began his screen career. He appeared in several films during the following decade, moving into television in the late 1960s. His skill as P.G. Wodehouse's bumbling Bertie Wooster and Dorothy L. Sayers' gentlemanly Lord Peter Wimsey demonstrated his talent for light English comedy of manners. He lived to be eighty-nine and died on February 5th 2010.

JUNE 19TH

1887: This year is remembered for the celebration of the Golden Jubilee of Her Majesty Queen Victoria. In Hull, the festivities began on this date with a Solemn High Mass at St Charles Catholic Church, Jarratt Street. The Mass was well attended and the participants included the Mayor, Alderman John Leak, civic officials and representatives from the Corporation of Hull. This was particularly notable as it is thought to have been the first Visit-in-State of any municipal corporation to a Roman Catholic Church since the Reformation. There followed many celebrations after this, throughout the country, and in Hull a magnificent reception was held at the Artillery Barracks. It was attended by around 15,000 residents and tea and entertainment carried on all week for the inhabitants of Hull and district.

───◆───

1940: On this day, Hull had its first bomb drop at 11.13 p.m. In total Hull had seventy-two air raids, the first warning being on September 4th 1939, sounding at 2.45 a.m. and the all-clear given at 4.08. a.m. There were in total 815 alerts in Hull during the Second World War; seventy-two were actual raids, resulting in thirty-five fatalities. A total of 1,185 people were killed and, despite the evacuations, about one fifth of these were children.

JUNE 20TH

2012: On this date the *Hull Daily Mail* reported that border officers had seized more than 2.5 million cigarettes, which were being smuggled into a Hull dock on Thursday 14th June. The contraband cigarettes were allegedly secreted inside jars of dried coffee in a trailer on board the ferry from Zeebrugge to Hull, but seized when the ferry arrived and was searched at King George Dock, Hull. If the goods had not been discovered, the border officers believed that the Treasury would have missed out on £575,000 in unpaid duty! It was believed to be the biggest seizure at the dock for more than five years. It was also reported that in 2010, more than 1.5 million cigarettes, worth £312,000 in unpaid duty, were found hidden inside concrete blocks in a lorry during a search by officers at the same Hull dock. Also, in 2009, officers found more than a million cigarettes hidden in a cargo of pint glasses. Earlier, in 2007, it was said that 2 million cigarettes were found in a shipment of dog food passing through the dock. The border officers certainly have to keep on their toes, wondering what hiding places will be used next!

JUNE 21ST

1887: A joint celebration occurred on this date: Queen Victoria's Golden Jubilee and the opening of Hull's East Park. Developed as part of a nationwide drive for healthier places for people to pass their leisure hours, East Park was a huge open area for picnics and relaxation. 'A more picturesque locality of that extent it would be impossible to find on the Eastern side of the Borough, or one more adapted to restore the jaded energies of the artisan or man of business when labours of the day are ended'. An 1886 engineers' report stated that 140 men were employed at East Park, being paid 18*s*, the equivalent of 90p, a week. In 1912, Thomas Ferens offered to fund a boating lake in the park, plus an almshouse for the elderly and playing fields for children. Flamingos were added to the park in 1913, but they did not survive long, so it was decided to stick to ducks for a while, although other birds were introduced later, in a special aviary. Much excitement was created when the splash boat/water chute was introduced in 1927 and an open-air theatre was added in 1950, opening with a performance of *The Merry Wives of Windsor*. East Park is now the largest public park in Hull and hosts a variety of concerts and events throughout the year.

JUNE 22ND

1631: This was the date that Hull-born Captain Luke Foxe navigated his ship, HMS *Charles*, into the Hudson Strait on his expedition to explore the North West passage and document new, previously uncharted territory. He developed a passion for arctic history at a young age and was soon regarded as a skilful seaman, adept at navigation. He became determined to lead his own expedition and in 1629 petitioned King Charles I to back his voyage. With this Royal patronage and support from prominent merchants, he and his crew of twenty men and two boys set sail in April 1631. Luke took his ship along the totally unexplored southern shore of Hudson Bay and northwards, to what we now know as the Foxe Channel and Foxe Basin. In all, Luke gave names to twenty-seven locations, eight of which are still used. In the September he reached a point further west than anyone had ever achieved, naming it Port Dorchester, then turned for home. The voyage had been nearly six months long and the first to circumnavigate Hudson Bay and beyond, and they returned home without the loss of a single man. Luke produced a book on polar exploration, possibly the first book ever published by a person from Hull.

JUNE 23RD

1971: A report was made in the *Hull Daily Mail* on this date about Hull's Dickey Sagg, who apparently had a reputation for being England's fastest walker. This would have been extremely useful, seeing as he was employed as Hull's sole postman, back in 1798. The article says that this hard-working man delivered all Hull's post in a day, covering one half of the city in the morning and then the other half in the afternoon. By all accounts Dickey was a small man who wore a swallow-tailed coat. He was well known by all Hull residents and his methods of delivering their post were certainly different from the way we receive our mail today! He would apparently take his stand in a square or court and call out the names on the letters for people residing there. The inhabitants then came out for their letters. If they kept him waiting, his language was said to be 'more vigorous than polished' and he would 'rebuke the slothful by taking the letters to his home, for them to fetch at their pleasure.' He died on August 24th 1828 and when his role as Hull's postman became vacant, a one-legged gentleman, John Stones, was said to have got the job! One leg versus the fastest walker in England? The mind boggles!

JUNE 24TH

2008: The *Hull Daily Mail* reported that the frozen food giant, Birds Eye, was opening the world's largest pea processing plant, in Hull, on this date.

The £10m site on the Brighton Street industrial estate in west Hull will freeze about 50,000 tons of peas during the harvest from June to August. The factory receives peas harvested from 24,000 acres of land in East Yorkshire and North Lincolnshire and freezes them within two-and-a-half hours of picking. They are then stored in one-ton blocks before being transported to Birds Eye's Lowestoft plant for packaging and distribution to retail outlets across the UK.

Frozen Peas have been produced in the UK since 1946 by Birds Eye, who still dominate the market today. Peas were the first frozen products to be taken to a mass market, but Birds Eye's famous fish fingers did not make an appearance until 1955. The opening of the reported factory was said to mark the return of Birds Eye to the city after the company closed its Hessle Road pea processing plant in 2007, with the loss of 600 jobs. The new jobs created increased employment, adding to the 1,250 people that the Birds Eye company already employed at sites across the UK.

JUNE 25TH

1790: This was one of the last dates that John Wesley, founder of Methodism, visited Hull. Always one to speak his mind, he was not shy to mention the state of the city walls in a previous visit in 1752: 'The miserable state of the fortifications, far more ruinous and decayed than those at Newcastle, even before the rebellion. It is well there is no enemy near.' In this visit he attended a service at Holy Trinity Church and then preached to a large crowd in the evening, but the night ended in disorder and Wesley was pursued by a mob into the town. Perhaps this gave him a dismal view of the place. He did express more positive comments on later visits. In 1759, he commented there was 'a far finer congregation' at Hull than at Pocklington. Then, in 1772, he described the new Manor Alley chapel as 'one of the prettiest preaching-houses in England'. By the time Wesley made his last visit to Hull in 1790, Methodism was firmly established in the city. Always the precise timekeeper, Wesley stopped at Beverley on his way to Hull, on this occasion to dine with some forty friends. Deep in conversation after the meal, Wesley apparently pulled out his watch and started to his feet. Saying a swift goodbye, he was off in his carriage before his friends knew it. They all hastened into action but it was only with difficulty that they managed to catch him up and escort him into Hull.

JUNE 26TH

1682: It was on this date that the Alderman George Crowle Hospital, in Sewer Lane, was founded. It could house twelve poor persons, who each received half a crown, with an additional allowance of coal. George Crowle followed in his family's footsteps, with a keen interest in politics. He was a member of parliament for the Kingston-upon-Hull Parliamentary constituency, being elected MP in 1724 and serving until 1747. He was a grandson of Alderman George Crowle, who was Sheriff of Kingston-upon-Hull in 1657, and Mayor in 1661. The Mayor and Aldermen were trustees of the house for the poor and it was left in a will that this institution should continue.

———◆———

2007: On this day, the *Guardian* newspaper reported that Beverley-born Katie O'Brien had become 'the first British player to reach the second round at this year's Wimbledon with a hard-fought victory over Germany's Sandra Kloesel. It was the British No.1's first victory at the All England Club in four attempts as she triumphed 6–3, 7–5 on Court 17.' Katie attended Hymers College, Hull from 1997 to 2002. Despite, or perhaps because of, her exciting and successful career, peaking at No.84 in the world rankings and being one of Britain's leading female tennis players in recent years, the BBC reported in 2011 that Katie was retiring from competitive tennis, aged just twenty-five. 'Having been completely committed to tennis for a long time I feel ready to explore different avenues of life,' she told them.

JUNE 27TH

1927: Hull-born Thomas Jacques Somerscales died in Hull on this date, despite being away for nearly thirty years. At the age of twenty-one, Thomas joined HMS *Cumberland* as a naval schoolmaster and enjoyed this career on various ships. He was discharged from the Royal Navy after contracting a fever in Valparaiso, where he began teaching in the Artisan School. Art was in his blood; his father sketched, his uncle was an amateur painter, and Thomas began to exhibit landscape paintings in Santiago in 1872. This was the start of a very successful painting career and he is remembered in Chile for the landscapes he created there. In 1879, when war broke out between Chile and Peru, he started painting naval battles and from this point on he became a marine painter first and foremost. His international reputation is based on his sea pictures. He moved back to England in 1892 and found the transition from being a celebrated artist in Chile to an unknown one in his own country unnerving. The next year, however, he took Britain by storm with his exhibition at the Royal Academy in London. The Tate houses his *Off Valparaiso* and Hull's Ferens Art Gallery holds four of his works.

JUNE 28TH

1661: On this date Holy Trinity Church was made a separate parish church by an Act of Parliament and the king became its patron. The church is much older, however, having been founded in 1285, with some mention of it made prior to 1204. In the *Guinness Book of Records* as the largest of all parish churches in England, it is an architectural gem in ecclesiastical building in medieval Hull. It houses some of the earliest surviving medieval brickwork and contains many features worth viewing: ornately carved Victorian pews, impressive stained-glass windows and a fourteenth-century font, where William Wilberforce, Hull MP and anti-slavery campaigner, was baptized in 1759. The poet Andrew Marvell is said to have come to Hull around 1625, when his clergyman father was appointed to this church. The building work took a long time from its founding in 1285. The land was consecrated in 1301 and construction continued throughout the fourteenth into the early fifteenth century with the addition of a 150ft-high tower beginning in the late fifteenth century. The windows were very large so as to lessen the weight of the church, as the land was marshy. The present building is said to be the third church on this site but contains many original and ancient features. The tower, with four clock faces, has a ring of fifteen bells. It is thought the earliest six bells date from 1648–1652 and gradually they were recast to make a ring of fifteen.

JUNE 29TH

1870: A picture painted by Frederick William Elwell can be seen in Hull's Guildhall which commemorates the visit to the city of wartime Prime Minister Winston Churchill in 1945. Elwell himself can be seen in the picture. Born in Beverley, near Hull, on this date, Frederick became an esteemed artist of considerable talent. Studying at the Lincoln School of Art, he won a scholarship in 1887, enabling him to pursue his passion full time. In the same year he won the Queen's Bronze Medal in the National Arts School Competition for his *A Still Life with Fish*. He was a student at both the Royal Academy in Antwerp and the Académie Julien in Paris, then, after having his first work accepted for display at the Royal Academy, he moved to London. Eventually he returned to Beverley and married fellow artist Mary Dawson Holmes. He established a successful reputation as a painter of portraits for wealthy Edwardian clientele and was even commissioned to paint King George V's portrait in 1932. Much of his work expressed his interest in recording Yorkshire life and he frequently used local people as models. He died in January 1958 and in his will he left £1,000 to the Royal Academy Schools to endow an annual prize for still life painting. Like any good Yorkshireman, he was still working up until three weeks before his death. Beverley celebrates its famous son with street paintings by him positioned around the town.

JUNE 30TH

1852: On this date the York and North Midland Railway Company obtained powers to build a railway line to serve Hull's Victoria Dock. Prior to this all goods had to be moved into, around and off the dock by horse-drawn carts and rullies. The railway line was built to serve the marshalling yards, which lay to the west of the River Hull. The company realised that goods could be transported more efficiently via a railway to the new dock. The line was 3.25 miles long and branched off the Hull-Selby line near Anlaby Road, running in a semi-circle around the outskirts of Hull at a low level and terminating at the Victoria Dock Station near Hedon Road. The line crossed all the main roads leading out of Hull and caused six level crossings to be built. The line was opened on May 16th the next year and a suburban passenger service began on June 1st, one of the earliest in the country outside London. Although this service dwindled in popularity and ceased in October 1854, the Victoria Dock Railway Station had become the passenger terminus of the Hull and Holderness Railway in 1853.

JULY 1ST

1908: This date saw the official opening of Hull's Garden Village. Sir James Reckitt was the man behind the idea and it was he who formed the Garden Village company, putting £150,000 of his own money into the investment. In a letter to Thomas Ferens, another generous Hull philanthropist, James stated:

> Whilst I and my family are living in beautiful houses, surrounded by lovely gardens and fine scenery, the workpeople we employ are, many of them, living in squalor, and all of them without gardens in narrow streets and alleys. It seems to me the time has come, either alone, or in conjunction with some members of the board, to establish a Garden Village, within a reasonable distance of our Works, so that those who are wishful might have the opportunity of living in a better house, with a garden, for the same rent that they now pay for a house in Hull with the advantages of fresher air, and such Clubs, and outdoor amusements, as are usually found in rural surroundings. The outlay would gradually be very large, but some revenue would be derived from rents.

Thus the idea came into being and Thomas invested too. Three lots of almshouses were also donated to the Village, with priority for ex-employees of Reckitt's company and elderly Quakers, who were charged no rent.

July 2nd

1849: The Sculcoates Refuge for the Insane was established in 1814 by Dr John Alderson and Mr Ellis, surgeon, with the ethos that 'every attempt consistent with humanity will be made to restore the patient'. At this time it was capable of housing eighty to ninety patients and was surrounded by large gardens for the enjoyment of the inpatients. The asylum lasted many long years, with numerous name changes, the last being De La Pole Hospital. The De La Pole Hospital was actually the merger of two private asylums, the asylum at Summergangs Hall, founded in 1798, and the Sculcoates Refuge. The proprietors of Sculcoates Refuge took over the running of Summergangs Hall in 1825 and built this new single asylum to replace the existing buildings. The new asylum was originally called the Hull and East Riding Refuge, and accommodated 115 patients. The Lunacy Act of 1845 made it obligatory for boroughs to provide asylums for their pauper insane and the Hull Borough Council purchased the Hull and East Riding Refuge at a cost of £11,000 in February 1849. It closed on July 2nd 1849 and reopened immediately as Hull Borough Lunatic Asylum. Eventually, in 1879, a proposal by the Justices to purchase the De La Pole estate, Willerby, for £12,770 was accepted and the residents moved. The number of residents began at a little over 200 in 1884 and steadily rose to 800 in 1930. The last name change occurred in January 1940, when it became De La Pole Hospital and the hospital eventually closed in 1997. A private crematorium has subsequently been built, which utilises the former asylum chapel.

JULY 3RD

2012: A *Hull Daily Mail* report on this day explained to readers with the heart-freezing fear of spiders that Hull's aquarium, The Deep, was running courses on overcoming arachnophobia. Breaking new ground, the first class ran on July 7th and was a combination of history and facts about spiders, a hypnotherapy session by a qualified hypnotherapist and then a practical 'Try and Catch a Spider' section. Kate Duke is something of a spider expert and talked about how influential spiders have been in many different cultures throughout history. She explained that there are 38,000 species of spider worldwide and 600 found in the UK. We are, however, apparently only ever likely to come across about eight, as many are so miniscule or are cave-dwellers. Spiders play a crucial role in ecology and we would not survive long without them. The newspaper report concentrated on Natalie Murphy's experience of the course and she believed the combination of science and the power of suggestion really helped her arachnophobia. By the end of the day she, along with all the other phobics, was able to catch a spider in a glass and move it – something she claimed she had never been able to do before. Could it cure your spider phobia?

July 4th

1597: It is thought that Drypool was once possibly a place where Saxon mission priests from a local monastery set up a preaching cross before they erected a church, on the spot later known as St Peter's Church, Sculcoates. There are records of this medieval church from 1266 but as it was rebuilt through the centuries, different parts of it were dated to different periods: for example, the round-headed north doorway appeared to have dated from possibly the eleventh century. It was built and rebuilt a number of times, but heavy damage caused by bombing in the Second World War left it a mere shell. The last part of it was demolished in 1954 but there are still some old headstones remaining in the garden, with a statue of St Peter. This particular date is shown in some of the earliest church registers, documenting a family tragedy. In the November of 1596, one Bartill Rutter was apparently buried, followed two months later by Isabell Rutter, widow. Then, in 1597, Anne Rutter, a single woman, drowned herself and was buried on July 4th. No doubt being driven to this through the loss of her family members, she was nevertheless denied a burial close to them, being a suicide. She was instead interred on the north side of the church.

JULY 5TH

1915: On this date a gun was installed on the factory roof of what later became Rose Downs and Thompson, following the first zeppelin raid on Hull. It was meant to afford protection to the city and act as a deterrent to the bombers. The gun, manned from 8 p.m. until 5 a.m., is said to have done its job well; stories claimed that when a zeppelin arrived to drop its bombs it suddenly turned and sailed away without discharging its load. However, it transpired that the Germans had been fooled – the gun was actually a dummy gun, made from wood! No wonder it was reported never to have fired a single shot. The foreman who saw the gun being delivered had his suspicions when seeing the gun handled, as he knew a thing or two about lifting heavy machinery. He thus guessed the gun was not real but the story did not come out until much later, as it succeeded in its job of scaring the Germans and also giving confidence to the people of Hull. It is said MP Alfred Gelder expressed his concerns about fooling the people in this way and perhaps it was his views that had the gun removed the following January.

July 6th

1837: In response to the new Poor Law, the Sculcoates Poor Law Union was created in Hull on this date. The Sculcoates Union Workhouse was built along Beverley Road, being somewhat misleadingly described in the *Hull Advertiser* as such: 'Not many passengers along the Beverley Road would imagine that the beautiful and immense structure which is in the course of erection, on ground just beyond the town, is intended for the reception of paupers. Its front aspect would not disgrace the residence of a nobleman.' In reality, the workhouse was the last resort for the poor, before starvation, as the regime was strict and harsh. During the 1862 American Civil War, cotton imports were restricted and Hull's cotton mills had to lay off hundreds of workers. All were loath to enter the workhouse and the Guardians apparently printed a report claiming former employee, Henry Allen, had entered and said it was very comfortable. Henry, however, replied rapidly, stating he had only entered the workhouse as a very last resort and urged others not to follow 'as long as they can obtain a crust to keep body and soul together'.

———— • ◆ • ————

1897: On this day, a Royal Charter was signed bestowing Kingston-upon-Hull city status. It then ranked as the third port in the country after London and Liverpool.

JULY 7TH

1932: On this date the *Hull Daily Mail* reported the death of Captain James Sutherland, world-famous elephant hunter, at Yubu. It was said that James, who was well-known in Hull, had 'been on the spoor of the elephant for 38 years, and he held the world record bag – over 600 bulls. He was reputed to have had a more extensive knowledge of Eastern and Central Africa than any other living man.'

Sidney Graham Woodward also made the *Daily Mail* pages on this date, as he had been found guilty at Hull Quarter Sessions on three charges of obtaining money by false pretence. Firstly he apparently obtained the amount of £2 10s from a certain William Blyth, then £1 from a William Hewson and lastly £2 10s from a William Shaw. Saved somewhat by his probation officer, who stated that Sidney 'was a good father and his character was very satisfactory', he was put on probation for two years.

Another story in the same paper told of John Alexander Tolmie, who went up before the Stipendary Magistrate charged with 'driving a motor car while under the influence of drink to such an extent as to be incapable of having proper control over it. John, a medical doctor, had apparently been involved in a collision and when the police arrived, he tried to drive his car away against their orders. He did not get far. In view of previous convictions for offences in connection with cars the Stipendiary inflicted a fine of £40, or three months' imprisonment, and £5 costs. Dr Tolmie was disqualified from driving for two years.'

JULY 8TH

1537: The Reformation years were ones of uncertainties and fighting for many. Hull played a fairly prominent part in this history. It had many monasteries, which were suppressed by Henry VIII, yet had brought nearly £200 per year. People were very dissatisfied with the oppression and a rebellion called the Pilgrimage of Grace broke out. Priests and monks marched and as Hull was then the most formidable fortress in the north of England, they were besieged by William Stapleton and his men, Hull surrendering in October 1536 into the hands of the Pilgrims. The king took steps to recapture Hull, which he managed in December of the same year. Many of the Pilgrims' leaders were arrested and in May they were found guilty of high treason and ordered to be executed. Sir Robert Constable, the third leader in the Pilgrim band, was amongst those to be hanged and his death was alluded to in a letter from the Duke of Norfolk to Thomas Cromwell on July 8th 1537: 'On Fridaye being market daye at Hull, Sir Robert Constable suifred, and dothe hang above the highest gate of the towne, so trymmed in cheynes, as this berer can shewe you, and I think his boones will hang there this hundrethe yere.'

JULY 9TH

2000: On this date the village of Swanland, lying a few miles west of Hull's city centre, officially became twinned with Lestrem in France. It was not until the 1960s that the housing boom really began in Swanland, but there were dwellings there for a long time before that. The congregational chapel was built in 1803 on the site of an earlier independent chapel, which opened in 1694. Tradition said that people always met in that area to worship even before any chapel was built.

Mere House, an old Victorian building near Swanland pond, has an interesting story attached. According to local folklore it is haunted by some sort of poltergeist. There is a well-known narrative from an eyewitness, Mr Bristow, from 1849, which states that the poltergeist activity occurred in the carpenter's shop, where he saw workmen being pelted with bits of wood. Each at first thought the other was doing it, but once that was settled, they could find no visible cause for the disturbances. They commented that the objects could not have been thrown because of the eccentricities of their course. This activity apparently lasted for a good six weeks and Mr Bristow exclaimed that it was 'the most remarkable episode in my life'. One theory the villagers had was that it was the workings of a deceased man whose affairs had not been settled to his liking.

JULY 10TH

2006: This saw the closing date for the Woodland Trust's initiative to encourage the people of Hull to rediscover the green spaces within the city. The Trust asked York-born actress Dame Judi Dench to help publicise and oversee the event. A main part of the event was an arts and photography competition, for people of any age to enter with their best image of 'Green Hull'. Ferens Art Gallery was also involved, promising to exhibit all the entrances in their Live Art Space in the September. The Woodland Trust wanted to shake off the title Hull had gained – the 'least wooded city in the UK'. The Trust was looking to plant over 56,000 trees, the equivalent of one for every child in Hull. Dame Judi, an honorary graduate of Hull University and supporter of the Woodland Trust, said, 'Our Green Hull art exhibition is a wonderful way of rediscovering Hull's hidden green spaces. I would encourage everyone to take a fresh look at the city to find and record these special places that act as a sanctuary for wildlife and people amongst the bustle of city life.' Dame Judi has been to Hull a few times; the second time was to open a theatre named after her at Hymers College, with which she was apparently thrilled.

July 11th

1818: Hull was famous for its whale industry in the nineteenth century and hundreds of ships and local men were involved in whaling expeditions, including two brothers, Edward and Philip Dannatt. In the season of 1818, a medical student called James Douglass took an appointment as surgeon on Edward Dannatt's ship, *Trafalgar*. He recorded the voyage from start to finish in great detail in his journal, which has now been published and gives a great insight into the lives of the whalers. He stated what a dangerous business it was and how a whale could kill a man instantly with one swipe of its tail. It could take hours for the crew to kill a whale and the dissection process could take at least another three. Icebergs and polar bears were a constant threat and the journal narrates stories of them being surrounded by the remains of wrecked vessels, ones that had been caught between heavy floes and crushed to pieces. During this five-month expedition, the *Trafalgar* caught twenty-one whales and eventually turned to home on this particular date, with nearly a full cargo; one of the lucky whaling ships to survive. Both brothers went out on more whaling voyages and when retired they were known as upright citizens of Hull, both being elected Humber Pilot Commissioners in their lifetime. They donated to many charities and were instrumental in lobbying the Admiralty to supply rescue ships when required.

JULY 12TH

1834: The *Yorkshire Gazette* declared on this date that the manuscript on the life of Snowden Dunhill, notorious thief, had been delivered and entrusted to Mr Pratt of Howden for publication. By September the *Hull Packet* was advertising the third edition of *The Life of Snowden Dunhill*. By his own admission in his book, Snowden concedes he was a thief from a young age, stealing corn, apples, eggs, etc. He believed his ensuing fate was largely due to the woman he married, Sarah Taylor, the widow of a man shot while carrying out a crime. They had a large family and lived in Hull and he claimed it was her influence on him which played a significant role in shaping his future career, a career consisting of robbing, stealing and money lending. In his book he details many of his crimes. Described as a highwayman by some, his reputation as a thief was unsurpassed. In 1812, he was caught and his punishment was seven years' transportation. He returned to Hull after this time, but he soon formed dubious new relationships with people in Hull and Lincolnshire. It did not take long before he was arrested for a 'paltry crime', for which he was tried and convicted in 1825. This time he was transported for life. Snowden was completely illiterate, but he dictated his life story to the man that he spent time with in prison, who wrote it down. Snowden was working in Port Jackson, Australia, when he met an old acquaintance from Yorkshire. The man, a sailor, was a former playmate from childhood. The sailor informed Snowden he was about to return to Hull, and he agreed to get Snowden's autobiography published. The sailor was as good as his word and deposited the manuscript with William F. Pratt, bookseller and printer of Howden.

JULY 13TH

1854: During this period the C & W Earle Shipyard did not have direct access to the Humber so their ships had to launch directly into Victoria Dock, which was a somewhat hazardous procedure. On this date the sailing ship, *Dowthorpe*, was launched. A huge crowd had forced their way through the dock gates to witness the event. An estimated 300 people were said to have boarded the *Dowthorpe* and once it was launched, the unofficial passengers ran back and forth across the deck, causing her to rock uncontrollably. The boat keeled over and scores of people fell into the dock. Four drowned that day, but it was not the unlucky omen for *Dowthorpe* as some feared it might be as she successfully went on to complete her trading voyage to Bombay.

———•◆•———

1987: This day saw Kevin McNamara become the Shadow Secretary of State for Northern Ireland. Educated at Hull University, Kevin was Head of History at St Mary's Grammar School then Lecturer of Law at Hull College of Commerce. In 1966, he became Labour MP for North Hull and was opposition spokesperson for Northern Ireland from 1987 to 1994. In 2006, Kevin received an honorary degree from Hull University in recognition of his forty years in politics.

JULY 14TH

2012: Hull girl Gay Yee Westerhoff returned to the area on this date to perform a concert at Brantingham Park, Elloughton. Alongside violinists Tania Davis and Eos Chater and viola player Elspeth Hanson, Gay Yee is part of the all-female classical style band, Bond. Their group has sold almost 5 million albums around the world and they have played on every continent. Gay Yee was one of thousands of students to have reaped the benefit of free music lessons, started by the schools' music service back in the 1950s. She received her free cello lessons at Highlands Primary School, Bransholme, then at Amy Johnson Secondary School. She also joined the Hull Youth Orchestra.

Having seen that classical music could cross over into the more popular music scene whilst touring with Vanessa Mae, Gay Yee helped to form the Bond girls with a friend and two girls from the London Music College where she studied. 'It wasn't really a conscious decision to go into music, I just couldn't see myself doing anything else and being happy,' she said. Although frowned upon by the classical scene for their sexy image, Bond have helped to spread a love for classical pop throughout the world and Gay Yee has had the pleasure of performing with the likes of Sting, Tom Jones, the Spice Girls, Pavarotti and Primal Scream.

JULY 15TH

1855: It was on this date, during the Crimean War at Sevastopol, that thirty-seven-year-old Hull boatswain John Sheppard set out on a mission that was to earn him the Victoria Cross, awarded for valour 'in the face of the enemy'. John apparently went into the harbour, under the cover of night, in a punt he had made especially for the mission. The boat contained explosive apparatus and it was his intention to blow up a Russian warship. He managed to pass unnoticed by the enemy steamboats at the entrance of Careening Bay but further advancement was apparently prevented due to a long string of boats, which were carrying enemy troops from the south to the north side of Sevastopol. He had to turn back but made a second attempt another day from the side of Careening Bay occupied by the French, but unfortunately this attempt also had to be abandoned. Although both efforts were unsuccessful, they were carried out in the face of extreme danger and described by Lord Lyons as bold acts of service gallantly executed. John was only the fourth ever person to be awarded the Victoria Cross and one of the first from Hull.

July 16th

1997: Lord Brian Rix was installed as the first Chancellor of the University of East London on this date. Born in Cottingham, the son of a Hull shipowner, it was his mother's enthusiasm for amateur dramatics that encouraged him and his sister to enter the world of acting. His sister came to fame as Annie Sugden in *Emmerdale* and Brian became well known for his *Whitehall Farces* and his staging of *Reluctant Heroes*. His trademark scene had him innocently involved with a woman in her bedroom, trousers around ankles, just as her husband arrived home! Brian appeared in eleven films and seventy farces for BBC TV and also made a handful of films for the big screen. He eventually moved into theatre management but one day saw an advertisement for the job of new Secretary General for MENCAP. There were some who apparently questioned his suitability for the post, but the Queen Mother said he was 'a most imaginative appointment'. Brian's own daughter was born with Down's syndrome and he had always used his name to promote public awareness and understanding of mental handicap, so the role seemed fitting for him. It obviously suited him, as in 1986 he was knighted for his services to charity. He also hosted the TV series *Let's Go*, the first British programme to be created specifically for people with learning disabilities.

JULY 17TH

1981: This was the date of the official opening of the Humber Bridge, by Queen Elizabeth II, although actual plans for the bridge were drawn up as far back as the 1930s. The Humber Bridge, the longest single-span suspension bridge in the world for sixteen years, is 4,626ft long. The total length of the wire in the cables of the bridge is said to be 44,000 miles, which is more than 1½ times the circumference of the earth. It is now the fifth largest of its type but remains the longest single-span suspension bridge in the world that one can cross on foot or by bicycle. The bridge, which spans the Humber and links Yorkshire with Lincolnshire, has always been involved in controversy about its finances. Running into debt when it was built, the toll was installed in order to recoup costs, at one time being the most expensive in Britain, although it was finally reduced in 2012. It was the only major toll bridge in the United Kingdom to charge tolls to motorbikes and, in 2004, a large number of motorcyclists held a slow-pay protest, taking off gloves and helmets and paying the toll in large denomination bank notes. Police reported a tailback of 4 miles as a consequence of the protest. More than 200 incidents of people jumping or falling from the bridge have taken place since it was opened, with only five surviving, but the bridge is a popular and picturesque place, also used by marathon runners and many charity walkers.

JULY 18TH

1888: A court case was held on this date at the Hull Town Hall to ascertain whether the fate of the smack, the *Gleaner*, could have been avoided. The ship apparently became stranded on the rocks to the eastward of the Island of Heligoland on June 13th. The *Gleaner* sustained material damage due to this stranding and the court decided this was attributable to the skipper having improperly attempted to navigate his vessel through the dangerous narrow channel between Heligoland and Sandy Island. The court found the skipper, Mr Wm. James Moss, solely in default, and suspended his certificate of competency as skipper for six months. Many of the stories that reach us of what went on at sea seem horrific and author Stuart Russell narrated one such tale, from second-hand, aboard the *Gleaner*. Edward Wheatfield would apparently beat young fisher-lad Peter Hughes systematically and sadistically, forcing him to endure humiliating and painful ordeals until he eventually died from being thrown overboard. His was not the only story of such cruel treatment of Hull fisher-boys, although few found justice for their ill treatment.

JULY 19TH

1843: This date saw the tragedy of the Hull steamer, *Pegasus*, which sank on its journey from Leith to Hull. Of the fifty crew members aboard, only six survived, three of whom were females, one being pregnant. Captain Brown, who did not survive, was said to have had great experience in the navigation of the coast, having sailed for many years as commander of one of the Leith and London smacks. He is known to have been considered an excellent seaman, so the disaster was something of a shock. The cause of the accident was apparently due to the boat striking the Goldstone Rock, which was submerged among the Farne Islands, and the *Pegasus* only managed another 300 yards before it quickly filled with water and went down in a depth of about 10 fathoms. This was reportedly only 5 miles from where the *Forfarshire* had previously met its fate in September 1838. This ship was wrecked on the rocks of the same Farne Islands on its way from Hull to Dundee. Over fifty people, including the captain and his wife, were said to have died in this tragedy, with only nine survivors. These nine owed their lives to Grace Darling and her father, who sailed out to rescue them from the Farne lighthouse.

July 20th

1574: These were severe times in Hull. The year 1571 saw a tidal flood destroy many houses and much property, then a few years later the plague hit the city, killing almost 100 people. The authorities in Hull had strict ideas about how the people should behave and one Reverend John Tickell stated that, 'The sins of fornication and adultery were so prevalent in Hull, that the magistrates were obliged to issue out the strictest orders relative to those vices and use all means in their power to suppress them.' The Archbishop of York was referred to for advice on how to deal most effectively with offenders, and on this date His Grace replied by letter, sanctioning punishment for these 'abominable and heinous crimes'. Church wardens and sidemen were ordered to search alehouses and streets and obtain names of those who were 'sinfully spending or idly wasting their time' when they should have been at church. He granted authority for the Mayor and Aldermen of Hull to eradicate the 'gross immoralities' by severe punishment, regardless of the circumstances. How times have changed!

JULY 21ST

1916: 'There is no wonder those who have a tendency towards drink try to drown their sorrows whenever they get a chance,' wrote Archie Surfleet in his war diary, on this date. Private Arthur 'Archie' Surfleet was at Serre the first day of the battle of the Somme with the 13th Battalion, East Yorkshire Regiment, one of four battalions raised by the city of Hull. Enlisting in the Army shortly after his nineteenth birthday, Archie kept a diary, from the start, adding details in later years providing a dynamic and explicit account of a young soldier's service. His diary details the daily life of the soldiers, the conditions, the rats, the food and, he said, the constant demands for working or carrying parties always provoked widespread 'grousing' among the infantry. Even before the Somme offensive, such tasks caused Archie to comment that, 'We all are as fed [up] as hell with this lot. The jobs we get are simply heart-breaking, almost inhumanly impossible but they have to be done, somehow, and I marvel, daily, that we stick it.' He commented that the chance to spend some francs from their pay on egg and chips or wine and beer in local establishments helped the men to briefly forget the terrors of the trenches, as entering the battle-zone for a tour of front line duty was always a sobering moment.

July 22ND

1987: On this date in London a political Palestinian cartoonist, Naji-al-Ali, was shot. When the police started investigations into the murder, a diary was apparently discovered in the loft of one Ismail Sowan, which contained information on international scandals of the 1980s and also had a Hull address! Officers in Hull were notified and when the address was duly searched, an astonishing arsenal of weapons was found. Six locked suitcases, when opened, allegedly uncovered detonators, four rapid-fire AK47 assault rifles, eight magazines loaded with 300 rounds of ammunition, nine hand-grenades, bomb-making equipment and almost 70lb of Semtex high explosive. The explosives found were nearly three times the amount used in the IRA bombing of the Grand Hotel in Brighton three years earlier, when Margaret Thatcher was the target.

Ismail Sowan was revealed by Scotland Yard to be a secret agent working for Mossad, Israel's intelligence service. He had moved to Hull twelve months earlier to study engineering and seemingly also managed to infiltrate a notorious PLO terrorist cell operating in Britain. Although Sowan denied any knowledge of what had been contained within the suitcases, he did admit involvement in Mossad and divulged the name of Abdul Rahman Mustafa as Naji-al-Ali's assassin. Mustafa, however, was never found and Sowan was sentenced to eleven years in prison.

July 23rd

1612: Not much is known about arctic pilot and navigator James Hall's past, save that he was from Hull. He piloted three of King Christian IV of Denmark's expeditions to Greenland, after previous explorations had apparently excited the king's interest. These three expedition ships, of which James was first mate and pilot, were sent out in 1605. During their expeditions they collected ore they wrongly thought might be 'silver-bearing'. They also took captive some Eskimos. In 1612, back in England, James apparently persuaded some merchants to finance another trip back to Greenland, searching for more mineralogical evidence. He sailed with the *Patience* and followed the west coast of Greenland north. On July 22nd 1612, he was evidently recognised by some Eskimos from whom he had earlier taken captives. One struck him with a spear and he died the next day. According to his last wish he was buried on a nearby island rather than at sea. The maps he had previously reported to the King of Denmark formed a valuable source of knowledge about Greenland, of which good use was made back in England.

JULY 24TH

1951: On this date the *Hull Daily Mail* reported how a police sergeant hid for over eight hours behind a piano in order to catch an intruder. He apparently concealed himself there, in the recreation room of the General Police Station, around 10 p.m., waiting until half past six the next morning, when he heard the intruder entering the canteen. The intruder was another police sergeant and he had come in to steal cigarettes from a machine in the canteen. Even though he tried to deny he was stealing them, it transpired he had done the very same thing just three weeks previously. He was granted bail, at £5, with one surety of £5.

The same paper reported that the Holderness RDC had decided to protest to the Yorkshire Electricity Board about their decision not to supply Halsham and West Newton with electricity before the end of 1952. One complainant said, 'People living in Halsham are surrounded by villages in which electricity is provided, but they themselves are burning smoky oil-lamps, candles and whatever they can get. Considering the time electricity has been in the area it is time something was done for these particular villages.'

July 25th

1937: The Hull trolleybus service opened for traffic on this date, two days after a ceremonial inauguration. This new system was introduced to replace the tramway network and consisted of seven routes and a maximum fleet of 100 trolleybuses. Prior to this, Hull had a tramway network but instead of needing tracks, the trolleybuses, often referred to as 'trackless trams', drew their electricity from overhead wires, connected by spring-loaded trolley poles. It was the trolleybuses which saw Hull through the war years. In 1941, over one third of the fleet was destroyed in the heavy bombing at the beginning of May and a bus cleaner was killed. All trolleybus and tramway overhead lines were destroyed on this occasion, as was the front of the depot on Hedon Road. Replacement motor buses were borrowed from Leeds and other cities. In 1942 they were renumbered, the letters removed and large blinds fitted for the blackouts. In 1943, gas trailer trolleybuses were tested in an attempt to reduce fuels, but withdrawn in 1944. The trolleybus service was closed in 1964 but will always be remembered in Philip Larkin's poem *Here*:

And residents from raw estates, brought down
the dead straight miles by stealing flat-faced trolleys.

JULY 26TH

1796: The *Hull Advertiser* printed an article in June 1796 showing that there would be horse racing in Hull on this date:

> Three races held over three days, prizes of fifty pounds for two of the races and the Town's Plate of fifty pounds for third. The horses to come to Mr Leonard's stables, opposite the first milestone on the Anlaby turnpike from Hull leading to the racecourse. Entrance three guineas each and Ordinaries and Assemblies as usual, horses to be entered at Mr Hollom's booth.

It is not a well-known fact that Hull was once home to horse racing, but Hull races are mentioned as early as 1754. Jeffrey's map of Yorkshire from 1775 shows the race ground in Newington just north of the Anlaby turnpike road. The races, apparently held every summer, encouraged much mirth and entertainment and pre-race celebrations included cock-fights and lively evenings. The prize money of £50 was a great sum in those days, but it seems it was partly danger money, as men were reported to have been killed after being thrown from horses during the races. The festivities attracted a rich clientele and this also drew pickpockets and opportunists, much as any such crowd, even today. After the races ended the site was still home to sporting events for many a year until the land was developed in the 1930s.

JULY 27TH

2012: The *Hull Daily Mail* reported the demolition of Hull's Orchard Park Bridgeman House tower block on this date. The Orchard Park Estate was originally planned in the late 1930s. The *Hull Daily Mail* commented at the time that living on Orchard Park would be like living in a new sort of world with its own parks, cinema and bomb-proof shelters. It was not until the 1960s that the park, built as a model urban estate, was constructed. It may not have included the hoped-for cinema and shelters, but it was built with the most modern television cable system available at that time already installed into its infrastructure. Rediffusion was a Hull-based firm that pioneered the concept of cable television. Each new home built on Orchard Park had television cables already pre-installed. The local school, Sir Leo Schultz High, was wired up and even had its own TV studio. The estate consisted of a number of high-rise blocks of flats, which received poor maintenance over the years and the area itself is known as having some of the highest social deprivation rates in the city. The changes were welcomed by residents, most of whom seemed pleased to see the blocks demolished. In their place there are plans for a £15m housing scheme which will include 115 homes and the refurbishment of 100 flats from other blocks. There were also plans in place for the construction of 680 new council homes; the first to be built in Hull for nearly twenty years.

JULY 28TH

2012: A *Hull Daily Mail* report on this date details a 'significant' find from the visit of Winston Churchill to Hull, after the heaviest bombing raids of the Hull Blitz during the Second World War. The bombings hit Hull very badly, with more than 1,200 people being killed and 3,000 injured in eighty-six raids on the city between 1939 and 1945. The 'significant' find was the itinerary of Churchill's visit, which, at the time, had to be kept a great secret for security reasons. The Prime Minister visited in November 1941, a few months after the worst of the raids, and is said to have surveyed the destruction and issued a rallying cry to the besieged residents. He then attended a gathering at the Guildhall, commemorated in a painting by Beverley-born artist Frederick William Elwell, which now hangs in the Banqueting Hall. According to reports of the day, as Churchill was touring the docks, the inevitable cigar between his teeth, a docker shouted, 'Chuck us the butt.' He did!

JULY 29TH

1932: Amy Johnson was the Hull girl who took the world by storm with her amazing feats of aviation, but it was not just through her career that she lived under the media spotlight. She met fellow pilot, Jim Mollison, during her world-famous visit to Australia. He had a reputation as a ladies' man, but also as one of the RAF's youngest officer pilots to see action in the First World War. After their initial meeting she did not see him again for two years, but heard about his flying exploits and sent him a telegram of congratulations. When they met for the second time, they really hit it off and were married on this date just two months later! With all the daring and record-breaking flights they made between them, they became one of the most famous couples in Britain. However, this competitiveness started to take its toll and there were rumours that Jim was having affairs. Once dubbed the 'flying sweethearts', they were now spending more and more time apart. After many public rows and humiliations they finalised their divorce in 1938. Perhaps it is inadvisable to mix business with pleasure!

JULY 30TH

1798: Hull newspapers in 1796 bore recruiting advertisements for the Royal Navy, inviting brave men to help defend the British way of life from French scoundrels. Promises of 'bountiful supplies of clothing, beef, grog and strong beer' along with guarantees of returning loaded with treasures abounded, but still Hull was unable to fill its quota of 731 men. As a result, press-ganging and kidnap were turned to and especially targeted were returning whaling ships, such as the *Blenheim*. It was on this date that the *Blenheim*, returning to Hull from Greenland seas, was set upon by the *Nonesuch* and *Redoubt*. They tried to board the *Blenheim* in Hull harbour but the crew, armed with large Greenland knives and spears, resolutely opposed their getting on board and in the midst of the struggle two members of the press-gang were killed. Another man belonging to the *Nonesuch*, named Bell, had three of his fingers cut off in attempting to board the *Blenheim*. He remained in Hull afterwards, and was nicknamed 'Three-fingered Jack'. The Captain of the *Blenheim* was taken to York Castle and was tried for the murder of the naval snatch gang's men, but he was acquitted. On his return to Hull he was received by the people with great celebration, and regularly chaired through the town.

JULY 31ST

1944: The death of Hull man Robert E. Sargent was reported in the *Daily Mail* on this date. A keen climber, Robert, a Hull LNER Assistant, was killed on Green Gable whilst on a climbing holiday in Cumberland. He was an old hand at climbing, having had such holidays in Switzerland and Germany, but on this tragic day he was leading the climb when he fell 60ft from his rope, taking teacher Evelyn Leak with him.

The paper also detailed the story of thirteen-year-old Keith Reynolds Allen, who discovered his mother strangling his seven-year-old sister, after he had been woken by her screams. Giving evidence in court, Keith described how his father had gone to work and he and his sister had gone to bed, in different rooms. He woke later to find his mother apparently sitting on the edge of his bed, saying they would all be better off dead. He told her, 'You are silly; we don't want to die.' Later that night he woke to hear his sister screaming and ran to find his mother strangling her. He could also see a cut on the girl's neck. He tried with all his might to stop his mother, but to no avail. Later, it was heard his mother was not of sound mind and had intended to kill Keith next, then herself, as she was scared of being separated from them.

AUGUST 1ST

1834: A fund was started in Hull after the death of William Wilberforce on August 3rd 1833 and money was raised from the public to erect a monument in his memory. The monument is 102ft high, the column reaching 90ft and the statue on top 12ft, carved from hardwearing millstone grit. The total cost of the monument was £1,250, equivalent to around £90,500 today. The foundation stone was laid on this date, in Victoria Square, where it stood for almost 100 years until the Queens Dock closed in the 1930s. A new road layout was proposed for the Queen Victoria Square area as the monument was making traffic flow very difficult. A new home had to be found and in 1935 the monument was moved to Queen's Gardens, where it stands today. It took four months in total to move the monument, apparently costing somewhere in the region of £1,500 (about £70,000 now). Whilst the work was going on members of the public were allowed to go up the scaffolding to enjoy the view of Hull for a 2s fee, both in its original location and the new one. The money raised went to giving poor children in the city a holiday, via the Mother Humber Fund.

AUGUST 2ND

2002: On this day, the well-known Hull-based chain store Jacksons opened its 100th shop on Blossom Street in York. Established in 1851, William Jackson opened his first small grocery and tea dealer shop down Scale Lane in Hull, as a celebration of his marriage. The business bloomed and steadily he opened more shops throughout Hull. In 1888, a new branch at Spring Bank was opened in conjunction with William's son George, and it was here that the company's first bakery was established. The firm flourished under the father-son partnership and in 1904 it became a private limited company, William Jackson & Son Ltd. By 1912 there were seventeen shops, a bakery, a jam factory, warehousing and stables. By 1916 there were thirty-two stores. William had died in 1912, aged eighty-four but had seen his business grow to be a great success and a household name. He was apparently active right up until his death, tasting tea at one of George's shops just the day before. The company, however, continued to thrive and the chain grew to 114 stores by 2004, when it was sold to Sainsbury's. Jackson's Bakery, however, survives, manufacturing the equivalent of over 1 million loaves of bread each week. It is said that if put end to end, the loaves would span 187 miles – the driving distance between Hull and London!

August 3rd

1569: Around this time Roman Catholics were heavily persecuted and the Lord President of the North sent many 'popish recusants' to the Blockhouse in Hull to be kept in close confinement. The punishments were cruel and harsh as Catholicism was being suppressed. The death penalty was given for ordaining a priest, for practicising confession and celebrating Mass, for attending Mass and denying that the monarch was the head of the Church. Hull Castle housed many of these 'offenders', such as Sir Thomas Bowlton, a priest, who was incarcerated for eight years and his fellow priest, Sir Henry Camberforth, who languished for ten years until he died. On this date the Archbishop of York wrote to Lord Burghley complaining of a certain Dr Vavasor, who had put the archbishop 'to shame' in a public disputation. He wrote, 'I, knowing his disposition to talk, thought it not good to commit (him) to the castle at York, where some other like-affected prisoners remain, but rather to a solitary prison in the queen's majesty's castle at Hull, where he shall only talk to walls.' Treatment in the vermin-ridden Blockhouse included starvation, torture and such neglect that the dead went unnoticed for some time. Sheahan and Wellan's *History and Topography of the City of York and the East Riding* paints a very dark picture of what occurred in our city.

AUGUST 4TH

1834: This date saw the birth of logician and philosopher, John Venn. Born in Hull, his father was the rector of the parish of Drypool and his grandfather had also been a rector at Clapham and had been well known in his own day as a campaigner for prison reform and fought for the abolition of slavery and of cruel sports. With religion playing such a large part in John's life, and losing his mother when he was just three, these male figures were important role models for him and it was expected John would also join the ministry, which he did for a short while. He was ordained as Deacon at Ely in 1858 but returned to his university at Cambridge to lecture in the moral sciences in 1862. John had a great skill, however, for mathematics and logic and he published texts on this subject. He also had a keen interest in building machines and one of his more famous inventions was a machine for bowling cricket balls! It is said that when the Australian cricket team visited Cambridge, John's machine clean bowled one of its top stars four times! John had a son who helped him write the history of Cambridge University. John is commemorated in Hull by the Venn Building at the university.

AUGUST 5TH

1916: John 'Jack' Harrison was a professional rugby league player for Hull who joined the army and was awarded a Victoria Cross for his bravery during the First World War. He began playing rugby in York when teaching there but was invited to play for Hull. When the war began he volunteered for the army, and on completion of his training he was commissioned as a probationary temporary 2nd lieutenant in the East Yorkshire Regiment, on this date. It was on May 3rd the next year that his actions led to him receiving his Victoria Cross. He and his brigade had been ordered to attack a wood near Oppy, Pas-de-Calais and during this mission his platoon became pinned down by machine gun fire. There was smoke and darkness everywhere that night, so it was impossible to see when it was safe to move in. Nevertheless John led his men in, under heavy rifle and machine gun fire, but they were forced back. After a similar failed attempt, John apparently made a dash for the machine gun on his own, to try and knock it out to help save the lives of his men. His body was never found but his wife back in Hull was presented with his award for the courage he showed and the self-sacrifice he made for others.

AUGUST 6TH

1831: The *Hull Rockingham* posted an announcement on this date, telling residents about the new gas lighting in the area around Anlaby Road, this being some of the first street lighting in Hull.

> We have the pleasure to inform the population inhabiting each side of the Anlaby-road, from Ocean-place to the West-parade, that the commissioners have given orders for laying gas mains the whole of that distance. It is calculated that in the whole there will be fourteen lamps. The residents in West-parade will also have the power of accommodating themselves with light by pipes from the mains.

The first place in the country outside London to be fully lit by gas lighting was Preston, in Lancashire in 1825, and by 1859 it had reached all over Britain. Gas was supplied to Hull by three companies: the Kingston-upon-Hull Gaslight Company, established in 1821, supplied the whole of the old town; the British Gaslight Company, founded in 1828, who purchased the Cottingham Gas Company in 1902; and the Sutton, Southcoates and Drypool Gas Company, formed in 1847, which was later known as the East Hull Gas Company. This new, brighter lighting enabled people to read better and for longer and was instrumental in speeding up the second Industrial Revolution.

AUGUST 7TH

1858: Argyle Street was once known as Asylum Lane, as it led north from Anlaby Road to Hull's Refuge for the Insane. By all accounts the road used to be in such an appalling state that drivers of carriages would often refuse to use it, especially taking elderly or frail patients over such a bad surface. A second entrance to the asylum had to be built, from Spring Bank, but as more building work was developed in the area the first road improved and received much more use. However, with the increase of buildings and residents, people began to complain about the name of the street, fearing it could somehow cast aspersions on their own sanity and, in 1861, the Board of Health resolved to change it. Some have suggested the new name, Argyle, was chosen to fit in with other royal sounding names in the vicinity, such as Victoria Terrace and Albert Terrace.

On August 7th 1858, the *Hull Times* reported that a drinking fountain was to be erected at the corner, aptly donated by Alderman Fountain. This was one of the earliest street drinking fountains in Hull and had a seat set into the wall nearby, for full comfort!

AUGUST 8TH

1475: On this date Hull Captain William Cummins set sail aboard his two-masted vessel, *Rainbow*, with a crew of twenty-three to search for gold and ivory in Africa. He had started out as a mate aboard the schooner-brig *Speedy* the previous year, yet things went somewhat awry. The ship sank off Heligoland after running into bad weather and William and a fellow crew member, Shepherd, were luckily picked up by a vessel called *Tyger*. This, however, turned out to be a pirate ship being hunted by the authorities. At Land's End there was a battle and the *Tyger* sank, William, Shepherd and the captain, Jinks, escaping on a little boat, with a chest full of treasure. Jinks was killed but William and Shepherd made it home to Hull, rich men. Hence William set sail in his own vessel, *Rainbow*, but fate was not on his side. The crew turned mutinous and the *Rainbow* ended up burning, with William escaping in a longboat. Legend has it he was betrayed by Shepherd, but foresaw this turn of events and had a plan in place. He managed to get a secret message to the young woman he had married in Hull just four weeks before he set sail. She apparently tricked Shepherd and managed to get a ship out to save her husband. William apparently made it back to Hull, where he became a rich and happy trader.

AUGUST 9TH

1865: Spring Bank's Polar Bear tavern appears to have opened sometime early in the 1840s, around the time Hull's Zoological Gardens opened. Numerous public houses sprung up nearby in order to refresh the visitors to the gardens and many of these took names from the exotic animals housed there. The Polar Bear was thought to have first opened at Carlton Terrace, further east along Spring Bank, before moving to its current site in the 1860s, being modified in 1895, 1911 and 1922. The building became listed in 2005 and is of special architectural interest, principally for the quality of its interior fixtures and fittings. These include a ceramic bar counter front, one of only about ten still surviving in England. This is complemented by the survival of features and interior fittings dating to the 1922 refurbishment. At one time the premises contained a shooting gallery, which was apparently well-frequented and, in 1861, a purpose-built museum was joined to the tavern. This was designed by William Botterill and was mostly made of weatherboarding supported by wooden posts. The museum was destroyed by fire on August 9th 1865. The tavern, however, remains and is certainly worth a visit.

August 10th

1849: On this date a deadly form of Asiatic cholera made its appearance in Hull. This horrific disease, caused by drinking dirty water, lasted one month in Hull, taking the lives of 1,860 citizens. This was at the rate of one in forty-three of the population, not to mention all the other poor souls whose lives were disrupted by this tragic epidemic. The late Reverend James Sibree is said to have discovered that the men employed in digging the graves for these victims had no respite but persevered with their grim task day and night. At first, single graves were dug ready for some eight or nine bodies but all too soon the demand became so urgent that double graves were constructed, with the coffins piled directly upon one another. There was, as can be imagined, much fear and alarm, causing market places to be almost entirely empty and few passengers visited by train, usually just for business matters. Five hundred Hull residents were said to have succumbed in one week in September. Many were buried in a mass grave in the newly opened General Cemetery on Spring Bank and there is a memorial built to commemorate those who died. The inscription states that the remains of 700 victims are buried near the monument and that it was erected to remember the one in three inhabitants of the town who fell victim to the disease. The epidemic peaked at one death every 24.1 miles, which was the highest rate in the country, undoubtedly increased by the fact that Hull was a thriving port with many immigrants arriving.

AUGUST 11TH

2012: On this date Hull boxer Luke Campbell won a gold medal in the London Olympics. The twenty-four-year-old was overwhelmed by his success telling the *Hull Daily Mail*, 'I am lost for words, very emotional. It's something I've worked for all my life. I can't believe it. Nevin's a top fighter; it was a very difficult fight, very technical. It was about outwitting each other.' By beating Ireland's John Joe Nevin, Luke became Britain's twenty-eighth gold medallist in the Olympics and the first boxer from the UK to claim top prize in the bantam weight category since 1908. Luke started boxing aged thirteen and just two years later he was representing England on the international stage. He took the silver medal in the 2011 World Championships, becoming No.2 in the world in the bantamweight division. His coach was very proud of him, saying that he is a great role model and his family had been a huge support. Luke talked about his hometown fondly and appreciated all the support he received from the Hull people. Hundreds turned out to see him bring the gold medal back home, which he showed off from the balcony of Hull City Hall. He also received an MBE, which he said was a 'great honour'.

AUGUST 12TH

2012: On this day the Hull's Dove House Hospice organised a ladies' sponsored walk, starting at midnight at the Princes Quay Shopping Centre, with a zumba warm-up and snacks available. Dove House is a special Hull and the East Riding of Yorkshire-based charity which provides specialist care for people in the area with a life-limiting illness, including cancer, motor neurone disease, HIV/Aids, Parkinson's disease and heart failure. The hospice has a yearly running cost of £5.6 million but for the patients there is no cost; all of their services are offered free of charge yet the charity is funded for the equivalent of just forty-eight days per year. Fundraising is essential to their continued work and the midnight walk is just one in a series of events organised to raise funds. A total of 585 women took part in the walk on the night, including the author and good friend Sally Stockhill, and it was estimated the event raised about £30,000. The parade was an amazing spectacle, with each of the ladies being supplied with pink flashing headbands and pink T-shirts, so that to passers-by the view resembled an extremely long, pink, flashing serpent!

AUGUST 13TH

1960: On this date the Hull fishing trawler *St Hubert* set sail on her fatal mission to the Arctic Circle. A spare hand aboard told that they had been fishing illegally during darkness and had picked up blocks of what they knew was explosive in the nets but it was dumped back overboard. However, on one of the last trawls the vessel brought up a long cylindrical object partly covered in concrete. The crew knew almost immediately that it was some kind of mine or shell and, having to leave the area before they were caught, they moved the object to the forward part of the vessel, meaning to dump it again in deep water away from the fishing grounds when they had the chance. A strong wind was apparently blowing and the ship was riding a big sea when, unfortunately, the bomb exploded and 'almost split the ship in half' killing four of the crew including the skipper, who tragically died just fifteen minutes after being rescued. For almost six hours after the explosion the crew battled to plug the damaged port side but in weather that was against them and because of the extent of the damage, they eventually had to abandon the vessel and launch the life-rafts. Struggling, she foundered in the rough seas, but the crew were saved by another Hull trawler in the area at the time, the *Prince Charles*. Skipper Ness' actions were commended at the coroner's hearing; '... although nearly half his face was blown away he continued to command the sinking trawler with his thoughts always for his ship and crew.'

AUGUST 14TH

2012: Richard Bean came home to Hull on this date. Born in the city in 1956, he had a unusually late start to his career as a playwright. He spent many years as an occupational psychologist, but in his own time he also lived the double life of a stand-up comedian. His first full-length play, *Of Rats and Men*, set in a psychology lab, was performed at the Canal Café Theatre and then the Edinburgh Festival. After this he adapted it for BBC Radio and it was nominated for a Sony Award. This was the start of his next career, and a very successful one it turned out to be. His plays have attracted directors such as Paul Miller, Sean Holmes and Richard Wilson, and have been performed at probably the three best new writing theatres in London: 'Remarkably few playwrights have been commissioned by the National Theatre, the Royal Court and the Bush at all. To work at each in such a short period of time shows that Bean has really made the grade.' He brought his work back to his hometown on this date, as a one-time only showing of *Smack Family Robinson*, which he rewrote to suit Hull, the family coming from Kirk Ella, instead of further north. Premiered at Fruit, the play was directed by Richard's long-time friend and collaborator Gareth Tudor Price, who has directed five of Bean's plays, including his breakthrough comedy *Toast*, set in a Hull bread factory. 'It's great to have Richard back in Hull,' he commented. 'Despite all the success he's had with *One Man, Two Guvnors*, and before that with many other shows, he's still the same bloke he always was. Down to earth and still incredibly proud to be from Hull.'

AUGUST 15TH

1644: Hull Corporation's Bench Book V makes mention that on this date it 'was ordered that a collection shall be made on Sunday next in both churches of this Towne for the reliefe of one Thomas Fisher who was borne at Dripole and has been a Captive in Algier about six yeares and a halfe in miserable slavery as by his letter now shown to this bench appears.' From around 1500 to 1800 this man-catching industry from the Barbary Coast caused great problems for European seafarers, whose navies were too weak during this period to put up much resistance. Perhaps in revenge for the Crusades, this Christian-stealing campaign was the blight of many and with Hull being a prominent port, the people were easier targets. Some managed to be ransomed back by their families but most were put to hard labour in North Africa or as galley slaves. It is said that,

> … from Hull to Plymouth and from Edinburgh to Cardiff, merchants and sailors, investors and bishops, royal courtiers and East India and Levant company stockholders all felt the impact of captivity: in sermons and homilies, during collections asking for charitable contributions to pay ransom, and in the tales told in public houses, Britons learned about the suffering of their countrymen in captivity.

What poor Thomas Fisher's fate was we do not know.

AUGUST 16TH

2012: The *Hull Daily Mail* reported a story about Dean Marshall on this date, headlined 'Cannabis-grower tried to call Queen and Prime Minister as witnesses in "bizarre" trial'. Dean was caught growing twenty-six cannabis plants in his Preston shed. Police apparently raided his home in June 2011 and discovered the plants had a potential yield of £8,220 and were capable of making 274 street deals. Dean, however, claimed he was not guilty because he was a member of the group Freemen of the Land believe that they should not be ruled by laws which governing bodies have created. They feel these laws are a control mechanism to dictate people's lives, whereas the only true law is common law, where there exists a mutual respect between people. However, Judge Jeremy Richardson QC was not swayed by Dean's claims, informing him that neither the Queen nor the Prime Minister could attend his trial. In fact, he told Dean, 'I ordered a psychiatric report on you to see if you were mentally ill or adversely affected by long cannabis use, but the report says there is nothing the matter with you.' Dean was given a twelve-month prison sentence, suspended for two years, and ordered to carry out 150 hours of unpaid work.

AUGUST 17TH

1991: The *Hull Daily Mail* reported the foolish gun prank of Thomas Blackadder on this date. Caught out not once but twice, Thomas was sentenced at Hull Crown Court to fifteen months in prison for his unwise behaviour, with a further nine months suspended for two years. In his first prank, Thomas apparently jumped out of the shadows at an unsuspecting passer-by, brandishing what appeared to be a real semi-automatic Browning pistol in one hand and a broken pool cue in the other. His joke was turned on him somewhat, however, as on this occasion the stranger was a martial arts expert who blocked the gun and knocked away the cue, whilst besting his attacker. 'I see you're a karate boy, are you?' Thomas is reported as saying as he fell to the ground. On the second occasion he pulled out another fake gun in a crowded pub in Hull's town centre. This time he was disarmed by the barman, after he had turned to the wall and pretended to reload the weapon. His defence counsel at court labelled Thomas a fool, explaining he 'gets himself into trouble by stupid actions, although there appears to be no intention to do anyone any harm.' Judge John Bullimore, however, was not impressed. 'If you thought it was funny, nobody else did or does.'

AUGUST 18TH

1808: Born on this date, Margaret Moxon was the only Hull-born person of her generation to work with freed slaves in Sierra Leone. She and her husband also worked as missionaries with Maori families in New Zealand. She became interested in missionary work when still at school, later marrying a Lutheran missionary, George Kissling. They moved to his CMS station in Sierra Leone where she taught in the mission school. George's health was always quite poor and Margaret took on a lot of the work to help her husband. After moving to a CMS station in New Zealand she started a school for Maori children, as well as assisting with the daily running of the mission station with George. Moving to Auckland in 1846, they established a Maori girls' boarding school and by the December of that year sixteen girls were attending. As one way to provide financial support for the school, Margaret organised the New Zealand Female Aborigines Washing Establishment, which many Auckland settlers used. She was known for her hospitality and sympathetic nature and took in visitors and many sick people, as well as being a mother to six! There is a street near St Stephen's Shopping Centre named after her, the Margaret Moxon Way, in memory of her good works.

AUGUST 19TH

1916: The *Hull Daily Mail* on this date printed a story about a Hull butcher who had been taken to court where the prosecution was said to have announced that 'unless the facts he would give to the Court could be disproved this prosecution was the most serious which they had had to bring for a considerable time.' Thomas Wilson, Hessle Road butcher, 'was summoned with respect to a quantity of veal found on his premises,' which was deemed unfit for human consumption. The veal had been found in Thomas' ice-chest but blood poisoning had set in and the veal, stored with good meat, was said to be 'in a highly dangerous condition'. Knowing he had been caught red-handed, Thomas tried to say the meat was only intended for his dogs, of which it transpired he only had one, yet large portions of the veal 'had been disposed of [and] he [the Town Clerk] invited the Magistrate to draw the inference that it had been disposed of to the public.' Thomas declared he had not intended the meat for human consumption and so the trial was adjourned for another day.

The same paper extolled the 'rough lads' on Hessle Road as being the stuff heroes are made of. It was apparently recorded that in the early days of the First World War this was one of the areas to send the most recruits to Kitchener's Army, 'and now the neighbourhood is celebrating the winning of two Distinguished Conduct Medals'. Both men were in the same East Yorkshire battalion, one 'carrying a wounded officer in under shell fire, the other for conspicuous trench work.'

August 20th

1831: This was the date of the first of the Hull Portfolios of social agitator, James Acland, who promised to record and report the vices and follies of Hull's Corporation to all classes of the people of Hull, 'to wit the downfall of corporate despots, the termination of magisterial misrule and the just punishment of the poor man's oppressors.' He apparently wrote these portfolios concerning the 'rights and interests of the people and town of Hull' from August until December, highlighting the undemocratic and corrupt rule of Hull and setting out campaigns to change the system. One of his campaigns addressed the Corporation's ferry monopoly over the River Humber and he even established a rival ferryboat, the *Public Opinion*, charging half the rate. He also disputed the legality of the market tolls and set up his own stall, selling gingerbread figures of the Mayor and Aldermen, and refused to pay the tolls and those on Hull's bridges. He was challenged by the Corporation and was up in court numerous times, even spending some time in prison, but his actions were not in vain. He had strong public support and managed to convince commissioners, on a visit to Hull as part of their national enquiry into municipal corporations, to investigate his claims. An overhaul of the local government was demanded and change was slow but sure.

AUGUST 21ST

2005: On this day, forty-two-year-old Graham Boanas waded through waist-deep mud, picking his way through perilous shipping channels and negotiating the Humber's notorious tides to help raise money for charity to help children with a rare skin condition. Thought to be the first person to cross the Humber unassisted since Roman times, Graham wore a specially designed suit, where the boots were moulded to the legs. Internal braces also helped to prevent the sticky mud on the riverbed from sucking the suit from his body and there were secure anchor points for the rescue team in case they did have to pull him from the mud or incoming tides. The Humber Rescue crew watched him the whole journey, as the Humber is notorious for its treacherous tides and shifting sandbanks. This date was one of only two per year where the tide's water levels would be low enough to try and walk across. With water travelling around 5mph around him, it is no wonder that he said, 'It is the most tiring thing I have done but it was worth it. I was just thinking about my family and about the children who I was raising money for.' Graham was raising money for DebRA UK, which works for people with epidermolysis bullosa (EB), a rare genetic condition causing the skin to blister. Children with the condition have been called 'butterfly children' because the fragility of their skin has been compared to that of a butterfly's wing.

August 22nd

1902: On this date Hull City Council, then known as Hull Corporation, was first granted a licence under the Telegraph Act of 1899 to operate a telephone system for the residents of the Kingston-upon-Hull area. This was a common occurrence during this era, with a number of such municipal telephone companies starting up around the UK. Hull, however, became the exception, as all the other companies in the UK were gradually absorbed into the Post Office Telephone Department, now known as British Telecom, or BT, but Hull remained independent. It was in 1904 that Hull opened its first telephone exchange at what was Trippett Street Baths. Hull telephone communications retained individuality, using white telephone boxes compared to the red ones the rest of the country employed. These can be seen even today, one being painted gold in 2012 when Hull brought home an Olympic Gold Medal. In 1914, the Hull telephone licence was renewed to keep this telephone corporation municipally owned, the only one remaining in the whole of the UK. In 2007, Kingston Communications, as it had come to be known, changed its name to KCOM Group. The ground, shared by the city's football club, Hull City, and Hull FC rugby, is sponsored by KC and even named the KC Stadium. KC serves over 200,000 customers in East Yorkshire and provides a comprehensive range of communications solutions to businesses and residents.

AUGUST 23RD

1601: On this date Lord Burleigh, the Queen's Lieutenant and Lord President of the North, visited Hull. It is said that, accompanied by many knights and gentlemen, they dined with the mayor, after which they were treated to a fine display of fireworks in the market place. The day ended in tragedy, however, as four people were killed when an old canon exploded.

———◆———

2011: On this day, the *Hull Daily Mail* ran a report on 'Superdog Sox', who saved his owners from burning in their beds during an arson attack on the family home. It is thought that burglars had broken into the garden shed and had set it on fire during the early hours of the morning. The whole family was fast asleep, apart from Sox, their Jack Russell, who barked so much that he woke them up. Linda Rose was the first to wake but when she saw the blaze in the garden she rallied all the family together and got them, and Sox, to safety. It is thought the loft insulation was only seconds away from catching alight, which could have burnt the whole house down. 'If it was not for Sox, I am certain we would all be dead,' said Mrs Rose's daughter, Kelly. A very clever dog and very thoughtless thieves, who could have become murderers, after burning the shed to hide forensic evidence of their robbery.

AUGUST 24TH

1759: William Wilberforce was born in Hull, at 25 High Street, on this date. In April 1784, aged twenty-four, he was elected MP for Yorkshire and it was during this time that he toured Europe, becoming deeply religious in the process. He became a back-bench MP in 1780, when Lord North was Prime Minister. Revolted by the drunkenness, swearing and immorality of the great mass of people in England, he established a Proclamation Society, set to encourage people to improve their behaviour. In late 1786, a Christian couple, Sir Charles and Lady Middleton, wrote to Wilberforce stating their abomination of the slave trade. They wanted a Member of Parliament who would campaign for the abolishment of the slave trade in the House of Commons. In this, Wilberforce found the cause to which he devotedly campaigned for the rest of his life. The Society for the Purpose of Effecting the Abolition of the Slave Trade elected Wilberforce as their spokesman in Parliament and after nearly two years of campaigning, on May 14th 1789, he had the chance to bring the Anti-Slave Trade Bill to the House of Commons. Unfortunately the matter dragged on, with strong opposition but, finally, at 4 a.m. 1807, it was passed by the Lords, with 16 against and 263 votes in favour. At last, through his efforts, the British Parliament had passed a Bill to abolish the slave trade throughout the British Empire.

AUGUST 25TH

1985: On this date, one of the two Hull rugby clubs was involved in the first ever rugby league match played on the Isle of Man. The Charity Shield between Hull Kingston Rovers and Challenge Cup winners Wigan drew a crowd of 4,066 to the Douglas Bowl. The final score was 34–6 to Wigan. Hull Kingston Rovers were formed in 1882 by a group of boiler makers and were nicknamed The Robins, after their traditional playing colours of red and white. The two Hull rugby teams originated from different sides of the city, the River Hull seen as the divide between them. The Kingston Rovers traditionally come from the east side; thus the majority of their fan base also originates there. Although having moved grounds over the years, their home is known as New Craven Park. The club played many matches before 1899 but this was the year they were admitted as full members of the Northern Union, the previous title for the Rugby Football League. In the September of that year they played their first official home derby against Hull, winning 8–2 in front of a crowd of 14,000. New Zealand visited Craven Park in September 1971. The Kiwis, playing their third game in five days, were unable to match the Robins, who beat them 12–10.

AUGUST 26TH

1941: This was the date that Sir Alfred Gelder died. Ask any Hull-born local what the name means to them and more often than not you will receive the answer that, although not entirely sure who he was, there is a street named after him! Deciding not to follow in his father's footsteps as a joiner, wheelwright and timber merchant, Alfred established an architectural practice in 1878 and in 1892 he formed a partnership with Llewellyn Kitchen, the Manchester-born son of a commercial traveller, and the firm of Gelder & Kitchen was founded. Alfred had entered the architectural profession at the time of the Victorian development of the city and quickly became its mastermind. The new town plan was largely his work, and was carried out while Alfred was Mayor of the city. The city centre was reconstructed and a new bridge built across the River Hull, the Drypool Bridge. A new road was built through the city centre to link up with this bridge, and was named Alfred Gelder Street. In the 1930s he was involved with the transformation of Queen's Dock into Queen's Gardens. Alfred was knighted in 1903 as Sir Alfred Gelder and it is said that under his supervision, Hull was hailed as one of the country's finest cities, with the slums and disorder of the Victorian city giving way to broad, straight thoroughfares.

AUGUST 27TH

1953: On this date, thirty-six-year-old Rufus Lord Noel-Buxton decided to attempt to wade across the River Humber on foot, as he claimed the Roman Britons did before him. Apparently dressed in grey flannel trousers rolled up to the knee, a checked shirt, canvas plimsolls and carrying a stout staff, he waded the one and a quarter miles from Brough Haven in Yorkshire to Whitton Ness in Lincolnshire. Accounts vary as to how long the journey took him, from between one and two hours, after which he was supposedly heard to say 'it was unexpectedly easy' to cross this treacherous distance of mud and sandbanks. He believed this to be the evidence that there was once a Roman ford across the river. His staples for the journey were a cigarette and a nip of brandy and a lifebelt over his shirt, and he claimed the water never rose above his hips. 'At no point was the water above my waist, and at many places on the sandbanks it was little more than ankle-deep.' He emerged, mud-spattered but triumphant, to a riotous crowd of cheers. It was an adventure which made headlines across the region. One report stated, 'For Lincolnshire "Humbersiders" it was the greatest ever locally staged event. For many, it was a sensation.' However, he did admit to having had a 100-yard boat ride across a deep shipping channel to start off.

AUGUST 28TH

1860: The grand opening ceremony for Hull's Pearson Park was held on this date. Known as the People's Park, the event was marked as a 'colossal fête' attended by tens of thousands of people, including many visitors from distant towns. The festivities were a two-day event with speeches, fireworks, hot-air balloons, displays of gymnastics, military bands and ceremonial planting of the first trees, by benefactor Zachariah Pearson and his family. Thirty-nine-year-old shipping merchant Zachariah donated twenty-seven acres of land for the park to be built to celebrate his first year of office as Hull's Mayor. Plans had been put in place for such a place of recreation in 1858, but fell through, giving Zachariah a chance to present this gift to his hometown. The people were at first in two minds about the idea of a park, liking the notion of having a natural place to use and appreciate but also wary that it might attract undesirable crowds and rowdiness. One of the conditions Zachariah stipulated upon his donation was that no musicians, refreshment stalls or public games were to be held on Sundays in the park and thus fears were allayed. Pearson Park lies about one mile north–west of the city centre and was the first public park to be opened in Hull. An ironstone monolith stands near the pond with a depiction of Zachariah and a plaque to commemorate his gift.

AUGUST 29TH

1914: The first Hull Pals Battalion, nicknamed the Hull Commercials, was formed on this date. They formed part of the East Yorkshire Regiment and within three months Hull had four Pals Battalions: the Hull Tradesmen, the Hull Sportsmen and the T'Others joined the Hull Commercials. When the First World War broke out, it was Lord Kitchener who was given the task of encouraging men to join the British Army and risk their lives for their country. The idea was suggested that more men would enlist if they had the comfort of knowing that they would be serving with someone they knew and so, with the promise that men could serve with their friends and work colleagues, the first battalion was formed in London, with over 1,500 men. The idea spread to Liverpool, then Derby, where the term 'battalion pals' was first used. Within the next month over fifty towns and cities all over the country formed Pals Battalions, with Manchester and Hull each having four. It was estimated that an average of 30,000 men a day during that period hurried to sign up and the office in Hull became unable to cope with the rush. The City Hall replaced the Pryme Street office and from its balcony banners were hung, bands played and speeches were given to entice young men. The Hull Pals won two Victoria Crosses in the First World War, but the tragedy of such close communities losing so many men at once was one of the terrible consequences of the idea of the Pals.

August 30th

1941: Thomas Wells was appointed Chief Constable of Hull on this date, while the city was suffering some of the worst bombings of the Second World War. Wells took early retirement in 1947, but for the next forty-four years the exact reason for that remained a mystery, a classified file residing in the Home Office. In 1943, Wells created the Hull City Police Boys' Club to help juveniles stay off the streets, especially when many fathers were away at war. He also opened another boys' boxing club in Garden Village and, on the first day of opening, 150 boys enrolled. During his career, however, not all his motives were to prove quite so honourable. During his time in office he clashed with some members of the Watch Committee, particularly Alderman Alfred Jacobs, owing to alleged corruption. The two men campaigned against each other, both ordering investigations into each other's affairs, until the media coverage became too damaging and they agreed to stop. Jacobs, however, apparently distrusted Wells and eventually forced an enquiry from the Home Office. It was the final report of this investigation that was banned from public revelation until 2027, although following renewed media interest it was finally made public in 1993. Apparently, it showed that Wells had acted improperly by conducting an unauthorised meeting with the Alderman which he then grossly misrepresented to the Watch Committee. Wells, however, obviously had friends in high places who colluded with his escape via a discreet cover-up and early retirement!

AUGUST 31ST

1976: On this date a five-day reign of terror erupted in Hull Prison. It was reported on the BBC News that the sixty-seven-hour rampage finally ended peacefully after negotiations with a senior Home Office official. Apparently, about a hundred prisoners began the riot in protest against alleged brutality by staff. The 140 prisoners who were not involved had been evacuated and the disruption started by the remaining inmates was by all accounts extremely violent and destructive. It had apparently been difficult to control the riot as many of the perpetrators had barricaded themselves on the roof, after destroying their cells and smashing doors and furniture. Once on the roof, they were seen hurling slates and debris at passers-by and firemen, who had been called to attend to the fires that had been started. One prison officer allegedly stated that at least two-thirds of the prison was completely wrecked. The jail had to be closed down for the best part of a year following the protest and it was established that the cost of repairing the damage caused would run into hundreds of thousands of pounds.

SEPTEMBER 1ST

1651: On this date the legendary, yet fictitious, Robinson Crusoe set sail from Hull, in the novel of the same name by Daniel Defoe. Robinson was an eighteen-year-old youth whose family lived in Hull, his father being an eminent solicitor. Robinson always dreamt of going on exciting sea voyages but his family were opposed to the idea, which forced him to run away with a friend. His ship set sail from Queen's Dock, Hull and there is today a plaque in Queen's Gardens, the former Queen's Dock, showing him on the island where he was eventually marooned. It was adventure he sought and adventure he received, right from the off: 'The ship was no sooner out of the Humber than the wind began to blow and the sea to rise in a most frightful manner; and, as I had never been at sea before, I was most inexpressibly sick in body and terrified in mind. I began now seriously to reflect upon what I had done.' We are not sure why Daniel chose Hull for his first novel, written in 1719, but some say it was autobiographical, Daniel himself being a great adventurer and a man of vast experience. *Robinson Crusoe* is also considered by many to be the first novel ever written in English.

SEPTEMBER 2ND

1643: It is said that by March 1642, the argument between King Charles I and the Long Parliament had escalated so much that the King moved up the country in an attempt to gather support from his northern subjects. Parliament, however, had taken precautions and Hull had been secured. In an infamous incident Charles was turned away from the gates of Hull in April 1642 by Sir John Hotham. Obviously incensed by this, and as Hull was housing the arsenal, Charles decided to lay siege to the city. He established his court in Beverley and the siege began. Dykes were cut around Hull and the Charterhouse was destroyed to prevent it being used in defence. Much fighting ensued, plus a failed attempt to blow up the gates. Hull's people had strengthened its defences with new earthworks and on July 6th they opened the sluices so the River Humber flooded the land for 2 miles around the town. Discouraged by the city's defences, Charles abandoned the siege and withdrew to York. On this date, however, a second siege of Hull began. This attack was not a success. The land around Hull was flooded again and the north blockhouse of the castle was accidently blown up by its own gunpowder store. Parliamentarian warships patrolled the Humber estuary so supplies could still reach Hull and again the siege failed. It was abandoned on October 12th and so ended Royalist hopes of an advance towards London by the northern army!

SEPTEMBER 3RD

2009: This date saw the death of Michael Hollingbery, son of George Hollingbery, who founded the nationwide company Comet. George set up the business in Hull in 1933 as a two-man operation, charging batteries and accumulators for customer wireless sets. As customers started to request replacement sets, George changed his focus to radio rentals. By 1939, Comet had 2,500 accounts and a small fleet of vans. He died in 1958, aged fifty-five and his son, Michael, took the business over. In 1968, Comet pioneered out-of-town retailing and the first discount warehouse, selling just radios and televisions from their boxes, was an instant hit. Seventy years on, Comet opened its second 'destination' store in Hull. Lord Alan Sugar is to have commented that this move 'changed the face of retailing'. He said that, 'this form of retailing signalled the demise of the small electrical shop on the street corner, which simply couldn't compete.' Michael was awarded an OBE in 2007 for services to the community. He donated money to various charitable causes, including the Postgraduate Education Centre at the University of Hull, Humberside Youth Association and cancer charities. Since the opening of the first store in Hull, Comet stocked over 18,000 products and employed thousands of people from the local area. Unfortunately, in 2012, Comet was declared bankrupt.

September 4th

1926: Hull is well known for its musicians, writers, poets and actors, but George William Gray, born on this date, should make Hull proud for the scientific advances he initiated. Born in Scotland, George forged a career for himself at the University of Hull from 1946 to 1990. His role was that of Professor of Organic Chemistry and he was apparently instrumental in developing the long-lasting materials which made possible liquid crystal displays, now known simply as LCDs, which are found on watch faces, calculators, etc. He created and systematized the liquid crystal material science and established a method of practical molecular design. The first book he wrote on the subject was published in 1962. George was the recipient of the 1995 Kyoto Prize for Advanced Technology and is a Commander of the British Empire. He has been a director of the International Liquid Crystal Society and they produced a medal named after him for those who contributed to the science. Hull Trains also named their first British Rail Class 222 'Pioneer' high-speed train after him, in recognition of his achievements.

SEPTEMBER 5TH

1941: Two Hull heroes were mentioned in the supplement to the *London Gazette* on this date because of their bravery during an air raid. The high-explosive bombs had demolished some houses and Lighterman Harry Cardwell, at great personal risk, tunnelled through the debris to try and rescue a fifteen-year-old girl trapped inside. He managed to reach her, staying with her for several hours comforting her, but as it was so cramped he could not get her any water. Fortunately, seventeen-year-old James Hodgson, who worked as a messenger for Hull Auxiliary Fire Service, was in the street and succeeded in wriggling further down the tunnel to the girl he recognised from school. In a report from the *Hull Daily Mail*, he said she was pinned under debris with a dead three-year-old child next to her and her dead father lying across her. He managed to get her some water but the poor girl died when the remainder of the building fell in. Harry was awarded the George Medal and James the British Empire Medal for their heroism and compassion.

SEPTEMBER 6TH

1991: On this date the *Daily Telegraph Third Book of Obituaries* printed a tribute from Dame Barbara Cartland about Hull girl Jean Rook. Born on Friday 13th November 1931, she was apparently told by the *Hull Daily Mail* that, at age twenty-five, she was too old to pursue the career in journalism she sought and had not got 'a cat in hell's chance of getting into Fleet Street'. She certainly proved them wrong! She managed to get a place on the *Sheffield Telegraph's* graduate trainee scheme, where her distinctive style of writing won her the job of columnist. After this she worked as Women's Editor for the *Yorkshire Post* then moved on to the fashion magazine *Flair*. She is best known for her regular column in the *Daily Express*, where she gained a controversial reputation for writing opinion pieces and interviewing the rich and famous. Soon she was known as 'the First Lady of Fleet Street' and her style was as brassy and forthright as her dress. As testament to her fighting spirit, she is said to have only missed her deadline for her *Daily Express* column on two occasions in twenty years. The first was when her son was born, and the second when she was told she had cancer. She died in September 1991 and her close friend Barbara Cartland said, 'I admired the way she always told the truth even if it was not particularly pleasant ... she will be a loss to the Press, which she raised to a very high standard of journalism, and her friends will never forget her.'

SEPTEMBER 7TH

1299: It was apparently around 1281 that a man walking along the shore of the island that once existed in the mouth of the Humber estuary found the remains of a shipwreck washed ashore. The wreck later became a hut where a hermit lived and gradually more people – fishermen, merchants, sailors – began to visit the island, known as Ravenser Odd. Eventually more than a hundred houses were built on the sandbank island and at one point the town was a more important port than its neighbour, Hull. However, there was a dark side to this community and Ravenser Odd became known as something of a pirate island. They would send vessels out to 'guide' merchant ships away from other local ports, especially Grimsby, and into their own. The island seemed to be governed by Isabella de Fortibus, Lady of Ravenser Odd and Lady of Holderness. She set up her own tolls, rules, laws and even gallows! The island became rich and made quite a reputation for itself. It was even granted a right to hold its own weekly markets and on September 7th 1299 it was granted the right to hold an annual fair. Other towns began to complain to the king about the island's activities but they need not have worried. Strong tides, currents and storms had been eating away at the island until, by the fifteenth century, hardly anything was left and all the people had scattered amidst looting and panic-flight.

SEPTEMBER 8TH

1890: On this day Tranby Croft House, at Anlaby, was at the centre of a gambling scandal involving the future King Edward VII – the Royal Baccarat Scandal. During this time the gambling game baccarat was illegal in England but was a favourite of Edward's. One of the guests, a certain Sir William Gordon-Cumming, was apparently observed to be cheating. He begged for it to be kept a secret once he had been caught but word somehow got out and Sir William was ostracised by society. He decided to take his case to court to attempt to clear his name and a trial was held on June 1st 1891. The prince was called upon to be a witness, a duty he was reluctant to perform, especially since he had been previously called as a witness in another case in 1870, where he denied having an affair with Lady Mordaunt. In the Royal Baccarat Scandal case the court did not find in favour of Sir William and his reputation was forever tarnished. He was dismissed from the army and never re-entered high society. The Prince of Wales is reported to have declared, 'Thank God! The army and society are now well rid of such a damned blackguard.' He apparently gave up playing baccarat, opting instead for whist.

SEPTEMBER 9TH

2009: The *Hull Daily Mail* published a report on this date about a Hull cheerleading team who gained success in an international dance competition. As cheerleading is not one of Britain's most celebrated sports, this international recognition was quite an achievement. Held at Loughborough University, the Electric Cheer and Dance Group performed their routine at the International Cheerleading Coalition's Nation's Best Championship, where they took third place in the Senior Co-ed Group Stunt Level Five Division. Sally Cimadoro, owner of the dance school, explained that the routine was very difficult to perform, consisting of dangerous stunts and tosses. It was also apparently the first group stunt for the team, called Electric Surge, which consisted of two men and three women, aged between seventeen and twenty-four. Sally added that the group had only ever competed at levels two and three, 'so placing so high in a level five division was an amazing achievement from our small team from Hull.' Electric Cheer and Dance is one of the leading cheerleading and dance programmes in East Yorkshire and certainly the home of Hull's first and most prestigious cheerleading team, the Electric Allstars. The school is a non-profit sports club run by volunteers to keep young adults fit, healthy and with a skip in their step!

September 10th

1541: On this date King Henry VIII made a visit to Hull with his young wife, Catherine Howard. It is said the object of his journey to Yorkshire was to attempt to allay the discontent many of the people felt about the changes he was making to Church matters and the dissolution of the monasteries. Great preparations had been made for their visit and they were met 'at the boarded bridge, near Newland' by the sheriff and a body of gentlemen. A great procession formed and marched to the Beverley Gate, where a platform had been erected, covered with scarlet cloth. The then mayor, Mr Thureross, and the Corporation met and welcomed the royal party here, after which the procession wended its way through Whitefriargate to the stately mansion built by the De la Poles, in Lowgate, then the mayor's official residence, the Manor House. Thousands turned out to see the king and the city was adorned with decorations, flags and streamers. The gables of the houses were bedecked with tapestries and the ships in the docks were festooned with ribbons. Henry is said to have remained for three days in Hull and was 'most magnificently and nobly entertained at the town's expense' and, on leaving, His Majesty graciously accepted £100 from the town's purse, presenting the town with a sword which remains in the city to this day. He returned three weeks later to check the city's defences, ordering various modifications to secure the town.

SEPTEMBER 11TH

1893: 'Sad Death of a Boy in Hull' declared an article in the *Eastern Morning News* on this date. Fourteen-year-old George Longman and two friends had apparently been playing tag when they collided with a group of lads running away from a local 'half-witted young man, named John Tans', whom they had been teasing. Tans had taken umbrage at this and given chase. Accounts say when the collision occurred John had turned to chase George instead, and the next thing anyone knew was that 'several persons were seen bending over the prostrate form of Longman, rubbing his hands and throwing water on his face.' The boy was unconscious and by the time he arrived at the Infirmary, he was dead. The cause of death was unknown, whether concussion – as there was a bruise above his eye – or from a heart disease he had been diagnosed with previously. John was arrested and George's parents, who were at chapel at the time, were understandably upset, 'particularly so as they were under the impression that he was at chapel himself.'

The paper also tells of two boys who had been fined between 5s and 8s for stealing a quantity of apples and pears from a garden adjoining East Park, plus 6s damage, each!

September 12th

1967: On this date BBC Radio Humberside's Steve Massam first walked into the newly built Sir Henry Cooper School on Orchard Park, along with around 1,200 other pupils. Forty-five years later he was interviewed in the *Hull Daily Mail*, as he had been asked to return to host the school's closing ceremony. The school was named after Hull-born doctor Henry Cooper, who worked as a surgeon and physician at Hull Royal Infirmary. He became Mayor of Hull in 1854 and when Queen Victoria visited the city later that year, he received the Order of Knighthood, on Corporation Pier. He had strong links with education, becoming a member and first chairman of the Hull School Board in 1871. When the Board Schools opened in 1876, in Bean Street, they were named the 'Sir Henry Cooper Schools' in his honour. Consequently, when they closed, it was decided to perpetuate this honour by naming the Orchard Park School after him in 1967. The badge of the school originates from the arms of Henry's forbears. The closing ceremony for this memorable school included singing, sports, arts, circus performers and talks. It also incorporated the handing over of the school bell to the local authorities after it had been rung for the final time.

SEPTEMBER 13TH

2009: On this date the Round the World Clipper Race set off from Hull. This was a big event for the city, with visitors arriving from all the countries represented in the race. The Freedom Festival provided music and entertainment throughout the weekend and the Red Arrows performed their magnificent display over the Humber. Each yacht covered 35,000 miles in a ten-month voyage which visited France, Brazil, South Africa, Australia, China, America and the Caribbean before heading back to Hull in the summer of 2010. The yachts measured between 10 and 20m in length and were manned mostly by amateur sailors from around the world. The fourteen crew members shared cabins but each had their own bunk bed. The Hull and Humber Clipper, which came second in the event the previous year, had all the latest navigational aids and could reach a speed of 16mph. Their skipper was thirty-one-year-old Piers Dudin, who was an experienced seaman. Unfortunately, during the voyage his leg was broken due to a huge wave smashing him on the deck, but despite this bad luck the team did very well, achieving an overall fourth position, with Australia winning the race. There were crowds of spectators creating a great atmosphere for the start of the race as the yachts set off on the first leg of the journey to San Rochelle in France. The partying culminated in a brilliant firework display from the tidal barrier on the Saturday night.

SEPTEMBER 14TH

1828: Thomas Thompson, one of Hull's wealthiest businessmen, died on this date whilst on a trip to France. His son, Thomas Perronet Thompson, is perhaps better remembered in the city for his campaign against slavery (Kingswood Academy was previously known as the Perronet Thompson School), but his father was a great benefactor and worked tirelessly for the poor and less fortunate inhabitants. Aged sixteen he began his career as a clerk at the counting house of William Wilberforce (grandfather of the famous emancipator of slaves) and worked his way up through banking, business ventures and politics. Apparently fired by his Methodist convictions, he became concerned for the less fortunate. He campaigned for the tithe system for farmers to be abolished and became chairman of the Hull Guardians of the Poor. He instigated the establishment of Hull soup kitchens in 1780 and it is estimated that one person in five took advantage of the free food. He was also troubled by the fact that pauper families were split up on entering the workhouse and in 1819 he fought for land to be provided in Cottingham where pauper families could settle and cultivate crops. This area, originally known as Pauper Village, was renamed New Village in 1829 and is now a thriving eastern suburb of Cottingham. Thomas had a large house of his own built in Cottingham, known as Cottingham Castle, now the site of Castle Hill Hospital, where he and his family resided during the summer. He was an MP for twelve years, but claimed his Parliamentary years had 'spoiled a very good banker and made a very bad MP'. If unpopular in Parliament, he will be remembered as an advocate of the poor.

SEPTEMBER 15TH

2012: An article in the *Hull Daily Mail* on this date reported that Hull-born 'guitar hero' conman, Marino De Silva, had been jailed in the US for up to eight years. As a guitarist in the 1980s in Hull, he performed under the stage name 'Marino'. He left Hull for America in search of fame and fortune. He achieved both, but not in the way he had envisaged. Describing himself as an 'award-winning guitar hero', he told investors he had remastered rare material by the Beatles, Jimi Hendrix and the Rolling Stones. However, once they had handed over their cheques, they found it impossible to find out what was happening with their money. Some had received poor quality recordings that were nothing to do with what they were promised. He even duped an old friend of his, Mike Dawson, who lost $38,000 to the scam. Instead of the promised new Beatles material, he received cover versions, including some recorded by Marino himself. In the meantime, Marino had been living a life of luxury in a $2 million mansion with his own personal pool in Las Vegas. His high life came to an end when he was arrested and this Greatfield lad will be spending a while behind bars.

SEPTEMBER 16TH

1829: Hull physician Dr John Alderson died on this date. His funeral was said to have been one of the most impressive Hull had ever seen. The hearse was accompanied by what was described as a seemingly endless procession and it was estimated that 15,000 people attended the funeral, held at St Mary's, Lowgate, to mourn a man who had done much to improve the health and culture of Hull. John was one of the founders of Hull's Literary Society, the Hull Mechanics' Institute and the Hull School of Medicine. He was president of the Hull Subscription Library and of the Literary and Philosophical Society. He was Hull's chief physician, acquiring a large medical practice in the city, and was elected physician to the Hull General Infirmary. John gave his services to the hospital for free and was honorary physician there for forty years. In 1814, he founded the Sculcoates Refuge for the Insane, for which it was claimed, 'every attempt consistent with humanity will be made to restore the patient'. He was made a Freeman of the City in 1813 and worked towards the provision of commercial education. Three statues were erected in memory of this man, who even dissected a sperm whale which was washed up on Tunstall beach in 1825 and whose skeleton now resides at Burton Constable.

September 17th

1991: Hull's City Hall concert organ was fully restored on this date. The subject of much controversy in its time, the organ is one of a kind. Norman Cocker was apparently heard to describe it as, 'not a concert hall organ at all, but it is one of the most ravishing cathedral organs imaginable; it has dynamic force, flexibility, immense variety, seemingly endless and glorious colour and certainly possesses distinction and meticulous regulation.' The initial cost when it was built in 1911 was £4,328 but, after certain relay boxes and luminous stops began to deteriorate in the 1970s, a restoration plan was put in place. It cost £300,000 to fully restore!

Also on this date the fishing ship *Norman* left St Andrew's Dock, Hull, for the last time. It became grounded in a deserted outpost in Greenland, shrouded in thick fog, and no one was answering the distress calls. After a failed attempt to launch the lifeboats she began to list and the crew feared she would overturn. They abandoned ship and all but one man were drowned in the treacherous tide. Young Norman Spencer was rescued seven hours later from the rocks he had scrambled onto, but the ship actually stayed afloat for another two days. If the crew had stayed on board they would have all survived.

SEPTEMBER 18TH

1793: Ye Old Black Boy pub, situated in the Old Town, is said to be Hull's oldest licensed premises, dating back to 1729. The building can be traced back as far as 1331 and, in its time, has been a brothel, a fish shop, a corn merchants, an insurance brokers and a popular meeting and trading place for merchants. Legend has it that it got its name from when it was a coffee shop in the eighteenth century and the owner employed a North African boy who boosted trade due to his mystique, but another theory holds that it was named after King Charles II, whose swarthy looks earned him the name 'the black boy'. It apparently houses three underground passages, which run to the River Hull and were much used by smugglers and press-gangs in times gone by. On September 18th 1793, an auction was held at the Black Boy to sell a brewer's dray. The poster of this auction was available to view at the pub (although it is not known if it is still there) and shows how popular it was even then. Today it has other reasons for its notoriety – that of the spirits which inhabit it, and not the ones on the shelves! Legend says that one stormy day the tunnels were flooded with seawater and several smugglers drowned: they are now said to haunt the pub. Whisky bottles have flown off the shelves and several people have allegedly seen ghostly hands materialise through panels on the wall.

September 19th

1893: On this date Thomas Sheppard joined the Hull Geological Society. Founded in 1888, the society, which is now an educational registered charity, concentrated on the geology of the area and the history of local geological studies. Thomas Sheppard was the president of the Society and published over 300 papers on geology. Perhaps his most famous contribution to local geological sciences was his *Geological Rambles in East Yorkshire* of 1903.

2000: On this day an article on Hull band Fila Brazillia appeared in the *Guardian* newspaper. The paper wrote of their 'deceptive music, full of hidden eccentricities that come from solid musicianship, subtlety and the silly streak that lands the tunes with names like "Here Comes Pissy Willy" and "Half Man Half Granary Thorax".' Fila Brazillia was named after a huge South American fighting dog which is now banned in this country, after the 1991 Dangerous Dogs Act. Formed in 1990 by Steve Cobby and David McSherry, they play electronica, ambient, techno, rock, funk and dub, and are often described as down tempo. Their music has been used on *CSI: Miami* and *Sex and the City* and even on cult films such as *Dogtown* and *Riding Giants*. Staying in Hull, the band maintained they did not want to be sucked down to the metropolis, like so many other London-based bands.

September 20th

1902: Stevie Smith, famous Hull poet, was born on this date, christened Florence Margaret and nicknamed Peggy by her family. She became known as 'Stevie' after being compared to popular jockey Steve Donoghue and the name stuck. Her father left the family when she was young and Stevie and her sister moved to London, where their aunt, the 'darling Lion of Hull', raised them to be independent strong women, without the need of a man. Her first work to be published was a collection of six poems, which appeared in the *New Statesman* in 1935. Later that year, she submitted further poems but was advised to 'go away and write a novel'. She did just that and produced *Novel on Yellow Paper*, which became an instant success. Her best-known collection of poems is said to be *Not Waving But Drowning*, published in 1957, and her popularity spread through Britain and America. She had a peculiar fascination with death and loss and it was often the theme of her work. It is also thought that Stevie had an affair with the married George Orwell, to whom she was close, although this was never confirmed. In 1966, she was awarded the Cholmondeley Award for Poets and then the Queen's Gold Medal for poetry in 1969.

September 21st

1964: On this day the legendary Rolling Stones played at the ABC Theatre in Hull. The ABC cinema opened in 1934 as the Regal, with a seating capacity of 2,553, plus a balcony. The large stage area also saw such stars as Cliff Richard and the Beatles perform there and it was on their fourth British tour that the Rolling Stones appeared to a crowd of thousands. Built in just seventeen weeks, the ABC was completed six weeks ahead of schedule and three years after opening it was taken over by Associated British Cinemas (ABC) and became their major cinema in the area – they owned four others in the city at various times. In 1959, a new projection suite was constructed at the rear of the circle and on reopening the cinema became known as the ABC, the name locals used for the site long after it was closed. Some say the richly decorated auditorium was ruined in 1976, when it was rebuilt as five smaller cinemas seating 569, 346, 261, 166 and 96. There was a suggestion at one time of converting the theatre into a rock venue, due to the popularity it saw with the Stones and the Beatles, but this idea did not materialise and the cinema was closed in 1989. The site saw a new lease of life, however, being demolished in 2004 to make way for the new St Stephens development.

SEPTEMBER 22ND

1778: This date was the official opening of Hull's first dock, named The Dock. Work had begun in 1775 as Hull's waterways were becoming congested due to growing commerce, so the dock was completed and became at that time the largest dock in the United Kingdom, measuring 518m long by 75m wide. The dock was renamed The Old Dock when the second Hull dock, Humber Dock, was built and then renamed again in 1854 in honour of the royal visit, the first since 1642, becoming Queen's Dock. The dock was used for over 150 years, closing in 1930. Over the following four years it was filled in and landscaped to become the pleasure garden we now know as Queen's Gardens. The gardens sit below the level of the surrounding streets as they were not fully filled in and they contain pools and fountains as a reminder of the former body of water once there. The year 1986 saw the addition of a Peace Garden at the east end of the park where peace events are held, and each year there is a commemorative ceremony to remember the bombing of Hiroshima and Nagasaki.

SEPTEMBER 23RD

2008: BBC Radio Humberside ran a report about Andrew Penny on this date, stating that his contribution to British music, although bringing him international acclaim, always bound him to the Hull classical music scene. Playing in youth orchestras in his younger days, he soon discovered a love for music and an amazing talent for conducting. This led him to study at The Royal Northern College of Music and from there his talent and subsequent career took off in leaps and bounds. Andrew has been Musical Director of the Hull Philharmonic Orchestra since 1982. The orchestra formed in 1881, starting with just twenty-seven players, but steadily increased over the years. In the 2006/07 season the society celebrated its 125th anniversary, performing a number of exciting concerts. Many believe it is Andrew's award-winning direction that has enabled them to tackle some of their most challenging works. The orchestra is now viewed as one of Britain's leading voluntary symphony orchestras and is a major feature of the city's cultural landscape.

September 24th

1951: Born in Hull on this day, actor David Banks has appeared in many leading roles in London's theatre scene but is better known for his TV appearances, such as Graeme Curtis in *Brookside*, *Canary Wharf's* Max Armstrong, and even as the photographer, Gavin, in *Eastenders* in 1992. However, David is best known for playing the Cyber Leader in the BBC series *Dr Who* in the 1980s. He played this character in all stories featuring the Cybermen, including *Earthshock* (1982), *The Five Doctors* (1983), *Attack of the Cybermen* (1985) and *Silver Nemesis* (1988). He even appeared as the Doctor in 1989 in place of Jon Pertwee, who was ill at the time. David is also a writer and director and has recorded over 100 audiobooks as a voice artist, including an unabridged version of Tolkein's *The Lord of the Rings.* He has written several books, including one concentrating on the conceptual history of the Cybermen, being somewhat of an expert, as he played the part for so long. An additional bit of trivia: David's first car was a black Morris Minor 1000 with flip-up yellow trafficators (the forerunners of indicators).

SEPTEMBER 25TH

2000: On this date the *Telegraph* newspaper printed a story about Hull-born Ronald 'Ras' Berry, who gained a reputation as an RAF Spitfire Ace. In 1940, aged just twenty-three, he flew with No. 603 Squadron when they were ordered south as losses in the Battle of Britain mounted. On August 31st, he was on the second scramble of the morning and found himself 'in the thick of a mass of wheeling, milling Me 109s.' He became embroiled in a dogfight but with his wit and skill he managed to shoot down three Messerschmitts in the one day. For this he was awarded the Distinguished Flying Cross and was hence known as 'the mighty atom'. By the close of the Tunisian campaign in May 1943, he had accumulated a score of fourteen enemy aircraft destroyed, ten shared, nine probables, seventeen damaged and seven destroyed on the ground, although inconclusive data and statistics would indicate that Ras actually had a much greater tally. He was awarded a Bar to his DFC, and then a Distinguished Service Order. He was appointed OBE in 1946 and CBE in 1965, and was one of fourteen former Battle of Britain pilots to lead the cortège at Sir Winston Churchill's funeral. His DFC citation stated, 'Through innumerable engagements with the enemy he has shown the greatest gallantry and determination in pressing home his attacks at close range. The skill and dash with which this officer has led his section have done much to assure their successes.'

SEPTEMBER 26TH

1339: This was the date that William de la Pole of Hull was appointed Second Baron of the Exchequer. This is a name well-known in Hull as an avenue and a hospital were named after him, the latter now being closed. However, not many people know that he was Hull's first ever mayor and also a key moneylender to King Edward III. Sir William was a very wealthy and successful wool merchant. When Edward went to war with Scotland, Sir William lent him the money to pay his troops as the king's bankers, the Bardi, were unable to do so. After this he lent the king money on numerous occasions in exchange for land, titles, favours and a licence to sell wool overseas. He represented Hull at court and, in 1331, persuaded the king to make Hull an autonomous borough instead of having a Royal Warden. However, in 1340, Sir William was arrested for smuggling wool and he was eventually forced to forgive the outstanding royal debts owed him, but he was still a very wealthy man when he died.

September 27th

2012: The *York Press* reported the death of a former bodyguard of Winston Churchill, Bill 'Happy' Day, on this date. Bill died, aged ninety-five, at his home in Victoria, Australia, leaving his wife Marie, and children Peter and Janet. Born in Hull in 1917, Bill went on to join the Royal Marines in 1934. At the start of the war he was promoted from corporal to sergeant and immediately volunteered for conflict, becoming part of the early Commandos. He apparently received training in demolition, parachuting, glider insertion and silent killing. It is said he came to Churchill's attention when he took part in the abortive Dieppe raid in 1942, which saw 60 per cent of the main force of Canadians either killed or captured. Bill landed with 40 Royal Marine Commando, 'which neutralised a battery of big guns on high ground and successfully withdrew.' Bill accompanied Churchill to the historic Tehran Conference in November 1943, where Joseph Stalin, Franklin D. Roosevelt and Churchill met to debate opening a second front against Adolf Hitler, a decision that helped win the Second World War. Bill was charged with the safekeeping of the Sword of Stalingrad, presented by Churchill to Stalin at the conference. Talking fondly of his father, Peter said that even until Bill died, 'he talked with great affection about Hull'. Bill was decorated with a Gallantry Medal, Six Campaign and Long Service Medals, and was awarded the second-highest possible British military honour, the Distinguished Service Medal, presented by King George VI. 'I'm proud of what he achieved,' said Peter. 'It wasn't bad for a depression-years Hull boy.'

September 28th

1976: 'Dawn for ship means sunset for 100 jobs at Hull yard' read the headline of one article from the *Hull Daily Mail* on this date. 'With a ship that sailed out of Hull today for her trials,' it reads, 'went the jobs of about 100 workers. Their work departed with the oil rig supply vessel *Stirling Sword*, the last ship built in a Hull city centre dry dock.' Fishing, trading and shipbuilding had been a massively important part of life in the city for so many years that this was to be a day remembered by many as the end of an era. The *Stirling Sword* was the last ship to be fitted out by workers at the Drypool Engineering and Dry Dock facilities at Alexandra Docks, meaning most of the workers employed at the Dock became redundant. The paper explained that the company was run by Mr R.J. Shepherd, who died in 1969, but there were further expansions after his death, 'involving the acquisition of Selby shipyard and then more business from the Beverley shipyard in 1973.' However, by 1975 the group ran into financial difficulties and although the Selby and Beverley parts were sold off, no one was interested in buying the Drypool facilities. It was a sad day for many, as the majority of the workers had been in shipbuilding all of their lives, but if they wanted to continue in the same line of work, which for many was all they were trained for, they had to consider moving elsewhere in the country. Representatives from the job centre were apparently on site interviewing each worker, however, and aiding their search for further employment.

SEPTEMBER 29TH

1885: On this date Hull's most well-known newspaper, the *Hull Daily Mail*, released its very first edition. Back then, the full title of the paper was the *Hull Daily Mail and East Yorkshire and Lincolnshire Courier*. The first ever edition, priced one halfpenny, carried mainly adverts on its front page for businesses. One of the stories was of three men who were charged with stealing 'a quantity of bottled ale and porter' from a merchant. Each was remanded until the end of the week, whence they were admitted to bail. There was also included a column about protests against the removal of the Patent Library at Hull's Mechanics' Institute, 'where it had been of great utility to the town generally'. The plans were to move the books to the Town Hall, but protesters believed they would be lost or that the public would not gain regular access to them. There seemed to have been a row over the order of the library in the Mechanics' Institute, whereby the librarian 'was rather annoyed [and] said he could put his hand upon any book in a moment.' The paper also contained a long script about its intentions as a newspaper, stating it would be Conservative: 'We shall ... not hesitate ... to pursue a policy of attack; to expose the fallacies of Radical doctrines; to correct the false and distorted descriptions of Conservative aims and policy which often pass current; and to place before the public the true issues between the two great parties which contend for supremacy in the State.'

September 30th

2010: On this day a special event, *Living Well with Dementia*, was held at the KC Stadium in Hull, offering advice and support to people with dementia and their carers. Well-known local author Valerie Wood was asked to attend and share her own experiences in caring for a loved one with dementia. Valerie, whose family moved to Hull when she was around thirteen, has written various novels, many located along the East Riding coast. When asked about her creative talent she says, 'My mother often told me that when I was small I had an imaginary friend and would sit on the stairs and talk to her. I do believe that a lot of children have imaginary friends, the difference is that they lose them or forget them once they get older, whereas I still have lots, all in my head, and these friends make up the characters in my novels!' She was invited to the event as she spent twelve years caring for her husband Peter, who sadly died in March 2009. She said: 'I am really keen to help raise awareness about dementia and its catastrophic effect on those it affects and their families. Dementia is a thief. It steals away the people we care about. It takes away their precious memories and any hopes for the future. It is also about the person with dementia losing the sense of themselves, of who they are, of who their family and friends are and where they fit into life in general.'

OCTOBER 1ST

1901: On this date the *Musical Times* ran a piece on the great organist and composer, Alfred Hollins. It stated that Alfred was born in Hull in 1865 and that, although he was born practically blind, 'this deprivation of the precious sense of sight has not clouded his sunny nature or darkened the earnest purpose of his life work.' From his earliest years he had an amazing ability of naming any note or combination that were sounded. He studied at the Wilberforce Institution for the Blind in York from 1874 to 1877, then went to the Royal Normal College for the Blind in 1878. In Berlin he studied under Hans von Bülow, who described him as 'one of those rare and true musicians among pianoforte virtuosi'. His first important public appearance was when he played Beethoven's Pianoforte Concerto in E-flat at the Crystal Palace, and he went on to play before Queen Victoria at Windsor in 1882, aged only sixteen! Mr Hollins had some interesting things to say regarding the different methods of working amongst blind musicians. It appears that some can only commit from Braille music; to others, committing from Braille is a slow and painful process. Alfred said his method involved a composition played over passage by passage, until he had learnt it by ear. He apparently never wrote his own compositions in Braille, but dictated them to his wife straight out of his head.

OCTOBER 2ND

1541: King Henry VIII visited Hull on this date in order to inspect the town's defences. He believed the city required some work to become less susceptible to attack. He decided Suffolk Palace was to become a citadel, the moat was to be scoured, the ramparts repaired and the gates to be provided with guns. He also ordered that the city's sluices be modified – so that the Humber could never again flood the surrounding area – and a new freshwater canal to be cut, from Newland to Hull. He sat with the Privy Council four times, deciding what alterations and defences needed to be made, and it was during this time that he apparently heard of the beauty of the wife of Lord Wake. There is some doubt as to the truth of this tale, but it is said Henry was so taken with the thought of Lady Wake's beauty that he insisted on dining with the couple one evening. Hearing of this, Lord Wake knew the dinner would only bring dishonour to his wife and probably death to himself, so he contrived a plan to avoid meeting with the king. He had his castle burned to the ground and when hearing of the misfortune, the king apparently offered him £2,000 towards rebuilding it. Never let it be said the gentlemen of Hull are not romantic!

OCTOBER 3RD

2011: Gavin Steed endangered the lives of dozens of people on this date when he ignored police demands to pull his car over and drove off, forcing them to pursue. The chase led through West Hull, ending when Gavin decided to abandon the car. Not only had he deliberately defied police by fleeing, but he then dangerously abandoned his car across the railway lines near Hawthorn Avenue, less than a mile from an oncoming train approaching Paragon Station. Fortunately, disaster was averted by a police helicopter, which managed to alert the train driver on his approach. Pilot Captain Kathryn Chapman, who coincidentally used to be a train driver, flew low above the train and apparently used lights to signal the driver to stop. The *Hull Daily Mail* quoted her as saying, 'We were just on the South Bank, looking across the Humber and saw the train going past the Arco building. I knew the train was getting close. I pulled the helicopter up to maximum speed, around 145mph. I was just determined to get ahead of the train.' Fortunately the driver managed to stop the train just 400 yards from the car. When searched, the car was found to contain heroin. Gavin pleaded guilty to all counts.

OCTOBER 4TH

1879: From *The Bellman* (a Hull publication) – a dark insight into the behaviour of certain Hull residents of that time:

> Hull numbers among its inhabitants two or three wretched, old, decrepit men and women who are, not exactly lunatics, but not quite so wise as that Scottish Solomon, King James of happy memory. The treatment which these poor creatures receive at our hands is a disgrace to our civilisation and a stain upon our public morality. Instead of pitying these unfortunates we make them a laughing stock ... As the poor, half-crazed, outcast passes along, men and women – or rather fools – laugh and mock at those whom the Almighty Father of all living things created as they are and those wrongs he will surely avenge.

———— • ◆ • ————

1864: On a lighter note, this date saw the drinking fountain of St Mary's Church in Lowgate inaugurated. The gift of Richard Sykes, Esq., the bowl and shaft were of polished red Peterhead granite and above the former were the arms and crest of the Sykes family. The inscription was from Proverbs: 'As cold water to a thirsty soul, so is good news from a far country'. The fountain cost about £150 and was from a design by Mr G.G. Scott, the eminent architect. The fountain was removed to just within the main gates into East Park at some point before the Second World War, and survived there until being removed during the construction of the new gates around the 1960s, but where it is now is not known.

OCTOBER 5TH

2004: The *London Evening Standard* ran a piece on twelve-year-old Hull-born Liam Mower on this date, stating that Liam had been chosen by director Stephen Daldry to be one of the three dancers to play the West End star role in *Billy Elliot*. Liam had been dancing from a young age:

> When I was little I was always dancing around the house. I started my first dance school doing disco, rock 'n' roll, ballroom and Latin. I was encouraged by my mum's friend to join the Northern Theatre Company where my interests grew for modern and tap, which I loved. My dance teacher Julie introduced me to ballet, and that's when everything changed. Ballet has become my favourite type of dance.

Liam had been persuaded by his Hull dance teacher to audition for the part of Billy. He went for the audition and landed the role, sharing the job with two other Billys, but it was Liam who starred as Billy on the opening night. Stealing the show, one theatre critic remarked, 'The beautiful blond boy playing the lead, Liam Mower, will surely become the biggest child star since Mark Lester played Oliver Twist.' His parents, bursting with pride, would travel from Hull to London every weekend to see their son in the part. When he left, Stephen Daldry said of the lad, 'Rarely does one ever come across a performer with so many skills and talents, particularly when matched by Liam's determination and good humour.'

OCTOBER 6TH

1862: Zachariah Charles Pearson is remembered in Hull for the park he donated to the city, Pearson Park, when he was at the height of his success. Born in 1821 into a shipping family, he developed a passion for ships from an early age. In 1825 he was orphaned and at twelve he ran away to sea but was discovered, although he did go on to become an apprentice at sixteen. Aged twenty-one, he got his first command and by the time he was twenty-five he was master (captain) of his very own ship. Before his fortieth birthday he was running his own shipping fleet and became Alderman, Sherriff and then Mayor of Hull. He headed up the business of Messrs Pearson, Coleman and Co., which ran mail packets between Australia and New Zealand. They also did much trade in the Baltic with Russia. However, a series of misfortunes and risky ventures eventually led him to bankruptcy. In 1862, Hull was hurting badly with the loss of the cotton trade due to the blockade of southern ports by the Federal navy during the American Civil War. Zachariah attempted to relieve the situation by running ships through the blockade to deliver arms and supplies, and to return with cotton. However, he lost ship after ship, all captured or sunk by the Federal Navy, and had to do all he could to avoid the inevitable bankruptcy. Always the moral man, he was determined to pay his creditors, as a personal letter from him, dated October 6th 1862, stated: 'I do resolve that if the estate does not paid [*sic*] 20/- in the pound I shall devote a portion of my future earnings to pay in full all the creditors in Hull.' He was finally declared bankrupt in 1864, living the rest of his life in a modest house on the fringe of his Pearson Park.

OCTOBER 7TH

1871: On this date the *Hull Daily Mail* celebrated the marriage of Hull-born Charles Henry Wilson and Florence Jane Helen, the eldest daughter of Colonel William Henry Charles Wellesley, nephew of the first Duke of Wellington. 'Never has there been a greater display of bunting in this port than that witnessed on Thursday,' claimed the newspaper. Charles and his brother Arthur took over his father's shipbuilding firm, becoming joint managers in 1867. It seemed to be their influence which led the company from strength to strength and by 1891, the Wilsons owned 100 ships with a profit of £2.5 million, a massive amount by the standards of the day. By 1903, the company was the largest in Hull, contributing significantly to the increase in Hull Dock acreage, from 5 acres in his father's youth to 150 acres. Then, by the early twentieth century, the business had become the largest privately owned shipping company in the world. It was sold in 1916 to Sir John Reeves Ellerman, reputedly the richest man in Britain at the time. Despite his stern manner, Charles had a very human side. During a strike at Hull docks in 1893, he apparently gave a generous donation to a fund for striker's wives and children, saying he 'could not bear to see little children suffer'. He served as High Sheriff of Hull and was elected as a Member of Parliament for Hull in 1874. When he died suddenly, in 1907, his brother struggled somewhat without him. Then, when Arthur died two years later, the large bell at Holy Trinity rang for an hour and a half, marking the end of an era.

OCTOBER 8TH

1985: On this date the famous international rugby winger Clive Sullivan died of liver cancer in Hull, aged forty-two. The people of Hull held him in such high regard that a section of the city's main approach road, the A63 between the Humber Bridge and the city centre, was renamed Clive Sullivan Way in his honour. Former Hull FC player and coach who played alongside Sullivan during the 1960s and '70s, David Doyle-Davidson, remembers his funeral service. 'There were thousands there, you couldn't get the fans into Holy Trinity and there were x thousands outside. So that in itself was a tremendous compliment to the man to say: "you are something special."' Although told when he was young that his knees, feet and shoulders, on which he had to have numerous operations, would never stand a sporting career, Clive persevered and was given a chance by Hull's rugby league club, becoming known for his exceptional speed and upper-body strength. His old injuries often caused him trouble, requiring constant attention and further operations, yet he played a total of 352 games for Hull, scoring 250 tries. In his 213 games for Hull Kingston Rovers, he scored 118 tries. 'From 60 metres out he was like a gazelle but from about 20 metres out he was like a wild bull: very, very strong,' said David.

OCTOBER 9TH

1937: 'Died After "Best Glass of Beer"' was the headline in the *Hull and Yorkshire Times* on this date, for a story about a Hull man who collapsed in a pub. 'He said it was the best glass of beer he had tasted for some time. He then put his glass on the table, made a rattling noise in his throat, and died.' Walter Siddal, aged seventy-eight, had gone along to the pub as usual, with a friend, Harry Chambers, seeming quite normal and in good spirits. He collapsed and died after his first pint, however; a pint he had evidently thoroughly enjoyed! His niece, Eva Peel, told how her uncle was in fairly good shape for his age, but the doctor had warned him at the beginning of the year to take things easy. The inquest heard that there had been no disturbance in the pub to upset Walter, they had not hurried to the pub and none of the others drinkers suffered any ill effects from the beer. The final verdict was heart failure due to natural causes – but if it was just his time to go, one is inclined to think there are worse ways!

OCTOBER 10TH

1896: October having long been known as the month of the famous Hull Fair even up to the present day, the *Hull and Lincolnshire Times* printed a local letter on this date extolling the joys of the fair back in the 1890s:

> Our good old 'carnival' is almost upon us and Hull is seriously beginning to wake up. Once, at least, in the year Hull rouses itself from its deadly apathy, and that time is when the Fair comes round. Many of the shops are then swept and garnished with extra care, and the windows, if possible, decked out with more tempting articles. The housewife, too, is extra busy … preparing good things for the friends from afar. We would not be without its old associations, its old, old memories, in spite of the fact of our bones being now too stiff to enjoy the pleasures of a mad ride on the hobby horse or the wild swish of the 'gondolas'. The time may be past for many of us when ice cream and 'Snaps' would have delighted our hearts, but there are others to take our place, and we may reap fresh pleasures again in watching their keen enjoyment and aiding them to go to our quaint and motley carnival.

OCTOBER 11TH

1643: There was a certain six-week period during the English Civil War that was particularly bad for the people of Hull. Charles I had been turned away at the city gates by Sir John Hotham and his hopes of raising a northern army against Parliament were becoming bleak. He laid siege to the town of Hull and for the next few weeks the inhabitants had a terrifying time. Red-hot cannon balls were shot into the town from the north to set fire to it. Their supply of mains water was cut off, so they had to rely on the brackish water from wells. The lands around Hull were flooded to keep the attackers at bay, but this meant that much of the townspeople's land was ruined, and so, therefore, was their livelihood. However, the folk of Hull remained strong and rallied together. Lord Fairfax, then governor of the town, had preparations in hand to face the royal siege. On October 11th, Fairfax took the initiative, using his now strong forces to advance out of the town, and after bitter fighting the Parliamentary troops over-ran the Royalists. Records state that the grateful citizens of Hull then brought out refreshments for the victorious soldiers – bread, meat and beer, 'which came very seasonably to them that had been fighting all day'. The siege ended the next day and Fairfax commanded that October 11th should be observed as one of general thanksgiving, its anniversary remaining as a holiday until the Restoration. This could possibly be why Hull Fair always commences the week closest to October 11th.

OCTOBER 12TH

1952: On this date Hull trawler *St Ronan* was lost at sea. Outward-bound for Greenland, it is said that the vessel passed through the inner sound between the Island of Stroma and the mainland. The channel was unlit and in an inquest later it was thought extraordinary that they had even decided on such a route. The trawler became stranded and was declared a total loss. The crew of twenty were saved, but at the inquiry it was found they had partaken in beer and spirits and the skipper was below at the time of stranding.

———◆———

1658: Hundreds of people in the Hull, Hedon and Holderness areas experienced a disturbing paranormal incident on this date. For a full fifteen minutes on a quiet, sunny afternoon the sounds and smells of battle filled the air. Cannon fire was heard, muskets and drums and plumes of smoke were even sighted rising over Hull. There were no troops in the area, no expected skirmish and no explanation for this strange episode was ever found.

OCTOBER 13TH

1926: On this date the Prince of Wales, later Edward VIII, laid the foundation stone for Hull's Ferens Art Gallery. The ceremony was part of a two-day visit, during which it is thought 200,000 people came out to see him. Before the start of the twentieth century, apart from civic portraits hung in the old Town Hall, Hull owned very few paintings. The first were given for Hull's permanent collection in 1902 by the Hull Society of Arts and Sir Albert Rollit. In 1905, Thomas Ferens began to contribute to the city's art collection by offering £5,000 in five annual instalments for buying works of art. These works were first exhibited in the Municipal Museum, but Ferens was unhappy with the space. In 1910 he opened a small suite of rooms, the Victoria Galleries, above shops in the newly built City Hall. He donated many paintings to this collection until in 1917 he felt the gallery no longer had sufficient capacity. He bought the land where the Ferens Art Gallery now stands and donated £35,000 towards building costs. Built in a classical style, it was opened in 1927 and named after its benefactor, being restored and extended in 1991. It is now a Grade II listed building.

OCTOBER 14TH

2008: There were ghostly goings-on in Hull's aquarium, The Deep, on this date when twenty-one-year-old Emma Place and her father visited the attraction. Whilst in a glass tunnel gazing at the sharks, Emma took a photograph which she noticed later had the eerie face of an unknown man reflected in the glass. The man's identity is a mystery. He was obviously not Emma's father as their appearances were very different, but there was no one else around who could have appeared in the frame. The aquarium bosses even searched CCTV to confirm this and tried to recreate conditions in the tunnel for the reflection to appear, but to no avail. The Deep was built on the site of an isolation hospital where smallpox victims were held and before that it housed Hull's Blockhouse, where many inmates met gruesome ends, possibly leaving behind many an aggrieved spirit. A nightwatchman also claims to have seen a shadowy figure within The Deep and others have reported hearing and even seeing the ghost of an inmate running along the banks of the river.

OCTOBER 15TH

1814: The PS *Caledonia* was the first steam-powered ship to be used on the Humber Estuary during this year. On this date a local newspaper report demonstrated the advantages of steam power, being able to work independently of either wind or tide:

> The steamboat *Caledonia* lately arrived here and has, during the week, been exhibiting her capabilities on the Humber; it appears that, with both wind and tide against her, her speed is considerable. On Wednesday she left for Gainsborough, and the weather being favourable, reached Barton Stather in an hour and a half.

This ship signalled a change from sail to steam, which revolutionised the shipping industry. It is ironic that the very first steam packet to be built was on the River Hull, in a yard in Wincolmlee in 1788. The vessel was bought by the Prince Regent, who transformed it into a pleasure yacht. The prince was apparently so pleased with the invention that he granted the patentees a pension for life of £70 a year each! Unfortunately, the yacht was destroyed in a fire shortly afterwards. It took another sixteen years for the *Caledonia* to be launched.

OCTOBER 16TH

1939: Hull's New Theatre opened on this date with the Hull Repertory Company production of *Me and My Girl*. Standing proud and magnificent in Kingston Square, the Hull New Theatre has survived many threats to its future, including a direct hit during the Second World War on the night of the 7th of May. The building, however, survived and has lived to see thousands of actors, performers and audiences come through its doors. There are, however, some spine-tingling tales about the place that were reported in the *Hull Daily Mail* in 1998. Actress Emma Morris revealed that she had seen a mysterious figure in a black cape and top hat down a narrow corridor. She was not the first to have reported such a sighting in the theatre, the spook apparently having been seen there for decades. Nicknamed Charlie, he seems to have a penchant for nipping ladies' bottoms! Emma escaped this treat but said she felt a cold presence when she saw him. First reported to have been seen in 1943, even two city councillors met the ghostly figure during a military band performance there. The newspaper suggested that he could have been the ghost of a man stabbed in a fight in the 1840s, or perhaps a builder who fell inside the walls while the building was being bricked up.

OCTOBER 17TH

1878: Anthony Bannister was a prominent figure in mid-Victorian Hull. He became a successful fish merchant and ship owner and became town councillor for the North Myton Ward in 1845, being elected Alderman in 1855. He also served as Sheriff, then Mayor and Justice of the Peace. In 1852, he was awarded a snuffbox of gratitude by the United Fisherman's Society for 'services rendered to their body'. With threats of war in 1859, Anthony formed a Hull company of Rifle Volunteers, established by the Hull Men's Working Club, and he also built a theatre in Humber Street. He was a greatly admired figure, very intelligent and forward thinking, and did much good for his city. He also helped instigate the plans for the Hull and Holderness Railway Company to develop coastal tracks, as he realised railways could bring further business and prosperity to the city. When Anthony died, a collection was set up a in his honour. On this date, the *Eastern Counties Herald* reported £15,000 had been raised to erect a marble statue in his memory, to be placed in the Town Hall, and the remainder of the money to be given to his family.

———◆•———

1862: Also on this day, the *Hull Packet & East Riding Times* printed a piece from the Hull Police Court:

> Breach of The-Bye-Law: Caroline Hough was summoned for a breach of the bye-law, by erecting a swing-boat in Osborne-street which projected 18 feet across the carriage-road. Judgement was respited on payment of costs.

OCTOBER 18TH

1957: On this date the *Hull Daily Mail* reported that a new wash house had been opened. It stated that after twenty years of the housewives of Hessle Road scrubbing and rubbing at their washing in the Regent Street public wash house, the Hull Baths Committee had opened the first part of its new modernised wash house:

> Aluminum sinks replace the old-type sinks set in wooden draining boards, and there is a constant supply of softened hot water. Housewives place their washing in one of the new machines (maximum 22lb) and wash their woollies and delicate fabrics by hand. All the clothes are placed in a spin dryer which extracts 60 per cent of the water before the laundry is dried as before.

The 'washing machine experts' attended for the first few days to show the women how to operate the machines. There were various opinions concerning the new machines from different housewives interviewed, some thinking the machines would be useful and save time, others reluctant to accept the change. Some were concerned that they would not be allowed to bring in dirty fishermen's bags, but the chairman of the Baths Committee assured them that 'there is no examination by the staff of what goes into the machines. If they put in seamen's dungarees, nobody will interfere.'

OCTOBER 19TH

1885: The *Hull Daily Mail* ran an article on this date telling the story of a Hull Police Constable who was charged with the theft of a gold keeper ring from the landlady of the Skinners' Arms, Cumberland Street. The narrative stated that William Ruddiford had gone for a pint after he had come off duty, still dressed in his police uniform, on the morning of the 12th. Mrs Woodcock, the landlady, had placed her ring in a vase in the room where he was drinking and whilst he was in there she said she spied him examining the vase. When he had left the premises she had gone to retrieve her ring, only to find it missing. Knowing no one else had entered the room she decided to confront the constable next time she saw him, but he denied the charge, even in front of his wife. However, soon afterwards Mrs Woodcock received a letter, containing her ring, stating:

> It was not the policeman that took the ring. I took it a good bit after he went. I have heard of him getting into trouble. The policeman is a friend of mine, and it was only a game. I think you would blame the policeman, but [this] is false.

Mrs Woodcock went straight to the police over the matter and the handwriting on the letter was compared with William's handwriting from police reports. With this evidence and witness reports claiming no one else had entered the room after him, William was 'committed to prison for two calendar months'.

OCTOBER 20TH

1962: 'Boothby Graffoe is a multi-talented, darkly hilarious, grade A British eccentric, who can twist your funny bone one minute and break your heart the next. A musical comedy act who is more musical than most musicians, and funnier than most comedians.' So says Stewart Lee about the Hull-born comedian, singer, songwriter and playwright. Born on this date, his real name is James Martin Rogers, but he adopted Boothby Graffoe as his alter ego, inspired by a village he drove past leaving a gig. He claims he is the only comedian in the world to be named after a Lincolnshire village! Boothby began his career working for BBC Radio Lincolnshire with his own two-hour long programme and has appeared regularly on BBC Radio 4 programmes. Apparently he caused quite a stir on *Opportunity Knocks* in the 1980s by wrapping sellotape around his head! As Lee says, Boothby's humour is dark, surreal and, frankly, off the wall. His song titles include, 'Planet Dog', 'Woof' and 'The Consequences of Living in a Container'. He has toured and worked extensively with comedian Omid Djalili, who says of Boothby, 'If I had to compare him with anyone, it would be Spike Milligan.'

OCTOBER 21ST

1904: One of Hull's greatest tragedies took place on this date. It was during the time Russia and Japan were at war and the Russian Navy were sailing to meet their adversary when they came across forty-five Hull trawlers fishing off the Dogger Bank. The Gamecock fishing fleet had sailed from Hull, completely unprepared for the horrors that lay in store for them. It was night-time and there was a fog, the fishing fleet had nets down and all hands were busy. This is when they encountered a fleet of warships they at first thought were British. The fishing fleet was suddenly floodlit by lights from what were actually Russian warships, claiming they believed the fishers were the Japanese Navy. They attacked, much to the shock and terror of the fishermen. Captain Whelpton is quoted as having shouted, 'Good God! This is not blank, lie down lads and look after yourself.' The scene was dreadful; injured men lay everywhere and two poor souls were decapitated. For twenty minutes they endured a barrage of fire, unable to run due to having their nets down. When two vessels limped back into St Andrew's Dock, the flag flying at half-mast signalled loss of life. The Russians should never have attacked; the trawlers and their nets were perfectly visible in the floodlights, their build distinctive. The incident caused a major diplomatic incident and almost started a war between Britain and Russia.

OCTOBER 22ND

1833: On this date Captain John Ross wrote to Captain George Elliot, requesting that some help be sought for funding the wages of his crew, suggesting the possibility of even making it a public charge. Captain Ross' voyage did not turn out as first planned when he set sail in 1829, on his second voyage in search of the North West Passage. The ship, *Victory*, became stuck in ice and the crew were forced to spend the next four years in the Arctic, not returning to Hull until 1833. They were the first such explorers to survive for so long and only lost three men in all that time. With the help of the native inhabitants, they apparently learnt to live in those harsh conditions and were finally rescued by the *Isabella*, an old flagship of Captain Ross'. At first the *Isabella*'s captain was apparently dubious as to whether or not it really was the missing Captain Ross and crew, as their appearance was so different from when they set out. Once convinced, however, they took them home and were met with a joyous reception in Hull. The rescue was said to have caught the imagination of the country at the time and attracted worldwide attention. Captain Ross was subsequently knighted for his achievements.

OCTOBER 23RD

1782: Hull's first infirmary was opened during this year, in George Street, but a new site was chosen the same year, on this date, at what is now known as Prospect Street. Then considered to be beneficial to the ill, the site was half a mile from the town, where fresh country air could be enjoyed, a strange notion to us now, as Prospect Street sits in the very heart of Hull's city centre. The institution was opened to help the poor and those unable to pay for treatment and relied mainly on doctors volunteering their services, such as John Alderson, whose statue now stands at the site of the present city hospital. The original hospital lasted 183 years, despite suffering bomb damage in the war, and it was claimed to be haunted by the ghost of a porter who had committed suicide there. When the Prospect Street Shopping Centre was built on the site, cleaners and staff complained of ethereal voices, shadowy figures and moving objects. The name Hull Royal Infirmary replaced General Infirmary in 1884, when their Royal Highnesses the Duke and Duchess of Edinburgh opened a new wing to the hospital.

OCTOBER 24TH

1925: On this date operatic singer Charles Kenningham died in Australia, aged sixty-four. Born in Hull, Charles was musically gifted from his youth, becoming a soprano soloist at eight years of age, at Holy Trinity Church. Then, only two years later, he was principal solo boy at St Paul's Cathedral in London. After his voice broke, he became the organist and choirmaster at St Luke's Church in Hull aged fourteen. Although he kept a keen interest in music, he enlisted in a military career for quite a few years, until he decided to turn back full-time to his first love and is probably best remembered for his roles in the 1890s with the D'Oyly Carte Opera Company, as a principal tenor. The *Sydney Morning Herald* reported Charles' death on October 26th, giving a glowing account of his life's works and explaining that he went to Australia in 1898 as one of the new artists engaged for the reorganised Royal Comic Opera Company. The article finished by stating that, 'In a wide range of parts during his Australian career, Mr Kenningham was always effective, and became very popular.'

OCTOBER 25TH

1980: On this date the official twinning of Kingston-upon-Hull and Freetown, in Sierra Leone, took place. There is a strong link between William Wilberforce and Freetown and it is said that the people of Freetown know more about William Wilberforce's works than the citizens of Hull do! Before receiving its current name, the port at Freetown was one of the centres of the slave trade in Africa. Thanks to the work of such tireless emancipators as William Wilberforce, the slave trade was abolished in the 1780s/90s and it was renamed Freetown and set up as a home for freed slaves. The year 2007 saw the 200th anniversary of the abolition of the slave trade in Africa, which Wilberforce fought for. Freetown remembers his efforts in street names, buildings and shop signs, even today. For the thirtieth anniversary of the twinning of the two cities, Hull City Council pledged to help improve the waste management system in Freetown. They have a population of 2 million, for which there were apparently only ten waste collection vehicles, compared with the sixty vehicles in Hull which deal with the waste of approximately 250,000 people. This promise of help ties in with the very reason the two towns were twinned in the first place.

OCTOBER 26TH

1952: The Poet Laureate of the United Kingdom from 1999 to 2009 was born on this date. Andrew Motion, however, broke with the tradition of the Laureate retaining the post for life, saying he wanted the post for ten years only. At the end of his post he told the *Guardian*:

> To have had ten years working as Laureate has been remarkable. Sometimes it's been remarkably difficult, the Laureate has to take a lot of flak, one way or another. More often it has been remarkably fulfilling. I'm glad I did it, and I'm glad I'm giving it up – especially since I mean to continue working for poetry.

Andrew was an English lecturer at the University of Hull when Philip Larkin was the librarian there. The two apparently became very close friends and Andrew wrote a biography of Larkin's life following his friend's death. This won the Whitbread Prize for Biography. It was also during his time in Hull that Andrew's first volume of poetry was published. He returned to Hull in April 2006 to give a prestigious reading, alongside fellow poet Alan Hollinghurst, to commence the new Creative Writing MA at the University. He also came to Hull in July 2010 to launch a bus in memory of his friend Larkin, commemorating the twenty-fifth anniversary of his death. Andrew apparently said, 'I think if he had been here today he would have been very pleased.'

OCTOBER 27TH

1916: The *Daily Mail* on this date contained many letters and articles about things war-related, as would be expected at this time. There was a column discussing 'The Meaning of War', which stated: 'As it is felt by many people that the war is an unmitigated evil, out of which no good can come, I submit the following observations for their consideration.' The columnist stated how conditions were before the war began, highlighting particularly that there was a state of unrest in the country, 'brought about largely, no doubt, by the uneven distribution of wealth'. He then went on to talk about the class divisions, the 'idle rich and the abject poverty', believing that 'free education contributed in no small degree to the awakening of the masses to a sense of injustice at the hardness of their lot.' However, with the onset of war all classes came together to face a tyranny united. 'We find the sudden disappearance of internal dissension and class antagonism, and a complete unity in face of the German menace which must have considerably surprised the Kaiser.' Our columnist also believes the role of women, so changed by war, can but be a positive outcome of this 'evil': 'Nobly have they worked in many and varied ways to support the men, and have, by their devotion, done more to earn for themselves the right to vote than could have been achieved by centuries of militant Suffragism.'

OCTOBER 28TH

2010: On this day, a little after 2 a.m., a number of Hull residents claimed to have heard a strange humming noise over the city of Hull. Controversy abounds as to what the noise actually was and the general consensus seemed to believe it was caused by a UFO! Hull resident, Mike, stated that he 'heard a loud roar as if a commercial airliner or military jet was heading over East Hull towards Humberside Airport. What was odd about this event was the duration of the noise, and how weird it sounded in relation to other engines we hear from passing aircraft.' Another resident commented that it sounded like an old Second World War bomber plane of some sort, as did many others who reported it. One man said it sounded as though it was a large aircraft with decent-sized engines struggling to gain altitude. However, there are no records of such a flight experiencing troubles over Hull and apparently no low-flying commercial airliners at that time. Damien Elvin, spokesman for the Ministry of Defence, said they were not aware of any military aircraft in the area and a spokeswoman for the police confirmed that the police helicopter was in Scunthorpe between 1.15 a.m. and 5.12 a.m. What the bizarre noise was remains a mystery.

OCTOBER 29TH

1863: On this date the Earl de Grey and Ripon was installed Lord High Steward of Hull. This was also the year the Prince and Princess of Wales married, so Hull had two big celebrations that year, the latter being remembered as a great occasion for the townspeople. As part of the day's festivities the statue of the Queen in Pearson Park was unveiled and four fine vessels from the shipyard of Messrs M. Samuelson & Co. were launched in the presence of the earl, the borough members, the civic dignitaries and the gentry of the town and neighbourhood.

By all accounts the installation ceremony, which took place in the Sessions Court, was most imposing and at its conclusion, a procession was formed and proceeded through the principal streets to the park, where the remainder of the ceremonies took place. The proceedings terminated with a grand banquet at the Public Rooms. The learned Recorder of the town, in his speech at the banquet, stated it was a 'most memorable and distinguished day in the annals of Hull', while the *Hull Advertiser* described it as 'a day in Hull memorable beyond all precedent, and successful beyond all expectation.'

OCTOBER 30TH

1970: The *Hull Daily Mail* reported the tragic death of Hull teenager Michael John Wolfe on this day. The fifteen-year-old lad, from Somerset Street, apparently disappeared whilst swimming in crocodile-infested waters on a trip to Nigeria. Michael joined the salvage tug *Neptuna*, on a six-month engagement in Nigeria, as a catering boy, in the September. Apparently it had been a life-long dream of his to go to sea and he had nagged his parents endlessly to allow him to go. Then, after relenting and letting their son sail away, the news reached his parents just a month later, on his sister's eighteenth birthday, that Michael had gone missing. They were told how he and fellow Hull lad Robert Platten had gone swimming in the sea, even though they had been warned of the dangers of doing so. They had apparently started swimming back to the boat together but when Robert next looked for his friend, Michael had gone. Sadly, news from Nigeria was very slow arriving, due to communications breakdown, so the family had to wait another five months to hear the exact details of their son's tragic death.

OCTOBER 31ST

1995: The *Hull Daily Mail* reported that Ye Olde White Harte pub was being opened for a Halloween charity stay-over on this date. Ye Olde White Harte in Hull's Old Town is a legendary building full of history, plottings and even ghosts. The pub was first built as a house sometime in the fourteenth century. In 1642, it is said that Sir John Hotham used the upstairs room known as the 'Plotting Parlour' for his plans to turn King Charles I away from the city gates during the English Civil War. 'Freda' is Ye Olde White Harte's resident ghost whose bony features peer down on drinkers. Is it Freda who leaves the mysterious smell of perfume? A human skull is kept in a Perspex case behind the small saloon bar. There are two theories as to whose skull it is. One suggests that the youth was the victim of an angry, alcohol-fuelled sea captain who hit him with the butt of his pistol, causing the fracture marks. The body was placed under the staircase, where it remained hidden until a fire in the nineteenth century unearthed it. Another story states that it was found in the 1881 renovations, the remains of an unfortunate maid who met a tragic end after (perhaps) some scandal, the landlord promising to hide the body and sealing it in the attic. Both stories appear to be based on legend, as no one seems to know who it belongs to. In English folklore the white hart is associated with Herne the Hunter and his pack of phantom hounds. Would you be brave enough to stay the night amid all these ghostly goings-on?

NOVEMBER 1ST

1881: This was the date the Hull Botanic Gardens railway station opened, under this name. In 1848, it was known as Hull Cemetery then changed to Hull Cemetery Gates in 1866. The position of this small country station was where Princes Avenue, Spring Bank and Spring Bank West met. The station itself was built at street level, near to the level crossing across the bottom end of Spring Bank, where the pub The Old Zoological (now known as Pearsons) is. It was the Hull to Withernsea and Hornsea railway line and remained known as Hull Botanic Gardens until its final closure in October 1964. The name commemorated a 49-acre stretch of land, which opened in 1880 as a Botanical Garden and which a Spring Bank pub is named after. This garden only survived a few years, however, as the site was used to establish Hymers College for boys. Hull Botanic Gardens railway station was an intermediate stop on the North Eastern Railway's Victoria Dock Branch line. Spring Bank contained another park, in 1840, the Zoological Gardens, hence the earlier name of the present pub. There was shrubbery and fountains, as well as lakes. Exotic animals were exhibited there too, including polar bears, wolves, elephants and tigers.

NOVEMBER 2ND

1611: William Gee died on this date, soon after making his will. Known in Hull as thrice mayor and local benefactor, William left bequests in his will to St John's College, Cambridge, and to the poor of Beverley. He was buried in York Minster as requested, where a monument to him was also erected. During his life, William had connections with Hull Grammar School, later known as the William Gee School for Boys, founded in 1330 and being the seventeenth oldest independent school in the UK. True to their motto, *Floreat Nostra Scola* (May our School Flourish), the school did flourish and was once one of the top schools in Hull. In 1486, a home for the school was built in Hull's Market Square and around 1578 William opened a subscription to repair it. A new school was erected, with William contributing a large sum towards the cost. It is this building, completed in 1583, that has a reputation for being haunted. At 7.40 p.m., a certain Mr Yates, supposedly a nineteenth-century vicar of St Mary's, is said to appear at the first-storey window. This appearance signals misfortune and there have been reports of fires and accidents after sightings of him. Dare you look up?

November 3rd

2009: On this day the *Jewish Chronicle Online* paid tribute to the Hull-born thriller writer Lionel Davidson, who had passed away in October. Lionel was one of nine children of an immigrant Jewish tailor. During the Second World War he served in the Royal Navy and acted as a freelance reporter, continuing this role after the war; he travelled widely and got to know Europe especially well. His first novel, *The Night of Wenceslas*, is thought to have been inspired by his travels, as it is set in Czechoslovakia during the Cold War. It tells of the reluctant adventures of Nicholas Whistler who becomes caught up in espionage. This first book was an instant success, bringing him a Golden Dagger award from the Crime Writer's Association in 1960. The *Jewish Chronicle* explains how he was the only person ever to have won three Golden Daggers and that in 2001 he was the recipient of the Diamond Dagger from the Crime Writer's Association for his lifetime contribution to crime fiction. In all he wrote eight novels, four of which could apparently be said to be his 'Jewish' novels, some written while he was living with his young family in Israel.

November 4th

1794: Prince William (afterwards Duke) of Gloucester visited Hull on this date, being the first member of the Royal Family to visit the town since its gates were shut against Charles I. On the following day he apparently reviewed the volunteer companies, Surrey Militia and Hanoverian Horse, after which he is said to have reviewed the invalids at the Citadel. He accepted the Freedom of the Corporation, and was made a Brother of Trinity House. The Prince was entertained at Sir Samuel Standidge's House in High Street and the following year he was knighted by King George III. It is probably his secret marriage to Maria Walpole in 1766 that Prince William is best known. The king was kept in the dark about the marriage, and he only found out after he passed the Royal Marriages Act of 1772 in the April, whereby no royal could marry without the consent of the reigning monarch. It is said his motive for passing the Act was the marriage of his brother, Prince Henry, to a commoner. One can image he was not best pleased when he discovered Prince William's secret!

NOVEMBER 5TH

1992: On this date the world-famous indie band Radiohead played at the Hull Adelphi Club. It would be a rare thing indeed to meet a Hull music lover who has not heard of the Adelphi Club, host to hundreds of bands throughout its years. As well as Radiohead, those who played there include Pulp, Green Day, The Stone Roses and The Housemartins, plus many established and countless local bands. Legend has it that the Adelphi Club's car park was created due to a hit by a Luftwaffe bomb. It was known as the Victory Club in the 1920s and the De Grey Club in the 1930s, becoming a sports club in the 1950s and a laundry in the 1970s. It was on October 1st 1984 that Paul Jackson took over ownership and made it into the legendary, international, diverse music hotspot it is now. The venue celebrated its twenty-fifth anniversary with an exhibition at the Ferens Art Gallery, the exhibition being made up of memorabilia dating back to when it opened and a series of gigs and special guest appearances occurring at the club itself. When asked about his relationship with the club, Mr Jackson said, 'It's mostly been a lot of fun, and a great privilege to have worked and played alongside so many talented young people from around the world.'

NOVEMBER 6TH

1961: The poliomyelitis outbreak in Hull began in September 1961 and was said to have lasted until the end of December that year. During this three-month period, 180 suspected cases of the disease were admitted to Castle Hill Hospital. Ninety-five of these were confirmed and two deaths were reported. The greatest number of cases was amongst pre-school children. At the end of the three months, thirty-nine cases showed no paralysis, twenty cases had minor paralysis, seven cases had significant paralysis and seventeen cases had severe paralysis. Differing from the 1947 epidemic, the cases on this occasion were said to be concentrated in a densely populated area near the docks. The previously used Salk vaccine was not able to halt the epidemic and the Hull Health Authority asked the Ministry of Health's permission to use the oral vaccine Sabin. There is a letter dated November 6th 1961 enquiring when the Minister of Health would make a decision concerning this. Within a few days 385,000 people were vaccinated in Hull and surrounding areas. By the end of October the epidemic was under control. This was the first time the vaccine had been used in Western Europe to halt an outbreak and following this success the Sabin vaccine became widely accepted in the UK. On October 24th 1961, the Ministry of Health announced the general introduction of oral vaccination with the Sabin vaccine as an alternative form, meaning Hull had been the forerunner in this preventative programme.

NOVEMBER 7TH

1944: In 1861, Joseph Henry Fenner opened a Hull business producing various leather goods, including hosepipes, strap manufacture and leather dressings. Then, in the 1870s, the company moved into the production of leather transmission belting to meet the demand generated by fast industrial growth. By the 1930s, Fenner's V-belts were sold worldwide and Fenner was becoming a household name. Some extracts from the minutes of board meetings of J.H. Fenner & Co. Ltd from 1937 to 1946 show that on November 7th 1944 conveyor belting was an innovation that was being considered by the company: 'This is a product that might well come within our capacity, though no decision has yet been reached, pending further investigations into the profit margin to be expected.' Conveyor belts are now a worldwide commodity, even used in such ways as flattening the grains of corn into the shapes we recognise as cornflakes and in MOT brake-testing equipment. Fenner's V-belts were also instrumental during the 1960s polio outbreak, when factories worked overtime to produce enough doses of oral Sabin vaccine. This was produced in sterile rooms, with airflow controlled by Fenner premium V-belt-driven fans. Fenner V-belts also formed part of the drives used on the 'bouncing bombs', made famous by the Dambusters' raids.

NOVEMBER 8TH

1930: Samuel Smith was a money lender and credit handler based on Anlaby Road. It would perhaps have been wiser if he had stayed with the fish and chip shop he used to own, as being a moneylender turned out to be a dangerous profession for him. On this date Samuel was found by his son-in-law beaten to death in his own home; he had been choked and left with a shoelace tight around his neck. He had been battered around the head, all for a wad of cash, a gold watch and chain. He was also owed £400 from his moneylending activities, which, back in the 1930s, was a considerable sum, so there was a motive for the murder. There were no clues as to who might have done the deed apart from the fact that all the houses in Samuel's street had the same key and he was locked in with no sign of a forced entry. Police wondered if the murderer had lived on the same street! A reward was offered but the murder remains unsolved.

NOVEMBER 9TH

1993: On this date Gerald Thomas, the man responsible for creating one of the most enduring and endearing British comedy series, the *Carry On* films, died. Born in Hull in 1920, Gerald was studying medicine when the Second World War began and he served in the British Army. When he left, he did not return to medicine, instead forging a career as a film editor, which included many films directed by his brother Ralph. Although he had quite a varied early career, he is almost exclusively remembered as the director of thirty *Carry On* films, the innuendo-laden British comedy series which was produced by his friend Peter Rogers. *Carry On Sergeant* was the first film in 1958. Then, for an intense twenty-year period, Thomas directed the *Carry On* gang through their eye-popping exploits. It is said some of the cast and crew of the films referred to Thomas as the 'Headmaster' or the 'Circus Ring Master'. He became good friends with many of them over the years and when he died Peter Rogers, his producer partner for over forty years, said, 'His epitaph will be that he directed all the *Carry On* films.'

November 10th

1279: Ask any man, woman or child in Hull about the Fair and they will be able to regale you with tales of bright lights, loud thumping music, hair-raising rides and more than enough smells and delights to fill the senses. This carnival of merriment is the largest travelling fair in Europe and one of the oldest, now over 700 years old! The first charter granting permission for a fair to be held in the locality of Hull was granted on this date in 1279. Later, King Edward I granted a further charter in 1293 for it to run from May to July and another in 1299 said it should be held after Easter. Then, in 1598, a new Royal Charter gave permission for Hull's Fair to be held in September, but, with riots over the loss of eleven days caused by the changes in the calendar in 1751, October became and still is the month for the Fair. It has changed its location many times and originally began as a market, with trade being the dominant function, but it slowly took on the character of a funfair and entertainment is now its main focus. Eagerly awaited and well attended, the fun of the Fair has never lost its magic!

NOVEMBER 11TH

2009: The *Hull Daily Mail* published an interview on this date with actor Barrie Rutter. 'There were two Road to Damascus moments in the life of Barrie,' it explained. 'The first came at primary school, when his English teacher propelled him towards his debut acting role – because "he had the gob for it". In the second, the Hull-born actor realised the value of a northern company performing classic plays in northern accents. "I'm a fish dock lad from when Hull was the biggest white fish port in the world," he said. "While my mates were working on the docks, I was singing and playing the piano and drums, so I could earn something to stand a round of drinks. I just had this affinity and enjoyment with being on stage. It is a glorious thing to do."' In 1980, he joined the National Theatre, where he worked closely with poet Tony Harrison, performing in all three of Harrison's adaptations, all written for the northern voice. It was this experience of performing in the northern voice that generated the idea for Northern Broadsides, his own theatre company, which is now a thriving success. 'Barrie's northern accent, fast-action, factory floor Shakespeare is as far from elitism as can be, though it has never dumbed Shakespeare down. What you get is the text, the poetry, the real thing, but with a northern vigour,' said former Deputy Prime Minister John Prescott.

November 12th

1973: Housed in Queen Victoria Square, Hull City Hall's foundation stone was laid by Her Royal Highness the Princess of Wales in 1903. By 1909 the City Hall was in use, and in 1911 a unique organ was installed in the main hall, but there appears to be no record of the City Hall having ever been formally opened. The City Hall plans incorporated space for an art gallery, which opened in 1910 and was used as such until 1927, when Thomas Ferens donated a new gallery to the city and the art was moved there. After this the space was used for a time as an exhibition suite for prehistoric antiques. Like many of the buildings in the city, the City Hall sustained considerable damage during the bombing of the Second World War, ruining the roof, main hall and the organ, which led to the building closing at this point. In 1950 the City Hall reopened and in the following year, the organ was restored. It is now a Grade II listed building, built in Baroque Revival style by Hull's City Architect J.H. Hirst, having been listed on November 12th 1973.

November 13th

1885: On this night, Chief Constable James Campbell was accused of making sexual advances to fourteen-year-old Edith Ann Creighton. Campbell, only the third person to hold the title of Chief Constable in Hull, previously had an excellent reputation, implementing many new laws. Ironically, when the 1885 Criminal Law Amendment Act, strengthening laws against prostitution and raising the age of consent from thirteen to sixteen, was passed, Campbell was proactive in implementing them. Edith's mother complained about Campbell to the magistrate, who called for an investigation. On this night, Edith stated that her father was away at sea and her mother and brother were out. Campbell apparently called round about 7 p.m. Realising she was alone he made her sit on his knee, placed his arms around her and tried to kiss her. He asked her to show him her leg and he allegedly pulled her skirt up to her knee. Then he gave her sixpence and told her not to tell anyone. When interviewed, Campbell admitted sitting her on his knee and giving her a peck on the cheek. The mother's story, however, was that he had pleaded with her not to let Edith go in front of the committee and to say that he was an old family friend who often visited and was close to the children. Campbell was asked to resign but the press were in two minds as to what had actually happened. Campbell and his family eventually emigrated to Australia.

NOVEMBER 14TH

1913: Dan Billany was born on this date. From a poor Hull family, he had a burning ambition to be a writer. Leaving school at fourteen, he fought to achieve his goals, attending evening classes at the Technical College after work. His tenacity paid off and he won a scholarship to Hull University, where he obtained an English degree and his teaching certificate. In 1938 he began teaching at Chiltern Street School, where he was popular and dynamic. Unfortunately, with the start of the Second World War, he had to leave and join the army. He became an officer in the East Yorkshire Regiment but never gave up his dream of writing. In 1940, T.S. Elliot, working for Faber and Faber, read his manuscript, *The Opera House Murders*, and published it. The book became a bestseller and spurred Dan on. He was a German prisoner of war in Italy until their surrender in 1943, when he fled to the countryside and continued working on his manuscripts, leaving them in the hands of a friendly Italian farmer who posted them to his parents in England. These were published along with *The Cage* and *The Trap*, but Dan never saw their success. Tragically, he and three friends were last heard of in 1943 making their way over the Apennines towards the allied forces. No one ever saw him again.

NOVEMBER 15TH

1915: This date marks the death of well-known Hull ship owner and developer David Parkinson Garbutt, most remembered for his creation of the Avenues Estate. This area was originally built as middle-class housing in the late nineteenth century and it is said 'that its popularity with left-wing intellectuals and academics, and varied leafy cosmopolitan ambience has caused it to be stereotyped as Hull's "Muesli Belt".' The area was once all green fields, known as Newland Tofts. Pearson Park was opened in 1860 and this gave the area a substantial advantage for creating this kind of estate. Princes Avenue was known as Derringham Dike and the 'road' along it, Mucky Peg Lane. To the west lay Ewe Lands and Chanter Lands. David developed all this area, the four avenues – Westbourne, Park, Marlborough and Victoria – for housing branching off from Princes Avenue. The estate was formally opened by David in 1875. As part of the original layout of the development there were cast-iron decorative fountains in the centre of the roads, with two more on Princes Avenue. The fountains on Princes Avenue were removed in 1926 due to increased traffic. In 1995, there were three car collisions with the fountains in Westbourne and Park Avenues, all coincidentally, in the November. Much damage was caused and a five-year restoration plan was put underway, costing £200,000.

NOVEMBER 16TH

1893: The *Eastern Morning News* gave a report on this date, concerning 'another effort ... to reconstruct the tram system in Hull, and to put it on a sound financial basis.' Although the 'principle proposals ... are as yet "in the air" ... the idea seems to be that the Corporation should be induced to buy up the existing companies and all their belongings; relay the main roads with a double track, and then lease the system to a company ... of local gentlemen, at term to be agreed upon.' The report suggests the previous year's proposal opened it up to a London syndicate, but this year's agreed the proposed lessees should be local gentlemen. 'Up to the present no formal advance has been made to the Works Committee. When it is made there is no doubt that the question will receive the most careful attention, and we hope will receive the solution best calculated to benefit the town.' The town's advancement seemed to be a priority then indeed!

The same paper gives mention to poor little Robert Matthews who was run over by a brougham carriage whilst he was playing in Park Street. He was taken to the Children's Hospital, where it was found that his right thigh was broken.

NOVEMBER 17TH

2005: On this day Hull-born actor Andrew Newton-Lee appeared on the Richard and Judy show to discuss his career in acting, which includes work in *Hollyoaks*, *Coronation Street*, *Casualty* and *Doctors*. He had an unfortunate start to his young career, being diagnosed with skin cancer at just twenty-four years of age. The doctor apparently blamed the heavy sunbed usage he employed to look good for his roles. Fortunately, treatment was successful and he was well enough to run the London Marathon in 2007. Andrew moved to Los Angeles with a celebrity-based business he had set up, and when asked what he missed about Britain his first response was, 'definitely not the weather!' He does admit to missing his family and friends but says whenever he visits Hull many of his friends are settled down with families and mortgages. As a single man, however, he is happy at the moment to follow his career, describing himself as 'ferociously ambitious'.

———— ◆ ————

1893: On this day the *Hull Daily Mail* included a story about two men who had stolen a pony from another man. The owner had apparently sent his horse and trap home while he was in the pub, but instead of taking it home the accused had taken the horse and swapped it for 'an old horse that could hardly walk,' for the price of £1. He was remanded for seven days.

NOVEMBER 18TH

1966: Born in Hull on this date, Jon Campling always knew he had to pursue his passion for acting, but at sixteen he became an apprentice within British Aerospace, helping to build parts of the Harrier Jump Jet, the 146 passenger jet and the Hawk (the plane the Red Arrows fly). He worked there for nearly six years before realising he could no longer ignore his love of acting, so with the support of his family he went on to achieve his dream. He has landed some important roles, including an appearance in *Harry Potter and the Deathly Hallows* (2010) as a Death Eater. Jon apparently revels in darker film roles and it is said he has developed a compelling, unique and very striking look. As well as being an actor, Jon is also a professional photographer and writes short poems. He is said to be able to ride a unicycle and has a rather unique claim to fame; during the filming of *Tax City*, Jon apparently had to fight former two-times World Champion boxer Steve Collins! Actors from Hull can certainly hold their own!

NOVEMBER 19TH

1835: On this date foreman of the Humber Dock gates in Hull, John Ellerthorpe, dived into the treacherous River Humber to save a man who had fallen in. John was working on the *New Holland* packet and on this particular day a dreadful storm was raging. The ferry had moored and as he was getting ready to leave he heard a splash, as a man fell in the water. With no regard for himself John apparently dived straight in and managed to drag the man to safety. After this John's reputation spread and he was given the job of watchman, to save anyone who fell in the deadly water. He was a self-taught swimmer and apparently excelled in feats of diving and swimming. John's first save was actually his own father, when John was just fourteen, and, during his life, he saved thirty-nine people from drowning. He was reluctant to accept any rewards for his bravery, but did accept a silver medal and certificate from the Royal Humane Society in 1835, and a gold watch and purse of 100 guineas from the Prime Minister. He campaigned for Hull to have a swimming bath and thought it every parent's duty to teach their child to swim.

NOVEMBER 20TH

2009: The *Hull Daily Mail* ran a story on this date about thirteen-year-old Jessica Newton, from Hull, who won the gold medal at the European Wado-Kai Championships in Dublin. Jessica was in the fighting kumite section and another Hull club member, Matthew March, won the silver medal in the kata form section of the same event. They are both members of the Shin Ken Dojo Club in Hull and this was the 37th annual European Championships in Ireland. Jessica had previously won the Ken Yu Kai Open Karate Championships in Manchester, but this international competition in Dublin was her biggest so far. Tony Dent of the Wado UK Hull Zanshin Karate Club was quoted as saying, 'It is a fantastic achievement for such a young athlete. This is Jessica's finest win to date.'

It was obviously a day for success in Hull, the same paper printing a story about Hull's Music Service being recognised for outstanding achievement and awarded the Major Trophy from the National Music Council of Great Britain. The Hull Music Service was formed in the late 1950s by the city's first instrumental teacher employed by the city council. This award is seen as one of the most prestigious that local authorities can obtain for their provision of musical education.

NOVEMBER 21ST

2007: This will be a year etched on the minds of every inhabitant in Hull as the worst flooding the area has seen for a long time. In June, the city experienced unusually high rainfall and the subsequent flooding caused widespread disruption, with damage to over 8,600 residential properties and over 1,300 businesses. It was calculated that over 20,000 people were affected. An additional 700 council staff were taken off normal duties to help the thousands displaced by the flooding; Council Tax information identified 2,681 households driven from their homes, records indicating over 600 having to live in caravans. On this date, an Independent Review Body reported that Hull flooded because the drainage system was overwhelmed. Although the sewer system is relatively modern for the UK, there were concerns as to whether the pumping stations were correctly designed. Also, the fact that Hull is a low-lying town adds to the worry of a repeat disaster, and it was thought it should have additional levels of protection above and beyond a one in thirty-year storm event. Additional pumping systems and regular unblocking of gullies would help, as well as rainfall flash flood warning systems. It was recommended that an independent Drainage Board for Hull be set up.

NOVEMBER 22ND

1913: On this day the *Hull Daily Mail* reported from the York Assizes during the past week that:

> Harriet Briggs, of Hull, a neatly dressed woman with a large picture hat, was charged with bigamy by going through a form of marriage with Arthur Barkworth, a trawler engineer, on March 5th 1910, her former husband being then alive.

She had apparently married her first husband in 1883, and declared herself a thirty-year-old spinster when she married the second in 1910. This would have made her just three years old when she married her first husband! She said she had not seen him in a great many years and then stated he had died in a lunatic asylum. Fortunately for Harriet she had a good defence; she stated that there needed to be proof that she had seen her first husband within the last seven years when the second marriage took place, and as this evidence was absent the judge had no choice but to discharge her.

There was also a case against four Hull dock workers who had been charged with beating a man to death, after he had intervened in an argument they had with another man. The men charged with his murder were said to be members of the notorious Hull Silver Hatchet Gang and received a penal sentence for their crime.

November 23rd

1846: Hull-born Methodist missionary, James Evans, died on this date. He and his family were one of hundreds who emigrated to Canada in the nineteenth century, where James greatly influenced the natives of North America. James had a natural inclination to teach and in the 1820s he was in charge of the mission and schools at Rice Lake in Ontario. He seemingly had a natural ability with languages and soon became proficient in Ojibway, the local native Indian language, into which he began to translate religious texts and other literary works. In the 1840s, James became Superintendent of the Methodist Mission at the settlement situated at the remote Norway House, where he continued with his translations into Ojibway, also producing a new alphabet for them so they could begin to write. This was a syllabic alphabet based on shapes which was easy to learn and eventually was used almost universally amongst the Canadian Ojibure and Cree. He also began a programme of printing texts and managed to campaign for a printing press, thus enabling the first ever books in the Cree language to be printed. He was on a visit to England when he died quite suddenly and was buried in Hull. Later, however, his body was taken to Rossville, near Norway House, his tombstone reading, 'He brought the Light'.

NOVEMBER 24TH

2011: On this day the *Hull Daily Mail* alerted audiences to the fact that the Hull-born heavy metal rock band, Salem, were to make a comeback and perform in their hometown. Salem was originally formed after the Hull band Ethel the Frog broke up in the late 1970s, when two of the members started a new band. When guitarist Paul MacNamara posted some of their songs on MySpace they were overwhelmed with the response and decided to reform, almost three decades later. Their debut gig was at Hull's Adelphi Club and was apparently a huge success, urging them to stay together. 'It's hard to believe, really,' said Paul. 'If we're honest, we probably thought the band had been consigned to the history books. So to be back now with dates lined up and an EP of new songs in the bag is incredible.'

1963: On this date the Beatles played at the ABC in Hull, to a crowd of hundreds. It was noted in the local press, 'Never before have I seen artists receive such a reception. The girls screamed until they could not hear the music.' Apparently, during the two concerts they played in Hull that year, twenty-three girls fainted.

NOVEMBER 25TH

1912: Francis Henry Durbridge, playwright and author, was born in Hull on this date. Apparently encouraged to write by his school English teacher, Francis sold his first play, *Promotion*, to BBC Radio aged just twenty-one. He went on to have a very successful career as a writer. His works include seven plays for stage production, over forty novels, twenty serials for radio, as well as series for TV and some films. Francis is best known for the detective and crime novelist character he created in 1938, known as Paul Temple. This proved such a popular creation that the stories were made into films, after initially being aired as radio plays, then as a TV series. In the 1960s, German radio apparently also picked up his Paul Temple serials and, just like the BBC, each part was said to have ended on a cliff hanger – or what the Germans called a 'strassenfeger' (street-clearer), i.e. they were so popular as to leave the streets deserted. A new character, Tim Frazer, was later invented by Francis, who died in 1998. His last novel, *Fatal Encounter*, was published after his death.

NOVEMBER 26TH

1970: The *Hull Daily Mail* printed an article on this date about the fact that the gold statue of King William III, which stands in Hull's Market Place, was not to be regilded after all. Erected by public subscription in 1734, the people of Hull made the unveiling ceremony quite a party by all accounts. According to one report the loyal inhabitants drank to the good King's memory 'till they lost their own'. The statue was described by one Hull historian in the last century as 'one of the best erections of the kind in the country'. The city's only equestrian statue, it is believed the last time it was regilded was in the 1940s, when it was brought back from its wartime hideaway at Sancton, and even then the regilding was apparently paid for by a private donor. However, the statue is well loved by the people. There is also quite a myth surrounding it. Legend states that if the clock in nearby Holy Trinity Church should strike thirteen, King Billy will dismount and go for a drink in the adjacent King William pub. Another tale says that the sculptor committed suicide when he realised he had not included stirrups!

NOVEMBER 27TH

1940: Born in Gainsborough on this date, the actor John Alderton was brought up in Hull and was a pupil at Kingston High School. Pursuing his ambition to act, John managed to land a role in an early television soap opera, *Emergency – Ward 10*. After this he took the lead in the sitcom *Please Sir!* which shot him to fame. This is one of the roles for which he is best known along with *Upstairs, Downstairs*. In the latter he was the chauffeur, Thomas Watkins, and played alongside his actress wife, Pauline Collins. They starred together in a number of projects and, after appearing in cult sci-fi movie *Zardoz*, John returned to television as vet James Herriot in the 1975 film, *It Shouldn't Happen to a Vet*. During the 1980s and '90s he had less visible roles but became a well-known narrator for the children's animated series, *Little Miss* and *Fireman Sam*. He reappeared on the screen in the 2003 film *Calendar Girls*, and then starred in ITV's *Doc Martin*. He was also involved in the BBC's adaptation of *Little Dorrit* in 2008, as the character Christopher Casby.

NOVEMBER 28TH

1901: Early in the morning on this date sixty-year-old Sarah Hebden was brutally murdered at 97 Hodgson Street, Hull. Being an upstanding, well-respected member of the community, her murder initially baffled the police. Sarah was one of three sisters and she earned her living by collecting insurance premiums for the Royal Liver Friendly Society from local fishing families, who put a little aside each week in case hard financial times should befall them. The motive for the murder appeared to be robbery, as Thursday was the day she was due to pay over the insurance money at the local Friendly Society offices, and most of the money had been stolen from her home. The perpetrator was found to be one Arthur Richardson who, surprisingly, turned out to be the illegitimate son of one of Sarah's sisters. He was, by all accounts, said to be something of a true villain, having served time in Lincoln Prison for robbing his own mother. He was eventually found guilty and was sentenced to death, despite protesting his innocence. He was hanged on March 25th 1902, but, before he walked to the gallows, he apparently dictated a letter to the prison chaplain finally admitting his guilt.

November 29th

1866: Hull mathematician and astronomer, Ernest William Brown, was born on this date. Educated at Hull and East Riding College, he then entered Christ's College, Cambridge, where he graduated with first class honours in mathematics. He continued with postgraduate studies at Cambridge until he left England to become a mathematics instructor at Haverford College, Pennsylvania. He was fascinated with the workings and motion of the Moon. His able understanding and intellect on the subject was shown in the publication of his first great work, *An Introductory Treatise on the Lunar Theory*, in 1896, when Brown was still less than thirty years of age. His project was to evolve a plan to create a completely new lunar theory and Ernest managed to secure an agreement with Yale for funding the massive task of calculating detailed tables of the Moon's motion, based on this theory. After a period of twelve years and a cost of over $34,000, Ernest's *Tables of the Motion of the Moon* was published in 1919. They were adopted by nearly all of the national ephemerides in 1923 for their calculations of the Moon's position, and continued to be used, eventually with some modification, until 1983, when the advent of digital computers changed things. There is a crater on the Moon named Brown, after him.

NOVEMBER 30TH

1904: The *Daily Mail* reported 'Whitefriargate Excitement' on this date, detailing an accident which occurred whilst the traffic on Whitefriargate Bridge was at its busiest. It said that the passage was fairly tight and at busy times became quite confined. 'A carrier's cart, heavily laden ... was proceeding over the bridge towards the Monument, when it collided violently with the post at the west corner. The animal, which was of the heavy type, fell with a thud, but never moved, having broken its neck in the collision. Traffic was considerably inconvenienced at this most awkward spot, for the dead animal lay in the roadway half an hour before it could be removed.'

———— ◆ ————

1946: On this day the *Hull and Yorkshire Times* ran a story about Hull blitz fighters not taking their Defence ribbons. 'Are Hull blitz heroes too modest?' the article enquired. The Defence Medal was offered to the thousands in Hull's Civil Defence services who fought the 'terror of the German bombers through weary nights,' but only 1,509 were issued. Much publicity was apparently given to the subject when the application forms for the medals were available, but perhaps it was offered to so many that it lost its appeal – or maybe Hull people *are* too modest!

DECEMBER 1ST

1913: On this day the *Hull Daily Mail* reported an incident which occurred the previous weekend, when four men were thrown into Hull's Victoria Dock, one of the poor souls succumbing to the waters:

> The mishap occurred whilst the steamer *Norge* was being towed into dock by the tugs *Southern Cross* and *Elsie Partiss*. Two of the men were in one boat, the other two in the second and when the steamer was near the West Pier the boats endeavoured to get to the steamer to get a job of handling the mooring ropes. When abreast of the piles near the pier the piermaster, Thomas Burton, shouted to them to get out of the way, as there was great danger of the small boats being crushed by the steamer. The four men, it is alleged, appeared to be having an altercation as to who should get to the steamer first. Hardly had the piermaster given his warning when the steamer caught the two boats, which were abreast of the entrance to the pier. Both were crushed on the piles beneath the pier, the little boats were smashed, and the four men were thrown into the water.

Three of the men apparently managed to hang on to the piles, but the fourth sank immediately and his body was not recovered.

DECEMBER 2ND

1536: On this date the rebellion known as the Pilgrimage of Grace ended in Hull with the king's pardon and the rebels dispersing. The Pilgrimage of Grace was the nearest thing to a civil war in Henry VIII's reign, when he began his Dissolution of the Monasteries and the people rose against him. Hull was drawn in due to the fear that the King would bring artillery into Hull to suppress the revolts in Lincolnshire and York. Hull, lead by Captain William Stapleton, became a fortress and the rebels made a blockade of the town. After a five-day siege the rebel force took control of the town in October, installing John Hallam as governor, and so the monks and friars were reinstated in their homes. A truce was agreed between the rebels and the king, but he became stronger and garrisoned Hull by force under Roger Constable. Thus the rebellion ended – until the New Year!

DECEMBER 3RD

1688: This was the night that Protestants, Aldermen and the majority of Hull citizens took the city back from the Governor and other Roman Catholic officers and declared the town in support of Prince Wilhelm. From thence on, December 3rd was declared a public holiday in Hull and 'Town-Taking' day was celebrated for over a century. Hull had played a major part in the troubles between the King and Parliament. John Hotham's decision to turn the King away from the city in 1642 was seen as the first act of civil war, with Hotham being declared a traitor the next day. The civil war lasted many years and much blood was shed, but the night the Protestant deputy governor, Captain Lionel Copley, along with members of the Corporation and Hull civilians, arrested the Catholic officers, no blood was shed. Then, as news spread of King James fleeing the country and William of Orange entering London, there was widespread rejoicing and the grandson of John Hotham, also called John, was appointed Governor of Hull. A subscription was raised and a golden equestrian statue of William III was erected in Hull's market place.

DECEMBER 4TH

1979: Peter Dinsdale, who changed his name to Bruce Lee, is known as one of the UK's most prolific killers. He apparently confessed to a total of eleven acts of arson and twenty-six counts of manslaughter; eleven were overturned on appeal. On this date a fire broke out in the house of Edith Hastie in Hull. Her son, Charles, managed to help his mother out of a back bedroom window, but her three other sons were trapped. The fire service got them out, but all three later died in hospital. Bruce apparently confessed to starting the fire, but held he didn't mean to kill them, saying Charlie Hastie had demanded money from him for sexual activities. Astonishingly, he went on to confess to more fires in Hull over the previous seven years. At first police thought he was a fantasist, willing to confess to anything, but after Bruce gave them detailed descriptions they realised they had a serial arsonist on their hands and, as a consequence, a murderer. Lee claimed that most of the fires were started at random simply because he loved fire, and that he did not consider whether he was endangering life. Only the Hastie fire was a 'known' house, as he bore a grudge against Charles. Bruce was imprisoned for life in 1981.

DECEMBER 5TH

1987: On this date the *Hull Daily Mail* told its readers about the new luxury hotel along the B1228 just outside Hull. This lavish bed and breakfast boasted black drapes, fully fitted carpets, divans, duvets, pillows, silk flowers, pictures on the walls, a choice of TV and radio, fresh towels daily and an intercom system. One may be tempted to think this is nothing unusual, as these things appear in any other hotel, but this particular inn was actually an extravagant boarding kennel and cattery! Run by Mrs Margaret Hill, she told the paper, 'People tell me they've never seen anything like it, and maybe the dogs don't understand the effort that's gone into it all, but I'm sure the owners appreciate it.' Margaret, a true animal lover, was also a dog trainer, taking over the Brooklands Country Pets' Hotel the previous summer and completely revamping the place. She even added a special pampering suite, the Prince and Princess, for extra-special clients. Barking mad? Certainly the dog's life for her!

DECEMBER 6TH

1856: On this day, the *Hull Advertiser* stated that a new street was to be made, running from Anlaby Road to Spring Bank, and was to be named Park Place, to replace Pest House Lane. This street is now known as Park Street but has had a series of different names and faces throughout its existence. Sources say a Pest House had existed down there, where people suffering from the plague were isolated from the town, and there is evidence to suggest it was also the site of some isolation cottages. The lane apparently had a poor reputation; one nineteenth-century writer stated:

> At nightfall it was not fit for a woman to go along, and in winter time it required a man with a stout arm to traverse the distance between Anlaby Road and Spring Bank, which twenty years ago and less was as destitute of life and light after dark as the most destitute region in the world.

Eventually the north end was developed and became College Lane and then, by 1861, the building registers record the name Park Street being used. More buildings and development changed the face of the area and Park Street encompassed the whole stretch through. Hull Fair was even held along Park Street at one time, on the Corporation Field, as were weekly markets.

DECEMBER 7TH

2010: The *Hull Daily Mail* reported the departure of John Godber from Hull Truck Theatre on this date. His plays have been the third most performed after Shakespeare and Scarborough's Alan Ayckburn. They are well-known across the world and he has won numerous awards for them. His works, such as *Bouncers* and *Up 'n' Under*, have proved immensely popular, even finding their way into TV and film. John seems to be as funny in life as in his writing, as shown in one interview where he was asked to comment on what the press say about him, '"17 stone John Godber", they never say "12st 9lb Tom Stoppard" do they? Or "5ft 6ins William Shakespeare", you can't be 17 stone and play a playwright apparently.' He is a big fan of the Humber Bridge and says about living round these parts: 'There's a real sense of freedom living here. It's that, the skies, and there's lots of space. I've been to most cities with my plays but I get back, look at Hull, and think, I'll tell you summat, this isn't a bad place to live.'

DECEMBER 8TH

1848: On this date a boat on the River Hull overturned near the ferry *Brewhouse Wrack*, between the Groves and Wincolmlee, and threw about thirty people into the water. The accident, which took place at 6 a.m., is said to have resulted in the greatest loss of life Hull had seen for many years. A total number of fourteen were drowned, all workers at Kingston Cotton Mills. The cause was thought to 'have resulted from the disposition of the persons in the crowded boat to frolic,' stated the local press at the time. 'An alarm was created by some of those on board moving to one side of the little vessel, which caused it to slant over. Upon this, a move to the opposite side was instinctively, though foolishly made, and then the boat at once capsized in the middle of the river.' The men and lads apparently 'plunged and struggled to reach the shore and the females, void of all self-possession, uttered shrieks which were heard at long distances in every direction.' It was a disaster which struck the hearts of many, as no real help could be offered quickly enough in the dark waters as the tide prevented the boats being launched immediately.

DECEMBER 9TH

1987: On this date the *Hull Daily Mail* reported a story concerning Philip Fussey, who apparently took his dog with him everywhere, costing him up to £6 a week on bus fares for the dog. He requested a special pass from the Kingston-upon-Hull City Transport staff, who were so surprised that they agreed. Cindy the dog could then travel the city for just £2.50 a week!

———◆———

1993: John Markham wrote an article for the *Haltemprice Advertiser*, published on this date, giving an account of the life and works of local writer Winifred Holtby. Born in 1898, she was very forward-thinking for her time, particularly in her rejection of the social whirl in which her mother apparently revelled, and strongly opposed the idea that a young woman's first priority in life was to find a husband! She never married, but rumours that she was a lesbian were discounted and when she died, aged just thirty-seven, it is said she was involved with a man, Harry Pearson, who apparently proposed to her on her deathbed. During her lifetime she was very well known as a journalist, political activist and social rights campaigner, who travelled Europe lecturing for the League of Nations Union and writing in support of women's rights. In 1988, Bransholme High School in Hull was renamed after Winifred Holtby and all new students and members of staff received a copy of her novel *South Riding*.

DECEMBER 10TH

1629: James Primrose was admitted a Licentiate of the College of Physicians on this date. Born in France, James moved to England in adulthood and lived and practised his faculty at Hull, where, as in most parts of the country, he was esteemed an eminent physician. He was best known for being an opponent of William Harvey's theory of the circulation of the blood, which caused a split in physicians of the time. His essay *Exercitationes et Animadversiones in librum Gulielmi Harvæi, &c.*, against Harvey's ideas, was derided by some; '... it abounds in obstinate denials, and sometimes in what may be termed dishonest perversions of simple matters of fact, and in its whole course appeals not once to experiment as a means of investigation.' On the opposite end of the scale, he was highly praised for many of his innovations, such as his theory refuting the doctrine that a hen fed on gold leaf assimilates the gold, so that three pure golden lines appear on her breast, or that the linen of the sick ought not to be changed and that gold boiled in broth will cure consumption. He died in December 1659 and is buried at Holy Trinity Church in Hull.

December 11th

1987: 'Puzzled police have drawn a blank after investigating reports of a huge UFO hovering over North Humberside', the *Hull Daily Mail* reported on this date. A witness told of seeing a 250ft-long triangular object flying above a farm, near Aldbrough. He said it was covered in red and white lights and was making a roaring noise. He was not the only one to report the strange sight; two men at Bilton apparently watched 'a series of large objects, also bearing lights, moving across the sky' late in the afternoon that day. These men, both in their thirties, claimed that the unidentified flying objects were moving slowly and a noise was clearly audible. One was quoted as saying, 'I have seen shooting stars before but I have never seen anything like this. I haven't got the faintest idea what it could have been.' Nor had the police, it seems, as a police spokesman stated, 'In this case, we have drawn a blank,' even after having reported the sightings to both the military and civil airport authorities as well as weather centres. The mystery remains just that.

DECEMBER 12TH

1864: Frederick Needler was born on this date. His family moved to Hull from Skirlaugh but his father tragically died in the typhoid epidemic in 1872. Aged eighteen, Fred landed a job with Edward Buckton, confectionery manufacturer, as his bookkeeper. The business, however, ran into financial difficulties and Fred was offered the plant for £100. His mother had savings, so he took the offer up in 1886. Fred's company was named Needlers Ltd and they made boiled sweets, toffees, praline chocolates, sticks of rock and health sweets. Fred made a real success of his business and looked after his staff very well, implementing welfare facilities way ahead of their time for his employees. He introduced a pension scheme, set up team sports, a choir, and bought a wedding gift for any girl leaving to get married! Fred died at the age of sixty-seven from Parkinson's disease, but the company lived on under his son, Percival. The factory in Sculcoates Lane was finally closed after Ashbury Confectionery bought the company in 2002. The site has been redeveloped and is now a housing estate called Needlers Way.

December 13th

1904: 'Young Man's Adventures at Hull,' stated the *Hull Daily Mail* on this date, under the heading 'Thoroughly Bad Lot'. The story concerned twenty-year-old Thomas Garner, who was sent to Hull gaol for five months for three charges of theft, including falsely obtaining money, clothing and a bicycle. Thomas had apparently obtained bogus advance notes from shipping offices, claiming to be a shipmate, then he took the notes to tradesmen whereby he obtained money and clothing on these false pretences. The lad was known to have a bad reputation, having been fired from his short-term employment for drunkenness, so it was a surprise he was allowed to 'borrow' a bicycle from a cycle dealer, especially after telling the dealer, 'If I don't bring it back, Dr Holder will pay.' Directly after obtaining the said bicycle Thomas apparently took it to a pawnbroker's along Waterloo Street, where he received a small loan for it. He then went to another shop on Beverley Road and hired a Singer cycle, which he then took to be auctioned. The audacious lad had also attempted to obtain money from the Post Office Savings Bank, even after admitting he held no money there. Perhaps it is no wonder he was caught!

DECEMBER 14TH

2007: The *Hull Daily Mail* reported the judge's verdict on the death of Michael Barnett on this date. Summer flooding devastated Hull in June, causing severe damage. Michael Barnett was a tragic fatality, drowning in the floods after his foot became trapped in a drain in Hessle. The jury foreman described Michael's death as a 'selfless act to help others, and without thought for his own safety'. Hull coroner, Geoffrey Saul, explained that all possible ways to save Michael's life had been attempted by the rescue services that day but they were not trained in underwater rescue. Firefighters and divers tried in vain to free Michael using hydraulic equipment. For four hours they tried but eventually they had to call a doctor to amputate his trapped leg, as the water was up to his neck and a diver had to hold up his head. The doctor stated that the operation was impossible underwater and in strong currents without a diving team. Michael was no longer showing any vital signs as the poor man had died of hypothermia. The coroner praised the bravery of everyone involved but wanted to highlight this gap in training provision. Michael's father said the emergency services did all they could and they were 'a brave bunch of lads'.

DECEMBER 15TH

1969: The *Hull Daily Mail*'s headline on this date read, 'Hull in grip of flu epidemic, says MOH'. The worst bout of flu seen by Hull in a long time brought many vital services almost to a standstill. A labour shortage of 239 was reported by the docks, 15 per cent of the Post Office staff were off ill (with the Christmas rush not far upon them), Hull Kingston Rovers had seven players affected and another four players were showing early symptoms. Between 20 and 30 per cent of schoolchildren were absent, nearly 200 railway staff had called in sick, and the Hull Royal Infirmary itself stated more than eighty doctors and nurses were absent, with the supply department down to about half the normal staff. On December 30th, Castle Hill Hospital said that 15 per cent of their staff – fifty nurses – were also off with the flu. Since the beginning of the month, 113 cases were apparently admitted to the infectious diseases unit at Castle Hill, where twenty-four died. A report from the 29th said that deaths from flu and pneumonia had risen from thirty-nine in December the previous year to 100 this year. Hull doctors, however, were confident that Hull was over the peak of the outbreak by the end of 1969.

DECEMBER 16TH

1986: On this date Hull indie pop band The Housemartins had their only UK No.1 single. The band was formed by Paul Heaton, vocalist, and Stan Cullimore, who played guitar, and the two of them originally performed as street buskers. Paul was apparently quite a devout Christian and many of their lyrics reflected this, as well as a belief in communist ideals. Politics and religion – two major controversial topics to sing about! The duo's demo tape was picked up by Go Disco and they recruited more members to start a proper band. Norman Cook, also known as Fatboy Slim, was the band's bassist for a period and The Gargoyles' drummer also did a stint with them. It is said that the band often referred to themselves as 'the fourth best band in Hull', after Red Guitars, Everything but the Girl and The Gargoyles. Their album, *London o Hull 4*, got to No.3 in the UK charts in 1986 and they had a loyal fanbase internationally as well as in Hull. Their No.1 single was a cover version of Isley-Jasper-Isley's 'Caravan of Love' but was knocked off the top spot on December 23rd, so they did not achieve the Christmas No.1 they so desired.

DECEMBER 17TH

1965: North Sea Ferries began operations on this date, sailing the Hull to Rotterdam route. Flying in the face of the critics, the route proved very popular and in the first year 54,000 passengers were carried. By 1974, the two largest ferries in the world, *Norland* and *Norstar*, were introduced to the route to meet the rapidly growing demand for capacity. By 1994 new super-freighters were introduced but turned out to be too large to pass through the locks to the King George Dock; thus a new river berth was built. Around 1996, P&O, who owned a 50 per cent stake in the company, bought out the other 50 per cent and North Sea Ferries became P&O North Sea Ferries. Two more super-ferries were built, *Pride of Hull* and *Pride of Rotterdam*, again the world's largest ferries, and the company continued to thrive. The company operates ferries from the UK and Ireland to France, Belgium, Spain and the Netherlands. The company has enjoyed great popularity through the years, but perhaps the price of cheap flights has had some adverse effect on their business.

DECEMBER 18TH

1824: Sir John Hall was born in Hull on this date, one of a family of five children. John was baptised at All Saints' Church, Sculcoates. After living in Prospect Street and Brook Street, the family purchased a house at Elloughton. Apparently after reading a book on sheep farming, he was attracted by the sheep-farming opportunities that New Zealand offered and emigrated there in 1852. John became extremely interested in politics and was a member of the Canterbury Provincial Council for most of his life. He was elected to the Second New Zealand Parliament in 1856 but returned to Hull for a couple of years in March. Whilst back in Hull, he married Rose Anne Dryden of Park House in Cottingham. Rose was the daughter of the Hull attorney, William Dryden, and the couple wed at Holy Trinity Church, Hull on April 3rd 1861. They returned to New Zealand, where John moved swiftly through the political ranks to become the twelfth Prime Minister of New Zealand, in 1879. John took an especially active interest in women's rights and was instrumental in moving the Parliamentary Bill that gave women in New Zealand the vote, being the first country in the world to do so.

DECEMBER 19TH

1934: Ethel Lillie Major was hanged at Hull Prison by infamous hangman Tom Pierrepoint on this date. She was the last murderer and the only woman to be hanged at Hull Prison. The story went that Ethel poisoned her husband, Arthur, with strychnine and her ghost is said to haunt the prison. Ethel became pregnant out of wedlock and to avoid social humiliation, the child was brought up by her parents, as her sister. She married Arthur Major in 1918 and it was not until 1934 that he began to hear rumours about his wife's 'sister'. When confronted, Ethel apparently refused to name the father and their marriage started to suffer. Then there were rumours that Arthur was having an affair with a neighbour. One evening Arthur became very unwell and Ethel blamed some corned beef he had eaten. Sometime later he died, but the funeral was delayed as the police received an anonymous letter suggesting Ethel had poisoned her husband. At the post-mortem, his body was found to contain a more than lethal amount of strychnine. When questioned, Ethel apparently denied poisoning him with strychnine, but as the police had not yet divulged the post-mortem results nor made any mention of the use of a particular substance, she was caught out!

DECEMBER 20TH

1804: James Clay, MP for Hull in the 1840s and '50s, was born on this date. Son of the musical composer, Frederick Clay, James is better known as a writer on the game of whist. His obituary in the Westminster papers stated that he was 'the acknowledged head of the Whist world', for at least the last thirty years of his life, where he spent much of his time and attention on whist and piquet. He apparently became chairman of the committee for settling the laws of whist in 1863. As MP for Hull, James was involved in a scandal, where accusations of bribery were levelled against him and because of this he was unseated for four years. The case against him at the time stated that the last election for Hull, for which he stood in 1853, was fixed. The report from the Select Committee at the time said, 'Corrupt practices have extensively prevailed at the last Election for the Borough of Kingston upon Hull, that the committee also found, that there is reason to believe that a system has existed ... bribing the poorer class of voters in great numbers, by a payment of about thirty shillings a head.' James, however, managed to regain his seat in 1857 and held it until his death in 1873.

DECEMBER 21ST

1970: On this date the comedy writer Derren Litten was born. Originally from Hull, he is said to jokingly describe his circumstances as improving from these humble origins to becoming a graduate of The Central School of Speech and Drama in 1993. After this his face soon became a regular on television, both in advertisements and shows such as *Perfect World*, *French and Saunders*, *Spaced*, *Eastenders*, *Green Wing* and *Pie in the Sky*, but it is for his writing that he is best known. The story goes that Derren's best friend from drama school was Catherine Tate, who asked him to write for her Edinburgh sketch show. Apparently he had never even written any comedy at this point, but was considered to be hilarious and was willing to help his friend for free! A lucky choice for them both, as *The Catherine Tate Show* became very popular and on the back of this Derren was given the opportunity, by Geoffrey Perkins, to write anything he wanted. Derren gave him the first two scripts that he had written for *Benidorm* and the series was commissioned rapidly, becoming a huge TV hit and winning various awards.

DECEMBER 22ND

1888: On this day Britain's chief maker and distributor of motion pictures, J. Arthur Rank, was born in Hull. The family were devout Methodists and there was a concern expressed by the Methodist community about the detrimental influence of the film industry on Britain and family life. This is said to have given J. Arthur the idea of producing films for religious and moral instruction. He established his own film company but quickly realised that this subject was unlikely to prove profitable. Realising that he had to widen the appeal, J. Arthur went on to produce many films at his purpose-built Pinewood Studios, including *Brief Encounter*, *The Red Shoes*, *Oliver Twist*, *Great Expectations* and *Henry V*. His organisation is said to have dominated the British Film Industry from the 1930s to the 1950s. In 1953, he also set up the J. Arthur Rank Group Charity to promote Christian belief, later becoming known as The Rank Foundation.

———◆———

On this date in 1883, a strange killing occurred in Hull when Charles Nowland, a pattern maker of 11 Granville Terrace, threw an iron spittoon at his wife. It caught her on the head and she died from the injury six days later. Nowland was sentenced to death, but later reprieved.

DECEMBER 23RD

1902: On this day William James Bolton, an engineer on a Hull trawler, was hanged at Hull Prison just two days before Christmas. William's crime was murder. He was seemingly separated from his wife when he met Jane Allen, described as a woman of 'the unfortunate class'. It is said he became very attached to her, but apparently she did not feel the same way. Jane allegedly announced to William that she was to marry someone else and this was not the news he wanted to hear. He lost his temper and stabbed the poor woman to death, then tried to cut his own throat. His suicide attempt failed and he was tried and found guilty of murdering Jane. William was only the second killer to be hanged in Hull Prison, his hangman being William Billington. The hanging attracted a large crowd, who gathered outside the Hedon Road gaol before 8 a.m. Reports say there were several policemen on duty to keep the crowd from the portals of the doors and soon after 8.30 Mr T. Morrow JP, representing the Hull magistrates, drew up in a dogcart and the people knew the time approached. The bell tolled and William met his end.

DECEMBER 24TH

1594: Christmas Eve is normally a time of love, celebration and forgiveness. But not this Christmas Eve, not in Hull, not for Catholics. This was a dangerous period to be Catholic, with Henry VIII's orders to kill and torture all and to destroy their religious institutions. Hull was no exception. Anthony Atkinson was appointed as Hull's priest-hunter, as well as customs searcher, watching out for smugglers and cheats. He had a heartless reputation as a man who thrived on the pain of others and he seemed to relish the war of hatred against Catholics. One example of his dedication to their persecution was on this date. He was on the trail of some Catholics and, with a posse of about thirty men, he smashed his way into a Hull house and made several arrests, including a Father Alexander Rawlings. All were imprisoned in the dreaded Hull Blockhouses. 'He was a man entirely devoid of character,' said one historian of Atkinson, who even went so far as to betray his fellow priest-hunters, just to save his own neck. This apparently happened when he got into trouble for disrespecting a Privy Council Member, but managed to avoid his sentence by giving them the names of others who had been with him. A true Hull villain!

DECEMBER 25TH

1925: Born on Christmas Day, Hull funnyman Norman Collier weighed a staggering 15lb 4oz. In an interview with the *Hull Daily Mail*, Norman described his childhood in Mason Street as hard work. 'There were eight of us in a two-bedroomed house, with an outside toilet and no hot water.' After leaving the Royal Navy in 1945 he found a labouring job. 'Coming home one night in 1948, Charlie Jacques asked me if I fancied a pint, so we went in to Perth Street Club. In those days, if the act didn't turn up, they asked for a volunteer. The next thing I knew, I was being announced. That was the first time in my life and it was as if I had been doing it all my life.' Norman's career as a comedian began, coming to national media attention after his appearance at the Royal Variety Command Performance in front of the Queen, in 1971. Norman had always been a very down-to-earth Northerner, known for his charitable works and strong family ties. His wife of over sixty years, Lucy, would always pack for his performances and be waiting up for him when he returned in the early hours. He sadly passed away in 2013.

DECEMBER 26TH

1866: The whaler *Diana*, which was a screw steamship, was the last whaling ship to sail from Hull. The ship left on February 1st 1866 for Greenland and the Davis Straits under the Command of Captain Gravill. It is said that the crew were trying to make their way home when the ship became stuck in ice around Melville Bay, which is north of Baffin Bay. Nothing could be done and the ship drifted in the ice for six months. The men were on rations, many of them suffering from scurvy due to the lack of fresh fruit and vegetables. The freezing conditions meant spending half an hour on the ice-encrusted deck would result in severe frostbite. Despite their circumstances the crew apparently managed to celebrate Christmas, with small portions of plum duff, meat and biscuits, which had been saved for the festivities. Unfortunately, the raised spirits were short-lived as on Boxing Day Captain Gravill died at the age of sixty-four. His was not the last death. In all, their nightmare voyage is said to have taken fourteen months. Captain Gravill's body had been sewn up in canvas and kept on the bridge for the remainder of the voyage and was eventually taken back to Hull. His funeral was attended by an estimated 15,000 people.

DECEMBER 27TH

1939: Born in Hull in 1889, Harry Duffin was a force to be reckoned with. Always a seadog, he joined the Royal Navy during the war and then afterwards became a fisherman, working on the trawlers. It was thought at one point that a ship on which he was working was bombed by German planes in 1939, but a report in *The Times* newspaper from this date modified this account and stated that his trawler, *Dromio*, collided with an Italian one and sank. Fortunately, all seventeen of the crew were rescued and brought home. That was not the end of his adventures, as later the trawler on which he was serving came under attack from German aircraft. Harry apparently responded so vigorously with the ship's gun that the Germans eventually gave up. Another time, as skipper aboard the *Yorick*, being part of a convoy en route to Iceland, they were again attacked, one trawler in particular. The crew of this ship were thrown into the sea and would surely have perished if it were not for Harry's efforts to reach them, even under heavy gunfire. He managed to save these crew members and for his bravery was awarded an MBE.

DECEMBER 28TH

1835: On this day, Hull seaman Anthony Ward was obliged to have both feet cut off at the ankle joints with a razor. This courageous and heroic man kept a diary during his arduous voyage, which began on the *Columbus*, setting sail in August from Hull's Old Dock. In November they hit bad weather; '… the frost was so strong that the ropes of the ship were three times thicker than their usual size with ice.' Eventually the crew had to abandon the *Columbus* and were taken aboard the *Robert of Lancaster*, which answered their distress signal. However, the *Lancaster* did not fare much better and became wrecked in St George's Bay, Newfoundland, at the beginning of December. Losing his shoes in the swim for shore, Anthony had to endure the deadly search for help over icy mountains and razor-sharp rocks in bare feet: 'As my feet were so badly cut by the rocks, they bled as I walked on the snow; the frost soon destroyed them of animal feeling'. Exhausted, freezing and starved, the surviving men eventually found help, but no one believed Anthony would live long. 'I was quite insane. All the toes were cut off both my feet and the flesh cut off the soles of my feet.' He lost both feet, plucking all four ankle bones out with a penknife. After much time and pain, Anthony made it home to Hull with a pair of artificial legs and found work French polishing. Unfortunately, the poor fellow succumbed in 1845 when cholera struck.

DECEMBER 29TH

1898: Elsa Gridlow was born in Hull on this date. Elsa was a poet who, in 1923, published the first volume of openly lesbian love poetry in the United States. It was called *On a Grey Thread*. When Elsa was six years old the family moved to Canada. As a child she did not apparently have any formal education, but helped her mother in the house whilst secretly nurturing her ambitions to be a poet. When she was sixteen they moved to Montreal, where she had her first passionate relationship with a woman. Aged twenty-one, she moved to New York and in 1927 to San Francisco, and continued to live, write and love for the rest of her days. Her autobiography gives a detailed and personal account of her existence seeking, finding and building a life with other lesbians at a time when little was recorded on this topic. She advocated alternative spiritualism and founded and lived in the rural retreat centre Druid Heights Artists Retreat in California. Her friend, Alan Watts, apparently said of Elsa, 'From the first meeting Elsa enchanted me, a witch casting a spell.'

DECEMBER 30TH

1878: Hull company Reckitt & Sons was officially registered on this day. Founded by Isaac Reckitt in 1840 as a small starch-making business, he slowly expanded it to include the production of black lead and washing blue. The company was originally called Isaac Reckitt Starch Manufacturer – late Middleton, as he had purchased the business from Charles Middleton. Although surviving, there was no real development in the business until his sons became old enough to help. Indeed, it was Isaac's son Frederick who became the company's first chemist and his other son, George, its first salesman. From this point on the business was known as Reckitt & Sons. It is now a name nationally and internationally renowned for its quality of production in household cleaners and pharmaceuticals, including such products as Dettol, Lemsip, Clearasil and Mr Sheen. When Isaac died in 1862, his sons carried on the firm and then in turn their sons carried it into the twentieth century. Offices have opened across the globe and the company is still going strong, having merged twice in its history. It became Reckitt and Colman in 1938, then Reckitt Benckiser in 1999. It is now the world's largest producer of household cleaning products.

DECEMBER 31ST

2008: This was the date that the New Year Honours list was released for 2009, which stated that Hull-born Alec Gill would be awarded an MBE for services to the fishing community in Kingston-upon-Hull. After graduating from Hull with a BSc in Psychology in 1977, he later gained an MSc in Environmental Psychology from Cardiff University. Alec began his study of Hull's fishing community in 1974 and, after six books, went on to found the Stand heritage group and instigated the annual Lost Trawlermen's Day service. His MBE, bestowed on him by the Prince of Wales, was awarded for his dedicated research. When the *Hull Daily Mail* asked what the award meant to him, he said:

> It's a wonderful honour and I feel like I am receiving it for everyone in Hull because Hull is a wonderful place to come from and it's wonderful to receive this award. I started taking photos of the community in 1974 and find them fascinating people. They have one of the most dangerous jobs on the planet, going out on trawlers, day in, day out. This award is in recognition of the work they do.